CLICK AND GROW **RICH**

CLICK AND GROW RICH

THE PROVEN FORMULA
FOR STARTING AND GROWING A *SUCCESSFUL*
AND *WILDLY PROFITABLE* BUSINESS ONLINE

BRETT FOGLE AND
E. DANIEL MILLER

NEW YORK

LONDON • NASHVILLE • MELBOURNE • VANCOUVER

CLICK AND GROW **RICH**
THE PROVEN FORMULA FOR STARTING AND GROWING A *SUCCESSFUL* AND *WILDLY PROFITABLE* BUSINESS ONLINE

Published in New York, New York, by Morgan James Publishing. Morgan James is a trademark of Morgan James, LLC. www.MorganJamesPublishing.com

ISBN 978-1-64279-436-6 paperback
ISBN 978-1-64279-437-3 eBook
Library of Congress Control Number: 2019930800

Cover Design by:
Chris Treccani
www.3dogdesign.net

Interior Design by:
Bonnie Bushman
The Whole Caboodle Graphic Design

In an effort to support local communities, raise awareness and funds, Morgan James Publishing donates a percentage of all book sales for the life of each book to Habitat for Humanity Peninsula and Greater Williamsburg.

Get involved today! Visit
www.MorganJamesBuilds.com

To all the people along the way who supported us, encouraged us, and mentored us when we were first starting out on this journey.

To all the creative and courageous individuals before us who have taken the bold step to start an online business, to try, fail, discover, innovate, succeed, and share what has worked and also what didn't.

To our families and all who supported and believed in us and the time sacrifices they made while we were traveling the world sharing these ideas.

To our students in seven countries (and growing) who have continued to encourage us to spread this message and create the financial #FreedomFighter movement.

And, of course, to Al Gore, who (sort of) invented the internet.

DISCLAIMER

You should know that the results shared in this book are not typical of the average person and may not be typical for you. You may achieve greater success or experience no success at all. As with many things, your results using this information will depend on your actions, and we are making no claims of future income that you may achieve using this information. Your success depends on your efforts.

Throughout this book we have done our best to portray accurate information. Some numbers shown or stated may vary slightly from the actual net totals, as refunds and adjustments may have been made after images were captured.

In parts of the book, personal experiences have been used to help illustrate key points and highlighted in "story boxes" to show relevant examples. However, in certain places "I" or "we" may refer to either of the authors, or prior business relationships depending on the context.

CONTENTS

FOREWORD

by Kevin Harrington

Hi, my name is Kevin Harrington, and you may know me from the hit TV show *Shark Tank* where I was one of the original founding "Sharks" on the show, now in its tenth season. It was a great experience, and I had the opportunity to meet a lot of smart, enthusiastic, and very driven entrepreneurs.

The one thing people always ask me is, "How did you get on *Shark Tank?*" One day Mark Burnett, the producer, called me and said, "Hey, would you like to be a shark on *Shark Tank?*" And I said, "You know, I've been hearing pitches for many years, so it makes total sense for me."

Over the last 30 years, I've launched over 500 products with sales of over $5 billion worldwide. I also had a joint venture with the Home Shopping Network, was CEO of HSN Direct International, and a pioneer of the "As Seen on TV" industry, with over 1,000 products on TV and the internet.

I did the first-ever infomercial and helped build several major brands on TV with people like Tony Little, Jack Lelane, the Jenners, Paris and Kathy Hilton, Kim Kardashian, Montel Williams, and even celebrity-branded artist 50 Cent's headphones. I saw just about everything during those years, worked with a lot of celebrities, and created a few myself. So, that's how I got on *Shark Tank*.

As a serial entrepreneur and investor, I've personally invested in over 100 businesses, so I know a thing or two about what it takes to succeed. I also was happy to write the foreword of this book because I truly believe that what Daniel and Brett are teaching in this book is today's "playbook" for success.

The MP^{5}MS^2 Formula for Success that Brett and Daniel have developed and put together in this book can transform any type of entrepreneurial activity, new idea, or even a business that you already own into a much more profitable company and potentially into a real online money-making powerhouse.

And if you're just starting out, this book will help point you in the right direction for starting a business online with the greatest chance of success. Just follow the formula you'll find in these pages.

I'm glad to be personal friends with both Brett and Daniel because I learn things from them about the internet, making money online, and just business in general. They're great guys, and I believe they are uniquely qualified to take you through the "Shark"-infested waters of building an online business.

You'll want to have an experienced guide who's been there before, faced tough business challenges, and pushed through them. Both have seen their share of successes and big wins, as well as failures. You'll want someone who's experienced both to guide you, because that's where the real lessons are learned. On *Shark Tank*, I always want to know if the entrepreneur can handle the setbacks and failures and still persevere. That's the entrepreneur I would most want to bet on.

I've always found that it's best to learn from someone who's already been there and made it happen. Brett and Daniel have generated tens of millions of dollars combined from prior businesses ventures, both online and offline, so these guys are the real deal and know what they're talking about because they've done it.

Twenty years ago, we sold a lot of physical products, like fitness systems and housewares. These days, it's a much faster-paced environment. It's a world of information products, digital downloads, and social media. It seems something new is coming out every day.

Today people are creating and selling their own self-created content, from digital information products to downloadable software, and even having physical products made overseas on sites like alibaba.com that they then can sell on Amazon for five, six, or even seven figures per month. It's big business, and people are doing this, in some cases, with relatively little investment. It's an age of people looking to create their own destiny, create their own freedom, and craft the lifestyle they want. It's a very entrepreneurial environment out there right now.

To offer some perspective, for us to make a million dollars from an infomercial back in the early days (even today), you would have to put up between a half a million to over a million dollars in production and media spend just to get it launched, with very little guarantee of success.

Today, you see people doing this online or on social media with very minimal start-up investment. It's a very different environment now that favors the entrepreneur and has really leveled the playing field.

Social media platforms are so powerful these days that you can build a massive audience and come out with a product very easily. Some people are literally taking their cell phones and essentially shooting mini-infomercials and then simply posting them online. Seemingly overnight, they have hundreds of thousands of views and followers they are able to sell products to if they choose.

I'm still seeing big opportunities for creating information online, selling digital products people self-create and put up on the internet to start making money easily and quickly. I see it every day.

Some of the biggest challenges I see, however, for those people who want to start online as an internet entrepreneur, mom-preneur, or solopreneur, are costs and where to find the money to start.

You have to be careful with controlling your costs and overhead. For example, let's say you get your new business going, and it starts to grow. Now you need a person or two to help out because nobody can do it alone, and you start hiring people the "traditional" way. In a small business, personnel cost can eat up a lot of your profits and revenue. It's one of the many reasons 95% of all businesses fail in the first year.

Using business automation software, outsourcing to virtual staff part-time when starting out, and following a proven success formula are some of the strategies that help you to succeed. This is all covered in this book, including which technology you can use to run your business. I'm actually a business advisor to one of the technology platforms these guys have built, and I believe it can make a big difference for you.

One of the other challenges in starting a business (especially alone) lies in not having the knowledge of where to go to find the best resources, what and when to get it, which steps to follow in the right order, and who to listen to in this endless sea of choices and nearly infinite directions.

If you look at Europe, China, and look at the rest of the world around you—and you look at the world of mobile—so many new things are happening out there. It's not just on your computer anymore. It's your tablet and mobile phone and anywhere with Wi-Fi, which is just about everywhere now.

I've always liked to start here in the United States and use that as a solid foundation to springboard into other markets. So, the principles and strategies in this book are even more valuable and timely because the global opportunities are endless. The internet is rapidly becoming a huge international opportunity.

Wherever your path takes you, enjoy the journey. With this book and the proven strategies being shared in these pages, you'll have a much better chance of succeeding online and creating more time and money freedom in your lives.

I look forward to hearing about your success!

OVERVIEW
(and *Why* You Should Be Reading)

Click and Grow Rich is the result of literally thousands of hours of learning, testing, trying, failing, stumbling upon, succeeding, and sharing these principles with other people just like you around the world who also aspire to create freedom in their lives and become online entrepreneurs.

Your journey begins here. You now have in your hands the "playbook" to create the income and lifestyle you desire, with no prior experience or expertise, and build your own highly profitable money-making online business that you can operate from virtually anywhere in the world, working as much (or little) time as you want, and creating true *freedom* in your life.

Whether it's time or money freedom you are looking for—or both—our nine-step formula, the MP^{5}MS^2 Formula for Success, will show you how to do it, just as we have done multiple times. It's the same proven process we've taught to thousands of people around the world, in seven countries and counting.

From all over the United States and Canada, from South Africa to Singapore, Kuala-Lumpur, Hong Kong, Mexico, and the United Kingdom, we've been sharing these ideas with aspiring entrepreneurs who are seeking financial freedom and creating their own destiny online.

We're on a mission to impact millions of people worldwide with one simple idea: you *can* create the life and lifestyle you dream of, making as much money as you want to online in the new global economy—without borders or limits.

If you truly desire financial freedom and time freedom, you're in the right place, and we encourage you to take the next step by learning this process. Discover how you can click and grow rich to create your own "laptop" or "mobile" lifestyle, as we and tens of thousands of other people all around the world are doing.

The time is now. The opportunity is growing. Roughly, just over half of the world's population is online right now, and that leaves enormous opportunity for you and everyone reading this book to start and grow an online business, to write your own story of success. And who wouldn't want to take control over their financial future?

Are you ready to get started?

The best part is, *you can.* In these pages, we'll show you how to identify impactful solutions to other people's problems, then simply market and sell those solutions. Imagine potentially earning more than your current full-time income while working part-time hours, whenever and from wherever you choose. Imagine improving others' lives with your valuable information, services, or products. We're about to show you how.

Our legacy is to help as many people as possible (including you) break free from the oppressive financial bonds that restrain them, that limit how much money they can make *and ultimately keep*, and that demand an increasing amount of *time* just to get by. So, if you also feel financially frustrated or constrained, with limited upside potential, read on!

Our rallying cry is *freedom*. Isn't it time you fought for your own time and money freedom? In this book, we're going to teach you the skills to become your own time and financial Freedom Fighter. Is it easy? It's not easy, but it *is* worth it, and you'll be hearing from some of our past and current students about how it's changed their lives.

But first, and before diving in, we'd like you to commit—if this makes sense to you—to put this information to good use. Nothing pains us more than giving our heart and soul to people, as we intend to do in this book, sharing our time-tested and proven online success strategies that can change lives, and then seeing that they don't use what we've provided. So, will you commit to us, right now, to use these powerful ideas and not waste them? Yes? We'll see.

In the First section, you'll be introduced to our Freedom Manifesto. We suggest you print it out—even frame it—and hang it up where you can see it. This will help you get into the daily mindset that will help make your financial dreams become a reality.

We invite you to join us in becoming Financial Freedom Fighters!

Welcome to *Click and Grow Rich*.

INTRODUCTION
What Is Click and Grow Rich?

Click and Grow Rich is the result of a 20-year journey, beginning in 1999 when the internet was first starting to become commercially available, and when the first websites started to appear in the world.

Al Gore wasn't really the "inventor" of the internet, but he was the first political leader to recognize the importance of the internet and support its development. In 1991 Gore sponsored The High Performance Computing and Communications Act, which was a major catalyst in opening up public access to the internet.

More importantly, thousands of people around the globe have been able to start with just an idea and turn it into a money-making online business that supports them and their families, with customers they've never met sending them money from around the world, over the internet. In this book, we'll talk about how you can start with just an idea and then, using our unique formula, determine the best way to monetize your big idea so that you too can live a "laptop" or "mobile" lifestyle.

You're about to learn the little-known secrets of how the insiders and gurus have been doing it for years, but in our simple step-by-step process that we've developed and proven to be effective. We must warn you, however, that part of this process is counterintuitive, and most people get it dead-wrong. In fact, 85%-95% of online businesses fail within the first few years because they failed to follow the right steps.

We'll cover the *right* way to go about it in this book. But before we dive into all that, it's important for you to know that it can be done…*and you can do it too.*

You don't need any special skills, expertise, or experience. Just one good idea…

You're potentially just *one idea away* from everything you've ever wanted in life.

That being said, it's important you also know that this is NOT a book about how to "Get Rich Quick." Your results will depend on your efforts alone, the quality of your idea, the market, timing, and your ability to implement, persevere, and invest your time to do the work.

This book will show you the path and the process we've used, and that you can follow. Tens of thousands of people around the world are living proof that the internet is a proven and reliable way to make money, regardless of geographic location, background, race, gender, or personal experience.

These days anywhere (which is now nearly everywhere) there is a Wi-Fi signal, you can start a business online.

You're just one idea away…

Section One

THE NEW ONLINE ECONOMY

WHY SELL ONLINE

Never before has it been so easy to take a new business from concept to revenue in such a short period of time. With little risk, and the potential to make millions of dollars.

You're just one idea away.

Before diving into this book, it's important to realize there are no easy shortcuts. The path to success online can be simple to follow if you follow *all nine steps* of our MP^{5}MS^2 Formula for Success outlined in this book. Our proven formula has repeatedly worked, both for us and our students currently following this methodology.

You truly can "Click and Grow Rich," but *again*, to be clear, this is not a "get rich quick" formula or a book about how to make millions by doing nothing. You have to do the work. If easy is what you're looking for, you are in the wrong place.

But if you'll take the time, you can learn the principles that have been the foundation for generating over $20 million online since Brett started his first website back in 1999. Daniel also used these concepts while building another organization that he helped grow to over $100 million in sales, which was later acquired by a major international bank for $606 million.[1] You can also create massive success in your life, if you'll take the time to implement this process.

The principles of the MP^{5}MS^2 Formula for Success, followed in the right order, will help you avoid the biggest mistakes and commonly unseen dangers that kill 95% of all businesses starting out, ultimately causing them to fail. If however, you'll follow our step-by-step process and put in focused time and effort, you can potentially achieve lasting success online.

Our earlier businesses were the inspiration for and foundation of the "accidental" formula we're going to reveal to you in this book. These concepts were responsible—whether we knew it at the time or not—for the results just mentioned and throughout *Click and Grow Rich*. All that we ask is that you make a commitment right now, to yourself and to us, that you will—at the very least—implement this formula and test these powerful principles.

We often share these same ideas and strategies in our live two-day workshops, which we teach to students around the world. Sadly, often we discover they're still having the same time and money issues they had before because they simply failed to take action and follow this process. But it doesn't have to be that way…

You may have heard before that "success leaves clues," and this expression has never been truer than on the internet. So you're in the right place, because we're about to peel back the curtain for you, and show you the *behind the scenes strategies* that the well-known experts and top moneymakers online have been using for years.

Now, if you'll agree with us that simply *learning* these ideas won't make you rich unless you actually act on them, we can begin. The good news is, it's a fairly simple process to follow.

But before we get started, it's important to share with you how we discovered this formula for success.

The Beginning: Origin Story—by Brett Fogle

In 2013 I sold the company I had grown from the proverbial "kitchen table," with no investors, no revenue, and little expertise, into the #276th fastest-growing privately held company in the United States, according to *Inc.* magazine, in three short years. Every year, *Inc.* magazine publishes its annual INC500 issue, listing the top private 500 companies in the USA.

I had grown my financial education company from $200,000 in sales the first year to around $3.3 million in sales during the qualification period of the prior three years. These numbers had to be verified to ensure they were accurate before our information could be published in the nationwide issue in 2008. We also made the list of the top 5,000 companies for the two years that followed, at #501 and #1001 respectively, which isn't easy for most companies to do. What's most important about this story is how we unknowingly used our "accidental" MP^5MS^2 Formula for Success to achieve it.

It's also important to note that I had no special talent or skills and certainly wasn't an "expert" in this market, and by all means, I *shouldn't* have achieved the level of success that we did by measure of experience or expertise. What I did have was the ability to persevere, watch what other successful people were doing, and model my efforts after what was working. I was also lucky to find a partner in this market who was an expert.

Fast-forward five years. After starting multiple successful related brands and information products in the financial markets (stocks, options, and Forex) and after generating approximately $17 million in revenue, in 2013 I was able to sell the initial company I started. There's an important lesson here also, which we'll talk about in section two when we talk about finding partners to help you grow your business, and later when we talk about selling your company.

A few years earlier, I had been introduced to Daniel Miller through a mutual friend and former business partner. Daniel and I soon became business partners in a software platform called Cydec, which was the technology I had used to generate most of the profits in the financial information company above.

One day, while brainstorming in my Boca Raton office, Daniel said, "Why don't we also teach people how to build a successful business online, as you have?" From there, we started whiteboarding ideas. I'll never forget the day he said, "We need to create a simple-to-follow formula so that people don't get overwhelmed. We need to give them the proper steps to follow."

I thought he was crazy at first. But as a former Six-Sigma engineer, Daniel knew the value of statistical process improvement and making things easy to follow. So, we went back to the whiteboard and started putting everything into categories, including all the things we had used and learned up until that point in our prior businesses.

Fairly quickly, we arranged everything into nine categories, which eventually became our MP^5MS^2 Formula for Success. Most important, we outlined everything in the proper sequence. The sad fact is that 95% of online businesses—and even brick-and-mortar businesses—quickly fail because they miss one or more of these important elements or follow them in the wrong order.

We'll take a deep dive into the MP^5MS^2 Formula for Success in the next section.

Why Now Is the Best Time

Why is *now* the best time ever to get started making money online and build your fortune?

Consider this. According to wearesocial.com, in 2018, for the first time ever, the world's internet users passed the 4 billion mark.[2] While this figure seems

The Internet Lifestyle

– Can Run From <u>Anywhere</u> in the World

– Now is the Best Time Ever To Start

– More Than 4 Billion People Online

– More Than 2 Billion People on Facebook

- Easier Than Ever To Start Selling Online
- Amazing Technology and Tools Available
- International Markets Just Starting Out
- Can Create as Little or as Much Income as You Want Online (You Decide How Much)

SPECIAL REPORT
DIGITAL IN 2018: WORLD'S INTERNET USERS PASS THE 4 BILLION MARK

massive, it's only roughly *half* the world's total population of 7.5 billion. And, for the most part, the internet marketing phenomenon we've seen in the United States over the past 15+ years is just starting to build in other countries. This means more opportunity for you as it will continue to grow for years to come both domestically and internationally.

Other countries where English is widely spoken are still three to eight years behind us in terms of how the internet is used to buy and sell goods, information products, and services. And this is more good news for you. This means a whole big world is out there, with billions of possible customers, and it's continuing to grow faster than ever. In fact, *Forbes* predicts that US digital marketing spend alone will approach $120 billion by 2021, driven primarily by millennial buying power.[3]

Let's face it. Times are changing faster than ever. Traditional ways to make money and build long-term wealth, like real estate, the stock market, or having a brick-and-mortar business, are all changing, too. These industries have all become ultracompetitive, and in the bell curve of opportunity, traditional paths to wealth have become or are becoming "laggard" businesses, meaning they are growing more slowly.

Let's start with the stock market. The concept of buy and hold is largely dead as we've seen with the not-too-distant market crashes of 2000 and 2008.

The stock market is just too volatile for many as your hard-earned money can disappear overnight. Unexpected market announcements, company earnings disappointments, and economic events can all send the stock market spiraling—and your wealth along with it.

Even more volatile are the newer financial markets, like the Foreign Exchange or "Forex" markets. Or consider the cryptocurrency markets, with bitcoin losing nearly half of its value in one month in December 2017.

People who bought bitcoin at $19,000, during the speculative run-up in the months prior to the collapse, may not recover these losses for many years to come—if ever. As of this writing, bitcoin has lost 84% of its value since the 2017 high. While many believe cryptocurrencies are the future, it's still not clear who the lasting players will be. Remember AOL?

Real estate can be equally volatile. With the collapse of the housing market following the subprime mortgage crisis in 2009, property values quickly fell by 50% or more. Many people lost their home to foreclosure, and many more were badly hurt by overleveraged real estate investments that lost much of their value.

Many experienced major loss—or worse, bankruptcy. Do you know anyone who was affected? We've personally talked to and know more than a few real estate investors who lost large personal fortunes during this collapse, all outside of their control. We don't know about you, but we don't want to spend five to ten years in anything that can suddenly crash and burn, especially if you haven't done anything wrong, only to find all your hard work, time, and energy was wasted.

Brick-and-mortar businesses (as we call them in the Internet Age and in contrast to online businesses) are equally at risk. We've been predicting what we call the "Amazon Apocalypse" for nearly five years now. Why? Because Amazon, as a result of their massive buying power and lower overhead, puts incredible pricing pressure on small businesses. As a result, many retail businesses have been closing their doors forever.

How many times have you walked into a retail store, asked the price, and then searched Amazon or other online options to see how much cheaper you could buy there instead? We all have, especially with the option of free shipping if you're an Amazon Prime subscriber. It's a no-brainer. Retail business owners know all too well just how hard it is to make a profit after paying rent, utilities, insurance, and salaries while carrying the cost of inventory. Taking even 10% of their profit margin away could spell disaster, and that's what's happening right now. If you own retail, it's likely time to get out.

Major chains such as Circuit City, Sears, Kmart, Macy's, and more have been closing their doors permanently. Developers are even tearing down strip-mall shopping centers in Florida, and it's starting to happen nationwide. Mark our words: a retail crisis is building, and the Amazon Apocalypse is coming.

Amazon is an amazing company that is changing how we live…making it easier (and cheaper) for us as consumers to buy goods *and services*, but we wouldn't want to be on the wrong side of this shift by owning a retail business. Do you?

We predict that the only brick-and-mortar businesses that will survive and thrive long term in the *new online economy* are specialty services, luxury brands, and convenience or grocery stores, along with fast-food and delivery brands.

According to NPR News, big-box retailers, like Sears, Kmart, and Macy's, will continue to close more stores in 2018 and beyond, partially because "more people are choosing to spend much more of their paychecks on their screens—on smartphone data plans, or streaming entertainment services like Netflix."[4]

Let's have a look at this curve. Notice where the internet and making money online is in relation to the three "laggards" (retail, real estate, and the stock market).

It's obvious. The traditional big-three ways of making money and building wealth in the last century—owning retail businesses, owning real estate, and investing in the stock market—are clearly in their laggard phase of the opportunity growth curve. That's not to say money can't still be made in these markets; however, more competition than ever before means less long-term opportunity for you. Plus, there are many *hidden* economic dangers with each of these, all outside of your control.

Have you read or heard about "Blue Ocean" strategy? This concept means you'll likely find the biggest wins and successes if you're "fishing" where nobody else is, where the water is still *blue*, versus over where the water is *red* with blood, from all the sharks feeding there.

Making money via an online business has passed through the most dangerous part of the economic opportunity curve, the "innovators" phase, in which only the most risk-tolerant innovators jump in to try new things. Because the risk doesn't always work out when launching a new business or industry, this phase is the riskiest and offers the least chance of success. Remember, "pioneers" are usually the ones with the arrows in their backs…

Fortunately, having an online business is now well into the early-adopters phase. It is just now hitting its *momentum* phase of the growth curve, which is the best place to be because the risk is much lower, and the potential long-term gains are much greater.

Imagine if you were surfing. Most surfers would agree that you want to be positioned *in the ocean* waiting for just that right wave to paddle after and catch so that you can ride it for as long as possible. To catch that *perfect wave*, you'll need to be well positioned to ride it for everything it's got…

But if you're trying to catch a wave that's already had its run, as with a laggard business, you'll miss the biggest part of the wave. By the time you jump in, you can only ride for a short time before it's over. Which part of the wave would you rather be positioned for: the beginning of the ride, or the end?

WHAT TO SELL ONLINE

Now that we've established that now is a great time to get started selling online, let's talk about what you can sell online. If you're reading this book, you probably have some familiarity with this concept or already have a website. Perhaps you know friends and family who have been making money online.

For those who are new to this idea, let's take a brief look at what's trending in today's online sales landscape, just as a quick review of our options. Later, we'll take a deeper dive into all of this and explain the specific types of online businesses you can build for maximum impact. In section three, we will provide examples of how we have personally made the most money online.

From Amazon to Alibaba and everything in between, there's virtually no limit to what you can sell on the internet. The landscape of what you can sell online hasn't really changed that much in the last fifteen years, but what has changed dramatically are the *distribution channels and ease of entry,* which now allow anybody to get into this global market.

Selling products from 1999 to 2003 on a "website" (still a relatively new term back then) and drop-shipping products from local or regional distributors became popular. This was just one step ahead of a mail-order or phone-order businesses, except that customers placed orders on the internet. The vendor would call, fax, or even place the wholesale order online to the distributor or manufacturer who would then ship the product.

Drop-shipping is still a viable way to sell products online today. Efficiencies and scalability are much greater today than ten years ago, with much bigger players in the game like Amazon, which is largely a distribution company. They are one of the best in the world at order fulfillment and getting products delivered, which has created huge opportunities for people selling their products on Amazon.

You also can choose to become a reseller of just about any products you like, have a passion or affinity for, or see a big market in. To find out how to get a license to buy at wholesale and sell at retail, just look online for a listing of distributors in your region or contact the brand or manufacturer directly. While this is not the model for making the *most* money online, it may be a good place to start.

Some of the most successful people online today are selling their own physical products, items for which they are the brand creator or product manufacturer. This is particularly true in larger hot markets like health or beauty (e.g., health supplements, like pills, powders, and shakes; topical beauty products, like anti-aging skin creams, facial lotions, and teeth whiteners). Health and beauty are both massive markets where many have built profitable businesses online. However, these sectors are now very competitive, and not where most people should start out.

That leads us to our crucial question: what should you sell online? Unless you have a unique brand you've already created, one that has already shown promise in the marketplace (like two of our students, Gunnar Monson and his wife, the founders of a great business called The Sasquatch Coffee Company, which we're helping to grow and turn into a national brand), the best place for you to start is likely digital and physical information products. We'll dive into these products in more detail in the next two sections.

Before we tell you about digital information products, it's important to tell you how we discovered these, and how we've generated millions of dollars from selling them.

In 2003, most people had become familiar with the concept of email, which just five years prior had been a big deal. Do you remember when "You've got mail" was exciting to hear? Until it wasn't. Imagine if you had to hear that every time you received an email these days!

But email was a life-changing paradigm shift for our society. Then somebody took that idea a step further and figured out that if people would read their mail in an electronic format, maybe they would also read an entire book this way, as an e-book, so that become the next logical extension of receiving digital information.

Ebooks became the first real digital information products that were widely accepted. Nowadays, they have evolved and been widely adopted by Amazon readers, are now commonly called "Kindle Books" and consumed on a Kindle device. While commonplace now, e-books marked the beginning of a massive wave of digital information. We're not talking about blogs or other free methods of information online but the type of digital information people were willing to pay for. This evolution birthed digital commerce and the current megabillion-dollar worldwide marketplace.

Once the marketplace became flooded with e-books, the next *big* shift occurred.

✍ BRETT STORY

I was at an internet marketing seminar in 2003 and heard that someone had just created a self-produced physical product. It was a video CD/DVD training, and a printed manual on the topic of Fibonacci trading. *I'll never forget that moment because it changed my life.*

It turns out, the creator was someone I was already familiar with; he and his wife later became mentors and encouraged me to release my own physical product as they had done. To be clear, theirs was a hybrid product. Not only did people receive the physical CD/DVD and accompanying manual via FedEx, but they also had access to an online library of videos, trainings, and other materials. Before that, *everybody* was doing digital products.

Following their lead and with their help, I was able to shortcut the learning curve, which likely made the difference between success and outright failure. Their mentorship and encouragement was the catalyst to starting a multimillion-dollar company from scratch. They shared some very valuable resources, from an introduction to a copywriter who wrote my first six- and seven-figure sales letters, which catapulted the growth of my fledgling company, to the graphic design team they used and who became one of my "secret weapons" over the years. I still use them today, fourteen years later. They actually created many of the graphics for this book!

So in 2004, I switched gears from e-books and started another company selling information products, also in the financial trading space. I found a partner who was an expert in the options trading markets, and we released our first product in March of that year. Since we were new and had no customers or email lists of prospects, we had found our first affiliate online. He agreed to promote for us, and within a few days we had our first $15,000. Half of this was commissions to the affiliate but, still, not bad for the first few days in business. This paid for the initial start-up costs, including the copywriter and design.

But most important, we were able to show these results to my mentors, and based on our strong sales conversion rate from the first affiliate, they agreed to promote the offer to their much larger list of stock traders. Within a week, we had over $185,000 in sales. Half of this was paid to them as affiliate commissions, but our profit margin was still very high at over $90,000. They were happy and so were we. We were then able to leverage these sales results and find bigger affiliates to promote the product, and that's how we grew into a multimillion-dollar-per-year company relatively quickly.

We'll talk more about the types of physical and digital information products later in the book, but it's also worth mentioning that one form of digital products that can be sold, which I've personally sold lots of over the years, is software.

I can barely spell PHP or MySQL. But I love *selling* software because, especially these days, you can find quality software programmers all over the world who can turn your idea into reality, and if your software idea can make someone else's life easier, they will gladly pay you for it. Imagine hiring someone to create a cool software solution for you, which you then get to sell over and over again for as long as people want to buy it.

You'll keep all the money, minus some ongoing costs for maintenance. We'll talk later in this book about some of the best ways to create and sell software, and how to get monthly recurring income for just giving people access to it, as well as where to find the best coders. You can find a list of our recommended resources for finding programmers in the resources section at the back of this book.

WHERE TO SELL ONLINE

T he internet marketing industry—also known as digital marketing—has evolved in many ways over the last 15+ years. The early days were a lot like the early Wild West, with few best practices and lots of early pioneers trying new things that didn't work out; some trailblazers even got in trouble with the law.

Fortunately, many discoveries were also made, and the word spread quickly about "what works" and "what not to do." So, this community of pioneers—of which we're proud to be a part of—thrived and innovated. They formulated the base for our proven methodologies and strategies, which are now working on a global scale. This space is always evolving, but we've proven to the world that these methods work and can provide a solid foundation for you. So, you're in the right place to learn these same proven strategies.

In the early days, people were mostly focused on getting their websites online, putting their products or services out there, and trying to increase their search engine optimization (SEO) rankings on Google and other search engines. Thus, website owners competed to outrank their competitors, creating a never-ending game of cat and mouse. It was exhausting to game the search engines for better rankings while the search engines got smarter and changed up their algorithms. This game is largely over and not worth the time for most people.

Affiliate networks such as ClickBank and JVZoo emerged as great alternatives to getting free traffic from search engines, and they continue to thrive to this day. If you're brand new, these resources are a good place to start looking around for ideas.

Affiliate marketplaces for physical products, like Commission Junction, Share-a-Sale, and even Amazon, offer commission programs for referring buyers to sellers, and you could be on either end of that transaction.

Today, many new websites, including educational portal websites like Lynda and Udemy, are also available to list your digital courses for sale.

We'll touch on that more later but will mostly focus on the real opportunities for those just getting started online, which is the focus of this book. If you're already selling online and already call yourself a digital or information marketer, feel free to skip ahead to the next section.

But we promise more valuable information awaits you in this book as well.

Who Can Do It? (You!)

The good news is, *anyone* with the desire to learn and implement the strategies in this book can be successful online. With no shortage of information available these days on how to start an online business, anyone with enough time, money, and resources can learn how to do this. The truly hard part is knowing what to do first and then what to do next (and even what to ignore). There is often an overwhelming amount of information and choices to choose from these days, so it's easy to get confused about which resources and strategies to implement in the right order. This is a big reason why many people don't succeed.

That is why we are writing this book, to cut through the noise and misinformation. We're here to share our proven process of what has worked for us, and outline the proper order so that anyone reading has a fighting chance to be successful. If you know the right steps in the right order, don't you agree you'll have a much better chance of achieving success? It's taken us nearly twenty years and hundreds of thousands of dollars to learn, implement, and test each principle, method, and strategy. If you go it alone, you will find the same learning curve applies.

But, again, success leaves clues, and we've distilled the clues to our success into an easy-to-follow manual—this book—that explains the MP⁵MS² Formula for Success: the right steps to take in the proper order. Think of it as your playbook—a valuable reference manual for building a business online. Read and refer back to it often, and use the resource PDFs we've included.

Anybody can do this. Anyone, *including you*, can find success online with the right amount of information, persistence, and action. You're really just *one idea away* from having everything you want in your life and having your own business. People say money can't buy happiness, but money *can* allow you a certain level of time and financial freedom, which is what most people crave: the idea of having more *freedom* in their lives.

We know from working with hundreds of people that achieving personal freedom is *the* core emotional driver for so many. Perhaps you're in a job you hate or you're stuck in a stressful relationship because of financial issues.

Could regaining your time or creating financial freedom open up more options in your life? Have you ever wished you could find more purpose, give back to the world or your favorite charities in a bigger way—be your own boss—and get paid for it?

If you like the idea of more freedom in your life, you're in luck. Because the core concept of this book is that *you are just one idea away from…*

- Getting Rich Online
- Achieving True Time and Money Freedom
- Earning the Respect of Your Friends and Peers
- Quitting Your Oppressive Day Job
- Giving Your Family the Lifestyle They Deserve
- Experiencing the Success and Happiness You Desire
- Leaving a Family Legacy You Can Be Proud Of

The most common reason we hear from people wanting to start an online business and make money online is the idea of improving their personal freedom.

To help you internalize this and create a powerful positive mindset, we've created The Personal Freedom Proclamation:

PERSONAL FREEDOM
PROCLAMATION

I ANSWER
To No-One But Myself

...

I BELIEVE
In Abundance and Wealth

...

I AM CREATING
Time and Money Freedom

...

I AM LIVING
Life on My Own Terms

...

I AM FIGHTING
For My Financial Independence

...

MY MISSION
Is To Fight For My Family, My Freedom
and My Financial Independence

...

I AM A FREEDOM FIGHTER
#FREEDOMFIGHTER

To download this as a printable image visit:
www.clickandgrowrich.com/book/Proclamation

We recommend that you print this Proclamation, along with the following Freedom Manifesto and Creed, then post these somewhere you can see them and refer to them often… Because change in your *outside* circumstances won't likely occur without change on the *inside* first. A mindset shift is often the first step for you to achieve true freedom in your life.

Our intention is to create a global movement around this idea of freedom and to help as many people as possible achieve this *who want to*. You are one of the thousands of people we've spread this message to, a number growing day by day. If what you've read so far resonates with you, we would like to invite you to become a part of this movement and share in the journey.

We invite you to join in our collective mission: "To Fight Against Mediocrity, Take Back Control of Your Time, Life, and Finances…and Become a Financial Freedom Fighter!"

On the next page, you'll notice the graphic of the full Freedom Fighter Manifesto. We suggest you take a picture and make it the background image on your phone as well as print it, and put it on your wall to continually remind you of why you're embarking on this life-changing journey.

And as a special bonus for reading this book, you can reserve your free (#FREEDOMFIGHTER) T-shirt by going to www.clickandgrowrich.com/FreedomShirt.

For a powerful motivational song to kick things off, search YouTube for the song "Freedom" by Pharrell Williams. Watch it right now and listen to it loud. Let it be your rallying cry. In fact, we recommend that you listen to it every day, before you start your day!

You'll thank us later.

Before moving on, it's important to talk not just about motivation but *belief*. If you don't have the right mindset and believe that you have the ability to achieve great things in your life, that's a problem you'll have to overcome along the way before you'll likely reach your goals.

Let's talk about the importance of having the right intentions, attitudes, and beliefs as these will ultimately dictate your actions, and therefore the results you experience. In fact, these are all interrelated. Most people go through life barely

THE FREEDOM FIGHTER
MANIFESTO

A FREEDOM FIGHTER is a **NEW BREED OF INDIVIDUAL**... Somebody Who Isn't Content Being Part of the "Status-Quo" and is **Determined to Rise Above Mediocrity**.

A FREEDOM FIGHTER is a **RENEGADE ENTREPRENEUR**... Who **Takes Action** to **Pursue Their Dreams** and Doesn't Let the **Opinions of Others** Hold Them Back.

FREEDOM FIGHTER'S Create Their Own **Destiny, Fortunes, and Futures** Crafting a **LIFESTYLE** Based on How Much **They Want to Earn** and How **They Want** to Live.

FREEDOM FIGHTER'S Don't Answer to 'Bosses' or Worry About 'Competition' -- They **Set New Trends, Forge New Markets, and Dominate Their Market Niches**.

FREEDOM FIGHTER'S Create Income by **Creating VALUE** in the Marketplace, **Creating SOLUTIONS** to People's Problems, and **Making the World a Better Place**...

FINANCIAL FREEDOM FIGHTER'S:

- Enjoy Time and Money Freedom
- Live a Laptop & Mobile Lifestyle
- Build Their Personal Fortunes
- Define Their Personal Legacy
- Follow Their Own Paths
- Heed Their Own Counsel
- Determine How Much They Earn
- Decide How Many Hours to Work
- Dominate Their Markets
- Provide Valuable Solutions
- Create Their Own Destiny
- Are True Pioneers in Life

FREEDOM FIGHTER'S LIVE BY THE CREDO:

"I AM JUST ONE IDEA AWAY..."

I AM A FREEDOM FIGHTER
#FREEDOMFIGHTER

To download this as a printable image visit:

www.clickandgrowrich.com/book/Manifesto

giving their attention to things around them, and as a result they become casual observers of the world.

To truly master your life, it's far more important to understand the power of intentionality and how this directly leads to becoming an active *experiencer* of the

THE CONSCIOUS
CREATOR CREED

If It Is To Be, It Is Up To Me...

I Am The Conscious Creator Of My Life:

My Intentions Will Dictate My Attitudes.

My Attitudes Will Dictate My Beliefs.

My Beliefs Will Dictate My Actions and

My Actions Will Dictate My Experiences.

Since I Am In Control Of My Intentions...

I Am The Conscious Creator Of My Life.

To download this as a printable image visit:
www.clickandgrowrich.com/book/Creed

world, as you'd like it to be. Intentions turn into experiences and let you become an active creator of your life. To help you understand this important relationship, we've created the Conscious Creator Creed.

Once you fully grasp this concept, you'll be unstoppable in your life and in your business. Go ahead and reread that a few times out loud right now. You'll start to feel stronger and more confident almost immediately. It feels good knowing you're in control, doesn't it? *You are.*

Keep an eye out for announcements from us about our upcoming Internet Freedom Experience live events, which will be held every year in the USA, or visit www.InternetFreedomExperience.com to find out more and to preregister.

THE LAPTOP LIFESTYLE

I magine how it would feel if you could work from anywhere in the world—from the beach, on top of a mountain, at your favorite resort, even from a remote South African game reserve. What if you could choose your hours, logging in to check with your virtual team, delegate projects, and check your sales for the day before going to do whatever you want with the rest of your day? Sound like a fantasy? It's not, we've done it. And it's perhaps one of the biggest reasons we do what we do—to show *you* how. Following these methods, you can also design a business that supports the lifestyle *you* choose.

Too many people have this backwards. They allow themselves to fall into a J.O.B. (otherwise known as just-over-broke), with predetermined hours and days to work. The job limits the amount of income they can earn and defines time and lifestyle boundaries for their lives. It doesn't make any sense, and it's why so many people are miserable these days.

In truth, we see no shortage of opportunity; opportunity is all around us. Most people are just too busy getting by to find the time and money needed to take advantage of all the possibilities around us. Or worse, they own a business that really owns them. If you're a business owner already and your top three employees are "me, myself, and I," then you definitely need this book. Possibly every bit as much, if not more, than someone just getting started.

Since the internet is virtually everywhere you would want to be these days, you truly can create a Laptop Lifestyle, running your business from anywhere in the world with Wi-Fi or cellular signal. In 2017, we were speaking in South Africa, and after an event in Cape Town, we decided to go off-grid for a few days deep in the South African bush where our local partners own a small game reserve.

To our surprise, a cell tower was on the property, so we were able to connect on cellular roaming and create a Wi-Fi hot spot in the middle of nowhere. The great thing is you can travel the world, visit exotic bucket-list destinations, and work anywhere there is Wi-Fi. Most luxury beach resorts, even in third world countries, have strong Wi-Fi all the way to the beach. We know because we've done work there many times and from many amazing locations.

In section two, we're going to show you how to hire and train highly qualified virtual employees to run the day-to-day parts of your business while you travel, or just to give you the extra freedom if you want to. All you'll have to do is check in from time to time and give them direction. Imagine for a moment how your life would be different if tomorrow you woke up in a tropical paradise with a cool but balmy breeze blowing by. After a relaxing, delicious breakfast overlooking the beautiful Caribbean Sea, you log on to the resort's Wi-Fi to check your sales from the day before. You made money while you slept, so you can go enjoy a nice, relaxing stress-free afternoon or do whatever you want.

Imagine a well-trained, international virtual team running your business around the clock for a fraction of the cost of finding qualified employees in America. Virtual employees don't require health insurance, benefits, payroll taxes, or self-employment taxes. (Note: Check with your legal and tax professionals to ensure you're operating well within your country's laws and regulations.) But this lifestyle is possible, and thousands are doing it right now all over the world.

In fact, we have many friends and students who are doing this. Some pick up and go to a new country for a month or two at a time, truly immersing themselves in the local culture. (Something you can never really do on a one-week vacation.) When they choose to go somewhere else, they pack up their laptop(s) and go. It's easy and flexible, with planes, trains, and automobiles to take you just about anywhere. The only thing stopping you is you.

If your dream is to travel the world but you'd given up because you're stuck in your job or your current business, *now* is the time to rethink your options. You can break free from these dead-end scenarios and create a lifestyle you desire. If you're stuck in the mentality that you can't do it, continually complaining about your current situation or where you live, keep an eye out the next time you're driving down the highway. *Big, green signs show you the way out of town.* You now have the vehicle—the information presented here—to create personal freedom and go anywhere you truly want to, with a little hard work and following this process.

Increasingly, everything is moving toward mobile. By the time you are reading this, we'll be talking more about building a "mobile lifestyle" than just a "laptop lifestyle." Every year our phones are getting smarter, faster, more powerful, and more capable of doing what you used to do on your home computer or laptop. People today are spending more time on their mobile phones than on their computers, and this trend shows no signs of slowing down.

In fact, on our way to South Africa a few years ago, we picked up a *USA Today* article that said that Facebook's advertising revenue was better than anyone expected. And that their mobile revenues were responsible for 61% of all advertising sales.[5] Today, this percentage is much higher and could be more than 85%. We predict that by 2020 we'll see people spending the majority of their time on mobile, and many websites as we know them will eventually all but disappear, becoming nothing more than an online business card.

The good news is, mobile phones are more portable than laptops and easier to take with you when traveling. You can run your business from wherever you choose to be, no longer shackled to your business or even a hotel room. Some mobile phones are even waterproof. We've literally been floating down an underground river in Mexico and having a video chat with our executive assistant in the Philippines, checking in on the day's tasks. That was our workday. *How do you like to spend your day?*

Now, we're not here to tell you it's all sunshine and rainbows. There is work involved in building your business. But we *are* here to tell you that it's worth it. And if you follow the steps and strategies outlined here, you'll have a much greater chance of success.

Your First Steps

Right away, let's get clear on three simple things. This will ensure you're starting off headed in the right direction. Before we tell you the three simple things, let us start with an analogy. Imagine you're a pilot about to take off in an airplane. Let's say there's no runway, just a wide-open flat space. Wouldn't it make sense to know your destination, or at least a general direction, before taking off? The hardest part in flying somewhere is getting the plane off the ground; you can steer fairly easily once you're in the air. The trip is much harder if you get airborne and realize you're going in the wrong direction.

At that point, it might be easer just to land, turn the airplane around, and take off again in the other direction. But why do that when you could just as easily have taken off in the right direction the first time?

So, let's use that analogy and compare it to your new business. Since getting the new business "off the ground" is also often the hardest part, wouldn't it make sense to first decide and define where you want to arrive? It sounds easier than it is, but it's absolutely critical to be clear on where you want to go. Then, you'll know which direction will likely lead to the greatest chance of success in your journey.

Since most people are notoriously bad at knowing what they want in life, they often find their path by ruling out the things that they *don't* want. Life is all about choices, and continually asking yourself, "Do I like this one better or that one?" Eventually, you figure out what works by process of elimination. This is true in relationships, occupations, travel choices, food, and just about everything. Wouldn't you agree?

To help people identify their best path forward, especially in their first online business venture, we've developed a simple exercise called the Interest, Experience, and Opportunity Worksheet, or I-O-E Worksheet for short. We've provided a diagram and download link below. but you can also find this interactive PDF online in the free resource section in the back of this book. This exercise is a very

IOE WORKSHEET

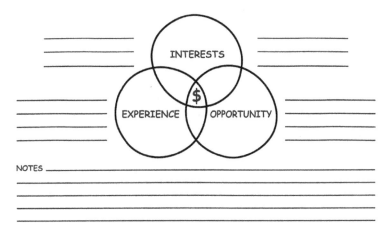

Download the I-O-E Worksheet Here:
www.clickandgrowrich.com/book/IOEworksheet

important first step in determining which *direction* to focus your efforts, even if you haven't yet decided what your big idea will be.

In the first circle of the worksheet is the letter *I*, which stands for *interests* or passions. List all of the things you love to do and would do all day long, even if you weren't getting paid for it, and assuming you didn't have to make a living doing it. Don't filter this list, just do a brain dump of your six to ten favorite hobbies or passions. Why is this an important place to start? Because life isn't just about making money. If you're not passionate about what you do in your new business, you're more likely to lose interest and quit early on when you run into your first challenge. And we don't want that. Stop and consider how many attorneys you know who are actually happy being attorneys. Chances are, not very many.

The reason we have so many "recovering" attorneys out there is because many people went into that profession for the money, only to realize they hated being an attorney. We have nothing against attorneys; they can be very useful for preparing legal documents and protecting you and your business from risk and compliance issues. Our point here is that you should choose a business for which you can maintain a level of passion and fulfillment for a long time. Your success depends on it. Take our word for it, interest matters.

In the next circle, you'll see an *E*, which stands for *experience* or *expertise*. Here, you'll want to list five to six areas in which you have the greatest amount of prior experience or expertise. This could be your current occupation, a prior one, or just something you're good at on the side.

In the final circle, you see the letter *O*, which stands for *opportunities*. Here you'll list five to six of the biggest market opportunities you think are out there, and again, don't filter these. Simply list out as many as you can think of. You may need to do some market research to come up with these but it's fairly easy to do online.

The last step is to look for areas where these three important elements overlap. This is the "sweet spot" where the most money is typically made and a long-term business can be built. Think of interests, experience, and opportunity as a three-legged stool. If any one of the legs is missing, a stool falls over. If you're not passionate about your business long term, you'll lose interest and quit and the stool will fall over. If you don't have experience or expertise in your market, people won't see you as an authority and are less likely to believe you can help them, so they don't buy what you're offering; the stool will fall over. Finally, without market demand (opportunity), you may find yourself with an *unintentional* nonprofit, and you don't want that.

So, start ruling out the less-good ideas. Maybe these ideas will lead to projects you can focus on in the future. But for now, rule out as many as you can until you get down to your top two choices. Then put the worksheet away for three days and come back to it with fresh eyes. Do this as many times as you need to, until your subconscious mind kicks in and gives you a clear vision of the best path for you. Typically, you'll be going about your day, doing something unrelated, and the idea will come to you. This is your light bulb moment, and this is where you should always start, with an idea that truly excites you and will motivate you to push forward and see your idea through to the end. Remember, *you are only one idea away*! So, make sure it's the *right* one.

In the next section, we're going to dive into MP^{5}MS^2 Formula for Success, which you'll be able to use to take your idea to fruition. Keep in mind the first two steps in this formula (Market and People) are critical, so don't skip over them. Your idea will need to pass these two initial filters, and you may need to adapt your idea to ensure everything aligns.

Section Two

MP^5MS^2
THE LITTLE-KNOWN FORMULA
THAT CAN MAKE YOU RICH

THE ACCIDENTAL FORMULA

Now that you have a good primer on online marketing and what this is all about, we're going to dive into the step-by-step process for how you can start, grow, and scale your new online business for the greatest chance of success. Are you ready to get started? Let's go!

Whether you are brand new to all of this or have already ventured into online selling, our "accidental" formula can make you rich if you follow the process, don't give up, and focus on coming up with the right idea.

Remember, you're only one idea away.

To make sure we get off on the right foot, let us clarify. We are not suggesting this process will be easy. It's going to take some work. But by following these steps in the right order, you'll have a much greater chance of success, can get there faster, and avoid the single biggest killer of up to 95% of all new businesses.

But before we get into that, it's important to review how this "formula" came to be. We "discovered" this process by examining all of the important things we had done to build prior successful businesses. We found that the seemingly endless number of tasks needed to build a successful business fit nicely under one of the following nine categories:

- Market
- People
- Products
- Places
- Passion
- Payment
- Marketing
- Selling
- Staffing

If you'll notice the first letter in each of these categories, you'll discover where we came up with the name for our formula: MP^5MS^2.

Breaking the process down into less than ten categories is easier to conceptualize and helps one fight the feeling of overwhelm, doesn't it? However, once the categories became clear, we were then confronted by two critical questions: Which of these areas should you focus on *first*? What's the proper order for the remaining factors?

To answer these questions, we looked back at some of our early failures. We considered not only our personal missteps but also other seemingly good ideas we had watched fail for one reason or another. As we analyzed these past ventures, a very obvious common problem became clear: not enough people wanted the products or services offered.

Have you ever heard somebody talking about how they have the next "big thing," a new idea that will change the world? They may be confident they're on the way to becoming a millionaire. A few months later, you run into that same person and ask how their new project is going. Then, they either quickly change the subject or make up some excuse as to why it didn't work.

Chances are, the person failed because they committed the number one mistake most business owners make when starting a business: they started with the product idea before doing any market research as to whether anybody's actually looking for this product or solution. Remember this: *It's very hard to create a market*, no matter how good your idea is and regardless of how much others should want it or need it.

Let's face it. When people have a problem, they go looking for a solution. And where do most people look first these days? The internet! But even if everybody out there *should* want the new idea and it would improve their lives, if they're not *looking* for it, then, chances are, it's going to be very hard to get them to buy it. And you don't want to be in the *convincing* business.

Another thing to consider is that people don't buy *prevention* nearly as much as they buy *solutions*. Keep this in mind as we go through the rest of this book. In our live events, we reinforce the idea that you can't create a market—unless you're Steve Jobs and have Apple's marketing budget. Do you?

This leads us directly to our accidental formula. We discovered this game-changing blueprint by reverse engineering our prior successes (and failures) and looking at other successful businesses. Let's go through the formula now.

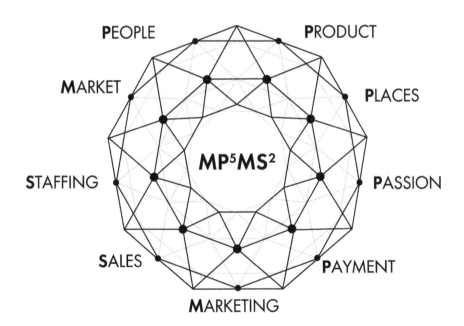

INTRODUCTION TO MP⁵MS²

A s mentioned earlier, when we first decided to teach people how to build a business to make money online, Daniel suggested we come up with a formula for success. As a former six Sigma Black belt engineer while working at Bechtel Corporation, Daniel was trained at using formulas for statistical process improvement to improve results.

Initially we struggled with the idea, believing there wasn't a repeatable "formula" used to achieve our success up to that point. However, when we started white-boarding all the different elements of growing a business, we soon identified nine major categories that enveloped everything we had done to succeed in the past.

When we started asking questions—like, what do you do first, and then what steps to do after that?—we realized that sequence was critical. As with many things, putting things in the correct order is important. You can't bake a cake by adding the icing first, can you? You can try, but chances are, the cake isn't going to turn out very well. *It's the same in business.*

WHY 95% OF ALL
ONLINE BUSINESSES FAIL

T he question of proper order leads us to the number one mistake 95% of all businesses make, which is choosing a product before first identifying a hot, trending market. We've talked about people who come up with a great idea only to abandon it later because they find nobody cares or is looking to buy that product. It's a very common mistake that we see all the time. You might even know someone personally who has done this.

So, we started out our formula with *market*. Choosing your market is the first and most critical step in the MP⁵MS² Formula for Success. Let's examine how to choose a strong market *first*.

MARKET (THE WHEN)

S ince all markets are cyclical, *market* is the *when* in our equation. It might sound counterintuitive to start with the when, rather than the who, what, where, or why, but it's the most important part of the entire process. Market trends are very important. Doesn't it make sense to put yourself where the money is being spent right now? Shouldn't you identify the hot areas in which people are already looking to buy?

 DANIEL STORY

All markets are cyclical. Make sure to remember this, as it's very important. Ideally, you also want to look for cycles that reoccur faster but always keep in mind that you'll be far more successful in a market that is currently trending, and is where people are spending the most money *right now*.

However, it reminds me of a story about a guy I knew who wanted to build a buggy whip company. I know about whips from growing up on a farm where we had horses, and sometimes you needed a good whip to snap for sulky racing to make the horse go faster. He had read about

Market (The When) | 39

the long history of making whips. His whips were going to be the best—beautiful, sleek, leather, lined with a copper thread. They were also going to be expensive because they were all hand made to order, and perfect. So, he believed he was going to be very successful.

Since choosing the right Market is the most important first step, I asked him "How many people do you know that have horses? Did you come on a horse today?" Let me ask everybody reading this: Do you "drive" a horse to work? Do you have a horse at all? I'm sure a few of you do, but for most of you I think you're probably happier with the horsepower from your new car. Am I right? Very few people these days are likely in the market for a new buggy whip.

Had he started this business a hundred years earlier, then the time might have been perfect, but today, it's unlikely to have mass appeal. However, all markets are cyclical and evolving, so always keep an eye out for when a market might be coming back in style.

Here's an interesting example. In 2011 British writer E. L. James (Erika Leonard) had aspirations to become a successful author, and wrote the best-selling book *50 Shades of Grey*.[6] From the genre of *romance and erotica* she was able to write a trilogy of very successful books that also resulted in an upsurge in sales of many products—one of them being riding whips. So maybe it is time to get into that business, because leather whips are not just for horses anymore!

Too often, new entrepreneurs identify a market that isn't being served well or at all and think they have a wide-open market they can dominate. The truth is, it's very likely somebody has already tried to appeal to that market and failed. That's why there doesn't seem to be anybody selling in that market.

Pro Tip: Check your potential market on Google. If you don't see any ads for this market, then there likely isn't a very strong one or perhaps not one at all.

Some see no competition in that space and think they've found a great opportunity, thinking they can be first. However, the opposite is actually true. Lack of competition usually means there isn't a strong enough market for anyone to succeed. Others have likely tried and failed. While exceptions exist, it's always best to identify a hot, trending market with lots of buyers already and then figure out how to position yourself there.

$$MP^5MS^2$$

Market (The When)

How to Determine Hot <u>Info</u> Trends?
Online Resources:

- **Google Search and Google Trends**
- **Amazon Popular Books & Categories**
- **Most Popular Magazines & Subscriptions**
  - **Can Sort by Category of Interest For Ideas**
  - **Ex: Crafts & Hobbies, Business & Investing, Health & Fitness, Professional & Trade, Etc.**
- **Most Popular For Kindle on Amazon**

The good news is, it isn't as hard as it might sound to find a viable market. For example, it can be as simple as googling "top trending markets or products." Two of our students, Mike Fatica and Laura Haxa from the United Kingdom, followed our advice and typed "top trending products in 2016" into Google. The top two results were *matcha tea* and *detox products*. Since they already had a background in natural medicine, these types of products appealed to them.

Following this trend, we created a brand together called *Eternal Vibrance,* which started out offering a matcha tea detox supplement that they white-labeled and had produced by someone else. By surveying this market, we later discovered that 76% of people wanting to detox were primarily interested in losing weight. This is another big secret to success: *asking* your market what they actually want most. Market prospects will often tell what they want, giving you great insight into their interests, fears, hopes, and desires. We'll revisit this later.

Weight loss is what we call an *evergreen market*. Evergreen markets are those that will pretty much always work because they appeal to people's core human emotions, interests, and needs. Some other examples of evergreen markets to consider are dating advice, health and fitness, making money online, real estate investing, financial investing, business opportunities, and making money with social media. That last market is, of course, a relatively new one and although it's emerged recently, it has great long-term potential.

MP^5MS^2

Evergreen Markets

- **Dating Advice**
- **Health & Fitness**
- **Make Money Online**
- **Make Money Investing**
- **Make Money in Real-Estate**
- **New Business Opportunities**
- **Social Media Marketing**

While this book offers many subtle success clues, we suggest you reread the three previous paragraphs. This concept is *that* important. By identifying what your market already wants and providing a solution to their biggest problem or pain, you have the potential to create a very powerful and profitable business—and in the shortest time possible.

On the other hand, if you choose to follow the most common path, which is to come up with a product idea first and then try to *convince* people why they should buy it, you will very likely waste a lot of time and energy, only to find yourself with nominal results. Even worse, you could go out of business, losing all of the time, money, and energy that you invested.

PEOPLE (THE WHO)

In thinking through who, what, where, and why, *people* is the *who* and the second step in MP⁵MS² Formula for Success. Finding the right audience for your product is essential. If you clearly define the type of person you are looking for, it is easier to find them. For example, if you pinpoint your ideal customers as aging male baby boomers living in the Midwest, it will be easier to find that population, don't you think? Fortunately, these days, it's fairly easy to target a specific population online.

For example, Facebook lets you run gender-based ads to males or females. You can choose a specific age range, region, country, state, or city. You can even set a limit on the radius in miles from a city or location. At the time of this book's publishing, you can zero in on an almost unlimited amount of personal interests, demographics, and psychographics. So, if you want to run ads in front of middle-aged, affluent men between 45-55 who like golf; live in the Southeastern United States, say, within 30 miles of Augusta, Georgia; are interested in losing weight; want to improve their golf game; and listen to country music, you can.

A demographic typically refers to age, gender, and geographic location. It's important to identify the population you will connect with and then target that

MP¹MS²

People (The Who)

Who Are Your Best Customers?

− **Find Commonalities Among Them**
− **Look For More People Like Them**
   • **Demographics & Psychographics**
   • **Targeted List Rentals and Solo Ads**
   • **Targeted Facebook & Google Ads**
   • **Newsletters & Magazines**
   • **Affiliate Email Lists**
   • **Offline (Still Works)**

demographic. Our point is this: people are more likely to buy from you if they feel a connection or affinity with you.

One example is a female student of ours who is Vietnamese. She has instant affinity in the Vietnamese-American market just by being Vietnamese. While you can't target your advertising toward a particular race, she was able to Google where the largest concentration of Vietnamese-Americans were located in the United States and then placed ads in these specific markets for her products. It is, however, much better to identify a bigger mass market where you can tap into the physical or emotional needs of the market, and provide a unique solution.

Psychographics encapsulates people's interests, desires, wants, aspirations, fears, frustrations, pains, problems, hobbies, and other emotional drivers. All of these are important, and the more you can find out about your ideal customer's wants and desires, the better you can find them online, particularly in the Facebook platform. Other advanced targeting ad platforms are out there, but, for most people, Facebook is the best.

But if you don't know your ideal customers' attributes, it's hard to find people like them.

Let's look at another example of how you can research people or groups who are most likely to be interested. Does your market niche have an annual trade show? The answer is, they probably do. So, how do you get the list of attendees? You can simply contact the tradeshow owners and say, "I'm thinking of being a sponsor or exhibitor at the tradeshow. Do you have any demographic data you can share with me?" They will usually send information to you *without charge* if you just ask for it.

You will gather all types of valuable information from these reports, including age range, interests, favorite magazines, and websites frequently visited—you name it. Tradeshow coordinators have already done all the work to compile this information. It's useful data because you can then target your ideal people in your identified market via online media like Facebook, Google, LinkedIn, Instagram, YouTube, and others.

MP^1MS^2

People

Resources & Research

- **Contact Magazines or Tradeshows in Your Chosen Niche and Ask For Demographics of Their Customers.**

- **Most Will Send To You Free If They Think You Are a Potential Advertiser.**

- **Once You Know Who They Are, You Can More Effectively Target Them**

- **Then Easier To Find More of Them.**

You can also call magazines and ask the same thing: "I'm thinking of advertising in your magazine. Do you have a PR or media kit on your readership?"

Typically, the magazine has already done extensive surveying of their customer base, which is great information that you can leverage, too. Again, just say you're considering being an advertiser or sponsor, which can be true if it's a good place to reach your ideal prospects in your market. Don't you agree?

In this example, once you know your ideal client's profile, associated companies will likely send you information for free, especially if they think you're potentially going to be an advertiser or sponsor.

This is why our formula, MP^5MS^2, starts with *market* first. Then, you identify your *people* and how you can reach them. Imagine, for example, that you have created the best hunting spear in the world. It is laser guided. It's heat seeking, and it'll hit any prey you throw it toward. Let's say your ideal customer is every hunter living in the Aboriginal outback; this group will 100% want one of these. But, guess what? How are you going to tell them about it? They're not likely on Facebook, LinkedIn, or YouTube. They don't likely watch TV. You need to get in front of them, but how?

It's crucial to *actually reach* the people in your market, not just identify them. Remember the old question, "If a tree falls in the forest and no one is there to hear it, does it make a sound?" This is essentially the same analogy. You can have the greatest product in the world, in a hot, trending market, but if nobody ever knows about it, then you're in trouble. It's not going to sell very well, is it?

Another reason you should research the people in your market is to make sure the population is large enough to build a scalable business.

Once you know your people, it's easier to effectively target more of them. But if you can't find enough people in your market, then your business is limited in how far it can go and how large it can grow.

Having a great idea without a population to sell to is like owning a Ferrari but living on a dead-end street. You can go fast for a little while, and then the fun is over because you run out of road. If you can't find a sizeable market, you're going to run out of prospects. Even if everybody is buying your product, without a large pool of prospects, you'll quickly run out of people to sell to. Bigger markets are your goal because they ensure more people who might buy from you.

One example is the golf market. With no shortage of people into golf, this global market is massive, with millions of dollars spent every year. It's an evergreen market because it's likely always to be there.

One great way to get started in your business and gain fast access to the right people in your market is to set up an *affiliate relationship* or *joint venture deal*. These terms are mostly interchangeable in our industry, and we'll talk more about this under "marketing."

✍ BRETT STORY

To illustrate the power of an affiliate relationship, I'd like to refer back to when I started my last business from scratch. With no prospects or really any advertising dollars to speak of, we had to somehow find our ideal client base and get our message out to them. So, I went to Google and typed in the term "option trading affiliate," and a long list of other companies selling related products came up. So, I reached out to the first one by emailing the owner of the site and asking if he would promote our products for a 50% share of the sales. He said yes.

We had no affinity with or authority in this marketplace and didn't know anybody, yet we launched a very successful company quickly. This is how you can shortcut this whole process: find the experts in your market who already have a relationship with your audience. People typically buy from you when they *know, like, and trust* you. If someone doesn't even know who you are, it's much harder to get them to trust you and buy what you're selling.

But let's say customers know and trust someone else already, and that person recommends you, letting you leverage the relationship he's already built with your ideal audience. It's a great win-win scenario where both sides benefit, and it's how many of the most successful online businesses have started out. The affiliate marketing industry is a multibillion-dollar-per-year industry and according to Statista, "A recent study published by Forrester and Rakuten projects a healthy

$$MP^1mS^2$$

People

Finding Your Ideal Prospects.

- ### Best Way is to Do Joint-Ventures With Affiliates in Your Niche.

  ### Ex: Offer "Free Report" or Free Webinar With a Backend Sale That Pays Affiliate Commissions On All Future Sales.

- ### Build a New List of Targeted Prospects and Buyers *(What You Really Want)*

60% growth for the affiliate industry from 2015 through 2020, with the industry at 6.82B in 2020."[7]

Let's say that Tony has a blog online all about fly fishing and gets 10,000 website visitors per month. Then Bob goes to Tony and says, "I have a free report. It reveals the seven biggest mistakes most fly fisherman make. It also includes three little-known ways to catch more fish than you can eat. If you'll send my promotional emails to your subscriber list and put a banner ad on your blog about my free report, I will pay you 50% of whatever sales come in from my fly fishing video series." Tony says sure, sends out the email, and puts a small banner on his fishing blog for Bob.

He's providing value to the readership in advance. In return, Bob is going to ask for an email address to stay in touch and build his own relationship with his new prospects. How many of you have ever done that, given your name and email address to get something free? Then, guess what? You're now on someone else's email list.

There's a right way and a wrong way to do that. But you should be able to earn a dollar per month from every person on your list if you're doing it right. If you only have five people on your list, it's enough to buy a coffee every month.

MP¹MS²

People

Goal: They Optin To Your Email List

Lead Magnet = Ethical Bribe
- **Free Reports**
- **Free Videos**
- **Free Webinars**
- **Free Content**
- **Free Information**
- **Free Service**

But if you have 30,000 on your list, you could potentially earn up to $30,000 per month. That beats a sharp stick in the eye.

In the example above, when people go to the free report page to obtain their copy of the fly fishing report, Bob then shows them a page that says, "If you're really serious about improving your fly fishing skills, then you might be interested in my $97 video course on how to improve your fly fishing skills and be the envy of all your friends." Let's say that 100 people take him up on the offer and purchase his Fly Fishing Secrets course for $97, for a total of $9,700 in sales. Under their agreement, he would then owe Tony 50% of these sales, or $4,850, which is pretty good for barely doing any work.

This is exactly how we took our business from zero to over $200,000 in sales in the first year, leveraging others' relationships with their email lists for a percentage of the profits. We built an email list of over 100,000 subscribers, and generated sales and profits from that list for years.

Ideally, the affiliate you choose will have an email list of 10,000-50,000 people. *If those email subscribers buy anything from you, you give the affiliate money.* This type of arrangement has changed how business is done online because nobody loses. This is a great way to start out when you don't have a list of your own.

What do we mean by "a list"? This means your email list and how many permission-based email subscribers you have and can send email to. However, email delivery rates and engagement are at an all-time low. Some believe that email is dying as a marketing medium. So increasingly these days, and with the rapid rise of social media, your *list* really needs to be more than just email subscribers.

The widely accepted axiom used to be: *the money is in the list*. But today we're seeing social media play a much bigger role in communicating with people who have an interest in what you do, so it's important to have a big-picture view of what social media offers. In our live trainings, we refer to online prospects as *audiences*, which include email lists, Facebook followers, YouTube subscribers, and users of any other medium you use to communicate with your ideal clients. The new trend is using automated messenger bots to communicate, an exciting new innovation. Whichever methods you choose, compiling an audience is of paramount importance when starting and building a business online. Fortunately, there are more options than ever.

Once you have people on your list or social media audience, it's a good idea to segment them into different sub-segments, showing the right message to the right audience at the right time. This is known as *message-to-market match*. If your message doesn't resonate with people, they're gone. It's wasted time. The message must immediately resonate with them and appeal to their WIIFM antenna, which stands for, "What's in it for me?" If you can create subgroups for exact-message targeting, your rate of response will increase. You do this by segmenting your audience into subgroups in your email software or online advertising campaign, ensuring you're sending the right message to the right audience, the message they want to hear at the right time. For example, sending dog owners an email about a sale you're having on catnip would likely be a waste of time, wouldn't it?

By building value, giving results in advance, and building that relationship first, you will sell more because people buy more when they *know, like, and trust you*. They don't care what you want to sell them. *They want to buy what they want to buy, and the best way is to ask them.* You do that through customer surveys, which again we'll talk more about later.

Another important element in getting your message to more potential buyers is finding similar audiences to your ideal client. One great way is with Facebook's "custom audience" feature, which lets you upload a list of people into Facebook. Using an algorithm, this feature will give you the option to find the 1 million to 10 million people who are most like your ideal prospects that you've uploaded. It's a very powerful feature, one many people don't know about, but it can let you get your message out to millions more who closely match your ideal prospect.

Facebook knows just about everything about its users, from websites visited, interests, behaviors, and even things they've purchased that are most like your products. They can track things we probably hadn't even thought of as part of their use of big data, including where and who you're spending time with, based on your mobile phone's GPS. These practices and capabilities are why Facebook is one of the biggest companies in the world.

While we don't recommend you "buy" email lists online, you can sometimes buy or trade lists online that you can use to create custom audiences. You can also buy solo ads where they'll mail it out for you, and you can then show ads to anyone who clicks to your page using Facebook's retargeting pixel. Always check with Facebook's terms of service to make sure you're compliant with their advertising policies, which may periodically change.

You should never buy an email list to send mail to for one good reason: you'll get hammered with spam complaints. Maybe some of you have heard of these "great deals" where you can buy five million email addresses for, say, a thousand dollars. Don't do it. They're useless because if you email those people without their express permission, it's not only illegal, it will most likely all go to spam, and your email service provider will likely shut you down quickly.

Gmail will look at the first hundred emails and see what most people do with them, and if the majority of people mark your email as spam or delete it, guess where the rest of the emails go? Likely they will all go directly into spam or into the promotions tab, equally as unlikely to be seen. But if subscribers are liking it and opening your emails, it builds a good reputation with Google and the other free email services, so your message is more likely to make it to your prospect's inbox and be seen.

By far, the best way is to build an email list from scratch, from paid-media advertising, social media, or affiliate promotions. Be sure to provide value in advance to acquire their contact information. Then nurture those people over time by sending them value in the form of information that can help them.

Pro Tip: The most critical part of this entire process is picking the right *market* first, the right *people* in that market second, and then finding a *product* or service that people actually want and will pay for.

One way to know what your subscribers want to buy and their market mindset is to visit a forum, chat room, or a Facebook group that's related to the market you are researching. Listen to what they're saying. What are they most frustrated by? What are their biggest problems or pains? What are their greatest wants and aspirations? Listen to what they're saying; then create a product or service around that. The market will tell you what they want most.

Another way to know your prospect's interest is by their actions. Even if they just visited your website to look at one of your products, that action proves some level of interest. Typically, it takes multiple exposures to your product before the consumer is ready to buy, especially if you're offering a more expensive product. Let's talk about how you keep consumers interested.

Ladies, how many of you have ever looked at a pair of shoes on the internet but didn't buy them right away? Did you then see them everywhere you went on the internet? It's a little like online stalking, isn't it? That's called "retargeting," and it's a very effective way to expose prospects to more of what they wanted. When a prospective customer goes to another website, it reads a little pixel on their browser that knows where they've already searched. Then, it knows to show them the same shoes on other sites. This type of technology is pretty sneaky, isn't it?

Retargeting can be effective and inexpensive. The concept works because we know it often takes *seven or more exposures to decide to buy something.* Let's say that after the second time you see the same shoes, you think, *Wow, these guys are everywhere.* You remember all the reasons you liked the shoes in the first place. After a few exposures, you're much more likely to buy them.

If you're selling your own products or services, this technology is ideal because it gives you the appearance of being a much bigger company, one with a giant reach online. The truth is, these retargeting ads are only shown to the people who originally clicked on your website or Facebook page. But the impression is that you're a much bigger business since your ads are on other major-brand websites and also because of multiple touchpoints. It's inexpensive and very effective. This is how you compete with the big companies out there, and it can level the playing field for you.

Now, before we move onto the next section, it's imperative to be crystal clear on your ideal prospects and audience. To help you, we've created two exercises you can download and use right now to define, based on your research, your ideal customer avatar attributes.

CUSTOMER AVATAR

AGE	GENDER	MARITAL STATUS
AGE OF CHILDREN	LOCATION	ETHNIC AFFINITY
OCCUPATION	JOB TITTLE	ANNUAL INCOME
EDUCATION	INTERESTS	BEHAVIORS
HOBBIES	SPORTS	TYPE OF BUSINESS
POLITICS	ENTERTAINMENT	HOME

GOALS	CHALLENGES	VALUES
PAIN POINTS	SOURCES OF INFORMATION	OTHER

Download the Interactive Customer Avatar Worksheet
www.clickandgrowrich.com/book/AvatarWorksheet

Download and fill out the customer avatar worksheet above or from the Click and Grow Rich resource section at the back of this book. A login is required, so simply register for your free account. Using the customer avatar worksheet, fill in any relevant information you know about your prospects already, either through existing customers or prospects from your market surveys. It's best not to guess here, because invariably you will miss something important. However, you can do that in the beginning and revise as you go along.

The important part here is to list as many demographic and psychographic attributes as you can to form a mental picture of your ideal customer. This will help you find more people like them. It will also help you target them either through social media or online (or offline) advertising mediums like Facebook, which allows you to hone in your ideal prospect by targeting various interests and behaviors your prospect has.

With the customer avatar *exercise*, you'll dive deeper into their psychological drivers, desires, pains, and frustrations. The way to use this exercise is to think about the things they want to move away from on the left side of the square, and where they want to move towards on the right. Now think about whether their reasons for wanting to this are immediate (real) or imagined and possibly off into the future.

An example of an immediate desire to move away from something would be a current pain or frustration that they're looking to resolve right now, which you would write down in box number one. Over to the right, and in box number two you'll want to list their immediate wants and desires, which is usually a resolution to a pain or frustration in box number one.

In box number three, you would list any of their known fears that keep them up at night worrying about, whether real or irrational. Their desire to resolve them is the same. And over to the right in box number four, you would list any goals or aspirations that they may have for the future. There is extra space down below to list these out, and the PDF below is interactive.

This is a very valuable exercise that we recommend you take time to do, and that will pay off for you in the long run by better understanding your prospects and customers. Simply by understanding their fears and frustrations, their wants and aspirations, as well as their core emotional drivers, you'll know how to sell better to them.

As humans, we're hardwired to avoid pain and seek pleasure, so this is the purpose of this exercise: to get dialed into what that looks like for your ideal prospect.

CUSTOMER AVATAR EXERCISE

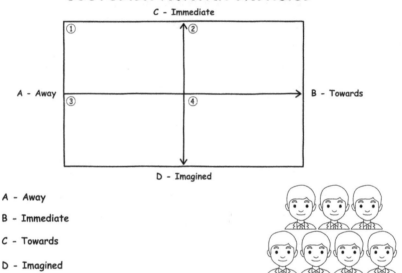

A - Away

B - Immediate

C - Towards

D - Imagined

Download the Interactive Customer Avatar Exercise
www.clickandgrowrich.com/book/AvatarExercise

 **DANIEL STORY**

If you want what others don't have, then you must do what others won't do. To create the life you want, you must be willing to do what others will not. Are you willing to make the time to find the right people—people who will help create your ideal life by being your best customers? You'll likely spend a lot of time marketing to and interacting with these people, so think about what you value most in your colleagues, partners, prospects, and customers. What characteristics should your ideal clients possess?

I own part of a premium cigar manufacturing company called Payne Mason Cigars. When creating that business, my partners and I had to choose who we wanted to be around, the kind of customer we would enjoy interacting with. We could have chosen to enter retail "cigar shops," like 97% of cigar manufacturers do. Or we could go after the 3% of cigar consumers who prefer ultra-premium, aged tobacco. We chose the latter, because we wanted to target the ultra-premium side of the market where there is less competition.

The average cigar smoker isn't willing to spend that kind of money. They want a cheap $3-$10 cigar (maybe $20-$40 for a special occasion, to brag about the Cuban they once had), which they can get from most cigar retailers. This is not our buyer. We market to the premium buyer who wants a status symbol *no one else* has. For example, we charge as much as $599 for a single Winston Churchill DNA 53 and that is why we are the cigar supplier for the NFL, PGA, NRA, Bugatti, and Gulfstream Jets and we supply 70% of mega-yacht owners worldwide. Every year, we are invited to be the only rollers for the Master Private players club and are in premium golf properties like Pebble Beach, Spyglass Hill, and the NIGA private player clubs. Because that's where our ideal buyers are.

I'm not saying this to boast—okay, yes I am—but I'm also pointing out that instead of choosing massive production, we chose to market to the elite. Thus, we have made up for not mass-producing cigars by instead offering our customers a handmade, 5- to 16-year-old-aged product that very few can afford. We want it that way. Let the Patels and Fuentes fight it out for the low and middle while we focus on people in the high-end market.

When you choose your people carefully and offer them what others don't, you and your products will have a loyal customer for life.

PRODUCT (THE WHAT)

Now that we've covered why you must first identify a hot, trending *market*, where a definable market segment of *people* are already looking to spend money, we can now talk about identifying the right *product* or service to sell.

As we've already mentioned, most people start with a product, and this error is the reason 95% of all businesses ultimately fail. Because they didn't identify a hot market for their products and services in the first place, they later realize there wasn't a strong enough demand to support their business idea. If nobody cares, it doesn't matter that everybody "should" want or need what you're selling. Nor does it matter that you could be "first" to this (non-existent) market.

People want what they want to buy, not what you want to sell them. So, it's imperative to first identify what consumers are already looking to buy and then give them more of that. While exceptions to the rule exist, our MP^{5}MS^2 sequence is a good method to adopt as you're just starting out.

MP^{2}MS^2

Product

What To Sell

- **Most Start Here - This is THE Biggest Mistake 95% of ALL Companies Make.**

- **People Buy What They Want To Buy, Not What You Want To Sell To Them.**

- **Identify What People Are Buying First. Make and Give Them What They Want.**

✈ DANIEL STORY

Once I was speaking on stage in Sydney, Australia, on the same day as Robert Kiyosaki, and I heard him say that he was "good" at real estate, and had sold a lot of education in this market. However, he followed that with a surprising statement; he said that his real love was *not* real estate. Rather, his affinity for real estate came from the life it afforded him and it was just a means to an end.

I often tell this story in our live classes, because I think this approach holds true for many. Even after considering their personal interests and skills, many entrepreneurs go for the biggest opportunity available, even though they may not love the product or market. The promise of greater profits sometimes outweighs the passion for a particular object or subject. In the end it depends on you. The best combination is both—a strong market opportunity and passion.

From what I have seen, I would say about 70% of successful entrepreneurs end up doing something because there is a huge market, and the opportunity is just too good to pass up. For example, two of our student partners have a company that makes alpaca clothing and socks. My love of socks is negligible because I live in Florida, so I'm in flip-flops most of the day. However, the number of people who love these socks and spend a lot of money on them is amazing. So, why not get behind this product?

A similar example is the story of UGG boots, which has now become a billion-dollar company. Founder Brian Smith, who we've met and spent time with, tells of how it all started. In this case, it was his passion for the product and the extreme loyalty and passion of the people that were buying them, mostly surfers in the early days. After years of staying small and relatively unknown, they bridged the gap from surfers to mainstream markets—becoming a huge success story, because everybody who tried them loved the products so much.

This is one rare example of how a unique product helped *create* a new market category where none existed before. If you find a market with people who want and need products you are really excited to make, then go for it. Maybe, just maybe, you will end up with a huge international growth opportunity that begs to be explored, because the product could potentially make so much money you can build a big business around it.

We recommend you consider these questions: Do you already have a product? If not, do you want to create one yourself or have someone else create one for you? For example, you can buy the resale rights to private-label products—products somebody else has created and is willing to give you a license to resell as your own.

While these typically won't generate large incomes for you in the long run, they might be a good place to start. Some people start with a private-label product to test out their market hypothesis, and if it works well, they can then create their own product, one similar to the product they purchased.

Another way to get started selling products online is via an affiliate. We talked about an affiliate relationship earlier, where one person can market and sell another person's product for a sales commission. If you are new to this concept, have a look at websites such as clickbank.com or jvzoo.com, which are affiliate marketplaces that match buyers and sellers around the world. Other sites are out there, but these are the biggest and sell hundreds of millions of dollars of products per year online.

These sites are also a good place to do your market research; simply look in the top-selling product categories to see which products and markets are trending. These sites specialize primarily in digital products, which can be downloaded, though ClickBank has started selling physical products. For more physical product trends, check the top-selling product categories on amazon.com and alibaba.com.

"On the Internet, nobody knows you're a dog."

You can also hire virtual writers to create information products for you as work for hire. You can even have these created under a pseudonym if you don't want to have your real name on the product. As this cartoon suggests, you can be anyone you want online.

For example, in 2001 an early online marketing pioneer named Eben Pagan created a very successful dating product called Double Your Dating, but he chose not to use his real name. Instead he used the name of David DeAngelo to sell his products online. At one point, he had grown his business to over $20 million per year in online sales. So, if you're a well-known professional or already have a brand online and don't want your name coming up in Google searches for your new business, you can use a pen name.

Next, we'll talk about two important types of products: primary products and secondary products. Primary products are what you sell first in your sales funnel, not including any teaser sales or free giveaways. Your primary product is your core offer, and the creation and marketing of it is what you will likely devote most of your time to.

With your primary products, you can offer a one-time payment or break payments up into multiple payments. Marketing legend Dan Kennedy says, "There is a person for every price, and a price for every person." While not everybody will be willing to pay full price for your product, they might still want it at *some* price. So, ask yourself, does it make sense to offer a slightly better deal or a one-time discount to turn them into a customer? The answer is typically *yes*.

One common misconception people have is the belief that the purpose of a customer is to make a sale. In truth, it's the opposite: *The purpose of the sale is to get a customer,* one who will buy over and over again in the future—*if* you take good care of them. As we also say in our industry, "The money is in the back end," in future customer sales and upsells.

Secondary products (or upsells) are what you offer after they've purchased your primary product. This is where the majority of income can be made, which most people don't realize. One way you can offer secondary products it is to offer one-time offers (OTO) as an upsell.

For example, after somebody buys the initial product you're offering and before you take them to the thank-you page, you show them a message:

"WAIT! Today only. Take advantage of this special offer. Get your copy of *XYZ Solutions* today for just $7—normally $47 (this offer expires once you leave this page)."

Several psychological principles are at play here. The biggest is the principle of scarcity, which is the tendency to value an item more if it is perceived as rare. We'll discuss this principle more under "marketing," but this strategy is an easy first upsell to ease the consumer into buying more. Ideally, you would offer additional secondary offers/upsells after this.

Another great example of a secondary offer would be to offer a monthly subscription to some kind of ongoing value delivery, like an online membership site or, for physical products, a monthly delivery of a new supply of products, like a box-of-the-month program, which is currently a very popular way to supplements, clothing, or any consumables.

This is also called a "continuity" offer because it creates continuity of income in your business. It's the best scenario because it creates passive, recurring income for you. It's also a great way to increase *the average customer value* of your customers, which allows you to spend more in advertising to acquire new leads and customers. Why is this important? Because in marketing, the person or company that can afford to pay the most to acquire a customer often wins. Keep that in mind.

Now, let's take a look at some real examples of how this works. Below, you'll see a screenshot of an actual launch we did in the Forex market where we were selling a $1,997 primary product. Notice that we did fairly well on this promotion, and 190 people took us up on our initial offer, which resulted in $379,146 in sales (excluding refunds) before paying affiliate commissions. Note: these are not typical results, and you should read our full disclaimer.

But also notice 53 people said *no* to the initial offer and, for whatever reason, wouldn't pay the full price. However, by offering them a payment plan, where they only had to pay $997 up front, with two additional payments of $500, we brought in an additional $52,841, not including the subsequent rebills. That's pretty good, for very little additional work, isn't it?

After that, well over 100 people who didn't choose to pay the $997 up-front fee opted to take the seven-day $7 special, which, after initial rebills, generated

Primary (Lead) Products

Products	Price	Sales	Volume
Forex Profit Predictor 10-Pair $2995 1-Pay	$2,995.00	4	$11,980.00
Forex Profit Predictor 10-Pair Upgrade	$1,000.00	13	$13,000.00
Forex Profit Predictor 10-Pair Upsell	$1,000.00	33	$33,000.00
Forex Profit Predictor 4-Pair $1997 1-Pay	$1,997.00	190	$379,146.00
Forex Profit Predictor 4-Pair $7 Special	$0.00	264	$144,624.00
Forex Profit Predictor 4-Pair 997 3-Pay	$997.00	53	$52,841.00
FPP Weekly Classes 30-Day	$0.00	44	$0.00
FPP Weekly Classes 60-Day	$0.00	242	$0.00

These results are not typical of the average person and may not be typical for you. You may achieve greater success or have no success at all. Like with many things, your result using this information will depend on your efforts, and we are making no claims of future income that you may achieve using this information. Your success depends on your effort alone.

an additional $144,624 in sales. *And again, that beats a sharp stick in the eye.* How would you like an "extra" $144,624 dollars next month? Every month? We've used this type of strategy multiple times with similar results.

Now, let's look at the secondary offers. You can see from the graphic below that after offering them our primary product, we immediately followed up with a $1,000 upsell into a more advanced version of our program; 46 people took advantage of this, generating an additional $46,000.

Secondary Products (Upsells)

Products	Price	Sales	Volume
Forex Profit Predictor 10-Pair $2995 1-Pay	$2,995.00	4	$11,980.00
Forex Profit Predictor 10-Pair Upgrade	$1,000.00	13	$13,000.00
Forex Profit Predictor 10-Pair Upsell	$1,000.00	33	$33,000.00
Forex Profit Predictor 4-Pair $1997 1-Pay	$1,997.00	190	$379,146.00
Forex Profit Predictor 4-Pair $7 Special	$0.00	264	$144,624.00
Forex Profit Predictor 4-Pair 997 3-Pay	$997.00	53	$52,841.00
FPP Weekly Classes 30-Day	$0.00	44	$0.00
FPP Weekly Classes 60-Day	$0.00	242	$0.00

These results are not typical of the average person and may not be typical for you. You may achieve greater success or have no success at all. Like with many things, your result using this information will depend on your efforts, and we are making no claims of future income that you may achieve using this information. Your success depends on your effort alone.

But that's actually not where the real money came in. As you can see in the figure below, we then offered them 30- and 60-day free trials of our weekly live webinar classes, which then rebilled at $297 per month, and 286 said yes to that.

Subscription/Continuity

Products	Price	Sales	Volume
Forex Profit Predictor 10-Pair $2995 1-Pay	$2,995.00	4	$11,980.00
Forex Profit Predictor 10-Pair Upgrade	$1,000.00	13	$13,000.00
Forex Profit Predictor 10-Pair Upsell	$1,000.00	33	$33,000.00
Forex Profit Predictor 4-Pair $1997 1-Pay	$1,997.00	190	$379,146.00
Forex Profit Predictor 4-Pair $7 Special	$0.00	264	$144,624.00
Forex Profit Predictor 4-Pair 997 3-Pay	$997.00	53	$52,841.00
FPP Weekly Classes 30-Day	$0.00	44	$0.00
FPP Weekly Classes 60-Day	$0.00	242	$0.00

These results are not typical of the average person and may not be typical for you. You may achieve greater success or have no success at all. Like with many things, your result using this information will depend on your efforts, and we are making no claims of future income that you may achieve using this information. Your success depends on your effort alone.

So, this is where it gets really exciting. The grand total for this promotion in the first 60 days, after these free-trial rebills came in, was $634,591, with residual recurring monthly income of $133,000 *per month*. To be clear, these figures may not be exact, due to refunds, and, in full disclosure, some people dropped out

of the recurring classes. So, these recurring figures dropped by about 10% per month because we didn't promote it again, but still, nothing to sneeze at, is it?

This promotion worked so well, we decided to use the same format when we launched a different product in the same market. As you can see from the image below, in this new promotion, we generated $1,408,388 in upsells alone from secondary products, not including the primary product sales, which were also significant at a $2,397 initial product price.

In this example, 310 people took our $1,000 upsell offer for a total of $309,953.44 in additional "extra" sales, and again, we offered free trials of our monthly recurring classes, which generated substantial monthly revenue, in addition to us then offering some of our older products to them, which at that point, weren't selling well anyway, resulting in another $21,276.

Results From a Single Product Launch
$1,408,388 in Secondary Sales After Initial Purchase

Product	Price	Sales	Volume
FM Live Trading Class 60-Day Trial	$297.00	2039	$408,256.74
FM 10 Currency Pairs Upgrade	$1,000.00	310	$309,953.44
FM Live Trading Class 30-Day Trial	$297.00	933	$244,751.26
FM Live Trading Class 90-Day Trial	$197.00	951	$165,440.00
FM Live Trading Class Special	$197.00	805	$158,488.00
FM Live Trading Class	$197.00	256	$50,467.46
FM Live Trading Class Turtle Special	$97.00	312	$30,264.00
FM Live Trading Class Upsell	$297.00	75	$22,275.00
FM Live Trading Class	$297.00	61	$18,117.00
FM Technical Analysis CD's	$197.00	87	$17,139.00
FM Live Trading Class Downsell	$197.00	21	$4,137.00

These results are not typical of the average person and may not be typical for you. You may achieve greater success or have no success at all. Like with many things, your result using this information will depend on your efforts, and we are making no claims of future income that you may achieve using this information. Your success depends on your effort alone.

Another key point is that your older information products become long-term assets that you can continue to sell to generate additional revenue. So, while these numbers certainly aren't typical, people are achieving similar, even greater results online, and you can too…

The biggest factor, again, is choosing a strong market where people are actively looking for a solution. Remember, if you're solving a pain or problem for other people, they will gladly give you money. The bigger the pain or problem you are solving, the more money they will typically spend with you, depending on the situation.

How do you find a problem worth solving? Research. First, you can look at what others in your market are selling, which validates the presence of a strong market. Once you have done that, we recommend you ask your market about their biggest fears, frustrations, wants, and aspirations, as we've talked about.

Next, go online and start looking for the best solutions available. Anybody can virtually become an expert at anything by spending a few weeks researching any topic online, just by going to Google. The best part is, you really only need to know 10% more than the next person, and then you're the expert!

Now, obviously, we're not talking about brain surgery here. But 97% of all information is already available on the internet, so why reinvent the wheel? Your prospect could do the same thing, but he is too lazy. The old adage, "Teach a man to fish and feed him for life," is wrong. People don't want to learn how to fish; they want fish perfectly sautéed in butter, with a side of asparagus and drizzled in lemon juice, on a plate, ready to eat right now. We live in a society that expects immediate gratification. So, if you'll take the time and effort to research, compile, and create a solution for them, *they will very likely buy it.*

Remember, you can offer *two types of products.* Your primary product is your core product, the one you'll build a brand around and use to make a name for yourself in the market. With your primary products, you can sell them at one price or have multiple price points for different levels of service (beginner, intermediate, advanced). Or, as we mentioned, you can also offer different payment options.

Secondary products are anything you sell after that initial sale, which can include a simple upsell of more of what they just purchased, an advanced version, a monthly membership, or even older existing products. You can even offer a bundle at a discount.

V SELLING

HOW TO
2X, 3X EVEN 10X
YOUR SALES

cydec

This is game changing, and if you really grasp this concept, which nobody else is teaching, you'll gain an advantage in your marketplace. We call it "V-Selling," which stands for "Value Selling."

What does that mean? Let's say someone comes to your website, and you have one standard price. They would like to purchase, but your price is out of their price range, a bit too expensive. What chance do you have of selling something else or upselling them—which is where the really money is made—if they leave your site? *Almost zero.*

In this example, wouldn't it make sense to try to offer them a slightly different offer, a slight discount or additional bonus material at the moment of their greatest indecision? While they're already on your order page—or at least have buying intent—wouldn't you want to make your offer as appealing as possible? Yes, absolutely, and we've proven this works. Using this V-Selling concept, you can actually recapture and reduce your order form abandonment by up to 80%, simply by offering a 20% one-time-only discount at the point of purchase—but only if they try to leave.

Remember, there's a *person for every price and a price for every person.* If someone makes it to your order page and leaves, it's not because they're not interested. It's because the price/value equation isn't quite right for *them.* Have you ever wanted to buy something, but it was slightly too expensive, so you didn't buy? Is it also true that you *would have* bought if the product was slightly cheaper or the site offered a payment plan?

We've all had this experience. And that's why V-Selling is so powerful. This often-overlooked area can be a hidden profit booster for most business owners. You're likely losing tens of thousands of dollars in revenue by not meeting your customers where they are and giving them a chance to buy at the price where they see the most *value*. To read more about V-Selling and to see some examples, visit our blog online at http://blog.cydec.com.

"Person for every price, price for every person"

You know when you fly in an airplane, everyone pays a different price for those seats, but the plane is always full because airlines know how to find that price/value equation.

Have you ever wanted to fly somewhere and tried to get the best price for your seat? Perhaps you called or went online months in advance, when the plane was empty and undersold, and reserved your flight for a cheaper price. But, let's say you need to fly somewhere at the last minute.

Now the plane is almost full, and the rates have gone way up because so few seats are left. But you really need to get to your destination, so the *value* of the seats has gone up for *you*, so you purchase the ticket. The price/value equation has tilted in favor of the airline, and they can now command a premium price. (Unless the plane is still nearly empty, and then the airline is willing to sell the seats for less than their price months earlier, just to fill the plane; it happens, believe it or not.) The airline wants to fill the seats because they need to pay gas costs for the trip, so they work with the passengers through discounts or bonus offers and they offer a price the customer will accept.

Or, in the case of a discount airline, like Spirit, they offer very inexpensive seats on their flights to attract the passenger looking for the best value.

These passengers don't care about all the extras; they just want to get to their destination. But once the flight is booked, what happens? The airline then tries to upsell you by offering upgrades, like Wi-Fi, mileage boosters, and early or priority entry. In the case of Spirit, you pay extra for baggage.

Why is this important to note here? Because the difference between success and failure in business is often in the small margin you're either making or losing. If you can cost-effectively buy advertising at a profit, you can grow your business. If you're losing money here, you have a problem. Many companies go negative on initial sales because their *cost to acquire a customer* (CAC) is greater than what they are making in initial return on investment (ROI). But, they are willing to do this because they know they can make it up with upselling after the initial purchase.

The important takeaway here is this: if you're letting your potential buyer leave without buying, you're losing a potential customer, who may have bought some, many, or *all* of your high-value upsells and secondary offers. We can't stress this point enough because very few people are getting this right.

So, how do you get a prospect—who has seen your product offer, has enough interest to click over to your order page, but, for whatever reason (usually price), has decided now is not the right time and tries to leave your order page—to stop in their tracks and reconsider their decision? How do you get them to then buy your product(s) and then buy another two times, three times, or even ten times more of your products or services right then and there *(because of a psychological phenomenon called consistency of commitment)?*

One way is with a visually attractive exit pop-up offer. Grab the would-be buyer's attention with a compelling "Wait, before you go!" video or even just an attractive image offering a 20% off, one-time-discount offer.

Now, some of you might be thinking, "I see these exit-page offers all the time, and they're annoying!" Yes, they are annoying—because they're in the wrong place (and ugly). If you're trying to show a "Wait, before you go!" offer on your *sales page*, where your prospect hasn't yet decided if he even wants your product (and sees no value), then why would offering them a cheaper price have any impact, other than annoying them?

But when your prospect has shown interest by clicking over to your *order* page, *then* if they don't continue to buy, it's because their personal price/value equation hasn't been met. So, like the airline, your objective is to find the tipping point for them *individually* and get them to buy your product at their price. Because *then and only then* will they have a chance to see your upsell offers, and as we've pointed out, upsell is where you both make more money and provide greater value to your customer.

Think of it this way: if you're not doing everything you can to persuade your customers to buy your products (assuming you are offering them valuable solutions), then you're really doing them a disservice by letting them leave without buying. This isn't sales "trickery." It's tried-and-true marketing advice that works, to the tune of $1.4 million in "extra" sales in the example above. How many of you could use an extra $1.4 million right now? Our examples aren't normal, but they *are achievable* by following these principles and putting in the work.

So, even if you have to present multiple offer variations to your prospect or if you have to offer them a "free" version in the form of a free-trial or free + shipping offer, it can still be very profitable for you once you factor in upsells and future recurring revenue.

For example, you might offer a free or $1 trial of your digital information product or membership site, which, after the first 30 days, automatically rebills at $47 per month. Once your prospect takes you up on your free offer, you can immediately upsell them on other slightly more advanced products, bundles, or services. The key is to get them to buy the first time and give you a credit card or other payment method. Then, you can more easily convert to secondary sales. The best way to do this is with a one-click upsell offer. Here's how it works.

Immediately after someone becomes a customer by purchasing one of your products, you should present them with another offer, typically for a larger purchase amount. Because they just bought one of your products and justified that decision logically and emotionally, they are in a prime state to buy again. So, this is the best time to show them a better offer, an expanded offer, a subscription offer, or other complimentary products and services. Typically, at least 10%-20%

of your customers will always take the next-level solution you offer, but *only if you offer it obviously*. But by not offering secondary products and upsells, you're leaving money on the table. And, as we've shown, this is where the real money is made.

For example, if someone orders your course on how to grow tomatoes, then you should immediately offer courses on other complimentary gardening skills. They key is *complimentary* offers that might enhance what they just purchased. So, if a customer orders one bottle of supplements, offer them three to six additional bottles at a better price. In their mind, they've already decided it's a good decision to buy your product. They've overcome the emotional hurdle of getting out their credit card to spend money with you. By presenting them with an offer that seems better *to them* logically, it's easier for them to justify the decision to buy *more*.

In our case, we started with investment-related educational and software packages. Once customers made the decision to buy a course on options or Forex, we were either offering them more of the same (Ten Forex pairs vs. only four) or other complimentary programs. If you have done your market research and found a passionate crowd to sell to, a large percentage of them usually want to get as much information as possible to solve their problems.

With technology, you can make this decision much easier, with less friction, by simply showing an order button that allows them to "click" once to add the upsell to the order, without having to reenter all of their personal and billing information again. This is nothing new in selling online, but if you're new to selling yourself, this is an important concept.

For physical products, like health supplements, skin-care and beauty products, or anything consumable that customers would likely need more of every month, arguably the best way to sell this is with a free + shipping offer. You might say, "Pay $0 today, plus a shipping and handling fee of $7.95, and we'll send you a free sample bottle of the product." Then, 30 days later, you would automatically ship another unit of the product for your regular monthly cost of, say, $39.99. This gets them into a subscription, or continuity program, that generates recurring monthly revenue for you, and that means passive income.

The $7.95 in this example is the shipping cost, which is reasonable for them to justify. But that should cover both your product cost and the shipping fees so that it doesn't cost you anything to acquire that customer. We'll get into sales strategy and more advanced tactics later on in this section.

Why should you consider this type of strategy? Because it's harder than ever to get somebody to buy from you the *first* time, but it's easier than ever to get somebody to buy from you the *second* and *third* time if you give them good value on their first purchase so that they start to know, like, and trust you. On this first purchase, they're really buying *you*. Once they buy from you and you give them value, then selling them more of your products and services becomes much easier. But you have to build the relationship first.

Now, let's talk about drop-shipping. Maybe you don't want to create your own products, but would rather resell a well-known product or brand in an existing market. After all, people are already looking for it, and you can easily have the manufacturer ship orders out to the customer on your behalf. Or, maybe you discover a hot product in a strong market and decide to have it manufactured in another country where the costs are lower, like China. Using a well-known website called alibaba.com, you can contract to have these produced and shipped to America to your customers. Many people are doing this and shipping items directly to Amazon, which then ships products out to customers.

MP^2MS^2

Physical Products

Create Your Own
- **More Work and Expensive Up Front**
- **Find Fulfillment Center to Pack & Ship**

Drop Shipping
- **Pro – Sell Well Known Products**
- **Con – Make Less Profit Margin**

Affiliate Marketing
- **Earn Commissions**

Amazon is no longer just a bookstore. They are primarily a fulfillment center, and they're the best in the world at shipping and logistics. With their Fulfilled By Amazon (FBA) program, you can literally ship your products to them and they'll handle all the orders for you. They will ship your products to your customers and then send you the profits.

One of the pros of drop-shipping physical products is you can create products that are already known in the marketplace and are a well-known brand with existing demand. You can sell well-known products that people are already looking for. The biggest negative is that you'll make less profit because you're not the one creating the product, but it can be a great way to get started.

Think of it this way; you can sell a product online to a customer who pays you the retail price, then your distributor or the manufacturer ships the product(s) to your customer on your behalf, then bills you the wholesale cost of the product. Typically, you'll have 30-60 days to pay, which is essentially an interest-free loan. You can use the float on the money owed along with the built-in profits to grow your business.

Let's say you have a favorite passion or hobby in a particular area, so you are familiar with a market you can sell to. Or, suppose you want to sell Gucci handbags or something high-end like that, something people already want. You could look into becoming a reseller and set up a wholesale account to resell goods online. Then, you just drop-ship your products from the distributor to your customers. Or, at the very least, you could then buy handbags for personal use at wholesale and write off your own purchases now that you're in that business.

Affiliate marketing is great way to sell other people's products and earn commissions on every sale, *without having to deal with any customer service on the products you sell.* Did you know that you can sign up as an affiliate for Amazon? If you send somebody your affiliate link and they buy a $3 item, you'll might earn a whopping 20% of that $3. But, if they then go buy a new HD flat-screen TV, along with all the cables and other electronics Amazon recommends to them as "Customers who bought this, also bought that," you'll earn commissions on these things also, as well as anything else they buy for the next 30 days. That's pretty good for not having to do a whole lot of work.

Digital products can also be sold as an affiliate. This is a great way to get started because you can focus on marketing, rather than creating a product yourself. Some people just want to be affiliates, and they earn a full-time income this way. If you have a popular blog, radio show, podcast, or website, then you can be an affiliate for other people by offering their products to your audience in return for a sales commission. For digital products, a good place to start is on ClickBank, which is a huge affiliate marketplace that matches affiliates and product owners together.

Another simple way to get started is to start selling private-label rights products, products created by someone else who gives you permission to resell these products as your own once you buy from them the first time. You can find marketplaces for these online also, and all you have to do is look on Google for "master resale rights" or "private-label rights" websites. Some examples include Bigproductstore.com, IDPLR.com, and Master-resale-rights.com, just to name a few, but you should do a Google search for other sites like these if this idea interests you.

The big advantage is all you have to do is buy these products once from the creator, then you can sell them forever and keep all the money yourself. They will provide you with proven products and sales materials so that all you have to do is focus on marketing. It's also a good place to research popular markets and get started selling products online.

You can even hire someone online to create digital products for you, such as downloadable books, home-study courses, software, or any valuable content that you don't have time to create. Many online resources are out there for finding great people to outsource work to, like fiverr.com, guru.com, and upwork.com. You own the product you pay to have produced; thus, you can focus on marketing and sales. However, in this case, you will have to handle customer support, billing, accounting, and management of the product delivery and downloads.

A variation of this strategy, which can be a very effective and profitable shortcut, is to find an existing expert in your chosen market and ask them to partner with you. Many book authors and noted authority figures are not very good at marketing themselves, so you'll be surprised how receptive many of them will be if you approach them as a marketing expert. (After reading this book, you'll know more than 90% of people out there.) All you have to do is contact them and say that you'll do the marketing if they'll provide the expert content, which they usually already have plenty of. We've used this strategy many times and created more than one multimillion-dollar business, as well as other very profitable joint ventures using this strategy.

Once you have built up a name in your industry and have your own list of followers, who have a positive relationship with, you can look into more of a publisher model. Instead of having one or two primary partners, you can then approach multiple experts in your niche and offer to promote or "publish" their materials and trainings to your list or audience (social media, email, blog, radio, etc.) for a share of the profits. The publisher model gives you more stability than a pure partner model because partnerships don't always work out.

One of the most successful examples of this model is a very profitable company that you've likely never heard of, Agora Inc., which generates well over $500 million per year, publishing a number of other experts' newsletters.[8] Though they promote various brands in the health and wealth markets, the

MP²MS²

Digital Products

Find an Expert to Create For You
- **Search For an Expert in Your Niche**
- **Partner or Publish**
- **Partnership**
  - Pro: **More Committed to Success and Quality**
  - Con: **Has Ownership and Harder to Separate**
- **Publisher Model**
  - Pro: **Keep More of the Profits and Control**
  - Con: **They Are Less Committed Long-Term**

company was started by two individuals in Baltimore, Maryland. This model has incredible stability because if one or more of your experts doesn't work out, you can just replace them with another because, these days, experts are everywhere and easy to find. In truth, *the marketing of the business* is *the business,* so if you have the audience and the marketing skills, you can win against all the other so-called "experts" in the long run.

In terms of creating your own products, or even when working with partners to create new digital products, one of the very best ways, which has generated millions in sales for us, is to simply record your screen using any number of the computer screen recording programs available, like Camtasia or SnagIt. If you can create (or your expert partner can convert their existing content into) a simple PowerPoint or Keynote presentation, then you can easily record that presentation and turn it into money by selling it as an information product. Both of these software programs have 30-day free trials, which you can download online.

The pros of creating your own products are that you'll have better control over the final product and they'll have a higher perceived value than selling someone else's product. Also, you'll be in charge. The downside of this method is that can be more difficult. For example, you might have to record, edit, and produce digital recordings to complete the final product yourself. Another drawback here is that some people may purchase your product, copy it, and then ask for a refund, which can happen. Some will even try to distribute and sell your digital product as their own, but it's not something to worry about or let it get in your way.

One of our favorite approaches—and, if we had to start all over again, we would start here—is to create and deliver live or recorded webinars.

One of the pros of running webinars is that they can be delivered "live." No editing is necessary, which is often the most time-consuming part of creating recorded video product. You can also record your live web webinars and sell access to the archives as part of an online members' website. You can even run webinar replays or recast them as "live," such that visitors don't know it's been recorded and replayed. The biggest negative of *live* webinars is that you have less

Digital Products

MP^3MS^2

Create Your Own

- **Recorded and Sold as Download**
  - Pro: Better Control of Final Product
  - Pro: Higher Perceived Value = Charge More $
  - Con: More Difficult to Record, Edit and Produce
  - Con: Easy to Copy and Distribute and/or Refund

- **Sold Live As a Webinar**
  - Pro: Can Deliver 'Live' So No Editing Necessary
  - Pro: Can Record and Sell Online Video Archives
  - Con: Less Control Over Final Product

control over the final outcome. However, it's still the best way. If you do make a mistake on a webinar, people understand because you're doing it live.

Remember, we began with the most important three elements of our formula (market, people, and product). Now that you have a much better idea of *product*—our third element in the MP^5MS^2 Formula for Success and our second *P*—let's move onto the next *P*, which is *places*.

PLACES (THE WHERE)

S o far, we have covered *market*, which is *when* to sell; *people,* which is *who* to sell to; and *product,* which is the *what* to sell. Naturally, *places,* our next element, is *where* to sell. Now, some people talk about online versus offline—which is better? The answer is, it depends.

The reality is, that the internet is just another form of media, like TV, radio, newspapers, etc. The most successful marketers use multiple sources, not just online. This book is primarily about how to make money online, but it's worth mentioning that you can—and should—consider using "offline" methods of marketing, which still work very well.

We recommend starting online because it's faster and usually cheaper to test new advertising to see what's working. Once it's apparent what works, you can then convert the best-performing marketing efforts into offline media, like direct mail, for example. Thus, the internet's biggest advantage is that it's easier, faster, and cheaper to test.

Unsuccessful testing is not a bad thing because it leads you one step closer to success. You don't always succeed the first time, so you want to fail quickly and then figure out what doesn't work. That insight will lead you one step closer to what *does* work. That may sound counterintuitive, but the reality is

MP³MS²

Places

Where To Sell
– Online vs. Offline
– Which is Better?

Smart Successful Marketers Use Both

"The Internet is Just Another Media, Like TV, Radio, and Newspapers."

that many, if not most, "winning" marketing funnels or paid-media ads started out *not* working. It was only through lots of testing and trying out new things (mostly that didn't work) that marketers ultimately find what works, and what works best.

The only way to find out what will work for you is to test multiple ideas. Much of marketing is trial and error, so testing online is really important. Fortunately, easy-to-use software and online tools can quickly tell you which of your marketing methods or ads are working and, more importantly, which aren't working. Then, it's a pretty simple process: eliminate the ones that aren't working and keep using the ones that are.

The reality is that most "big, dumb" companies know that only 50% of their marketing is working. The problem is, they just don't know which half. As entrepreneurs without million-dollar marketing budgets, we need to know exactly which ads and strategies are working and which aren't. Then, the next step is easy. If it's working, keep doing it. If it's not working, stop doing it. *Make sense?*

You must learn it's okay to fail and, ideally, to fail quickly. Rule out what's not working and focus on what is. That's the biggest reason to *start* with marketing your products and services online vs. offline because it's easier, faster, and cheaper to test and see what works.

Ideally, you'll test improvements in your offer as often as possible. Once it's optimized, profitable, and working well, then you can go ahead and test it offline, to see if it still works. You'll find less competition these days offline than online. Many entrepreneurs have stopped spending as much money on things like direct mail because they perceive the internet as the "new" media and as less expensive. So, with less competition offline these days, you can be very effective—especially if you've honed your marketing message online.

MP^{3}MS^2

8 Steps To Selling Online

1. **Create Your Business Brand**
2. **Buy a Domain Name (URL)**
3. **Build Your Business Website**
4. **Create Your Business Entity**
5. **Apply For a Business License**
6. **Open Your Business Bank Account**
7. **Register For Payment Processing**
8. **Setup Your Ecommerce Software**

Create Your Business Brand

First, you'll need to know what you're going to call your new company. Choose your brand wisely as people often "judge a book by its cover," especially online, where you have just milliseconds to capture someone's attention. Think about it. The next time you're searching on Google for a solution, how long do you spend analyzing and evaluating which company or website you want to do business with? It's often a very quick decision, at least as far as narrowing down website(s) that seem good enough to click on and visit. Before you can capture someone's *interest* and *desire* to buy your products or services, you first have to get their *attention*.

We'll talk more about the A-I-D-A Formula in the *sales* section in the following pages, but, for now, let's focus on capturing initial *attention*, the first element in A-I-D-A.

The very first thing that often captures someone's attention is your company brand, so wouldn't it make sense to have a strong and powerful brand name? Fortunately, we've come up with a formula and have isolated three elements of a million-dollar brand:

1. A "hot-cognition," easily identifiable big benefit.
2. A clearly definable market or market niche.
3. (Optional) A word or phrase that conveys credibility, expertise, or authority, such as *Global, International,* or *Labs/Laboratories*—as long as these labels are truthful and not misleading.

THE FORMULA:

1. A HOT-COGNITION IMMEDIATE BENEFIT WORD
2. THE MARKET NICHE DESCRIPTION
3. A CREDIBILITY OR AUTHORITY ELEMENT

EXAMPLES:

EAGLE VISION LABS

ETERNAL VIBRANCE

NATURALLY ENERGETIC

AGELESS BEAUTIFUL SKIN

LIMITLESS LABS NUTRITION

VITAL INFUSIONS TEA

ANCIENT CHINESE REMEDY

NATURALLY ENERGETIC

Case Study: Dr. Greg Griffith, Eagle Vision Labs

One of our platinum mentoring students, Dr. Greg Griffith, came to us with an idea for a line of supplements and vision products to help prevent premature macular degeneration. His initial idea was to call the company Blindness Prevention Kit, which did a fair job of telling what the big benefit of using the products was. However, that title didn't convey a strong company brand message to attract people. So, we applied our Million-Dollar-Branding Formula and came up with Eagle Vision Labs, which carries a much stronger brand message, doesn't it? What do you think about when you envision an eagle?

Eagles are typically known for being independent, enjoying a great sense of freedom, and possessing amazing eyesight, able to see even small prey from up to a mile in the sky. So "Eagle Vision" satisfies the first two elements of our Million-Dollar-Branding Formula. The big, clearly identifiable perceived benefit (the hot-cognition") is that you'll be able to see like an eagle, with crystal-clear eyesight. Notice, we're not making any medical claims here; the person hearing the brand will likely make the connection instantly, even subconsciously. Think about how you can convey your brand's biggest benefit to your customer and tie that message in with imagery and the right choice of words.

"Hot-cognition" refers to things we immediately "get" and understand. Millions of years ago, when the first creatures crawled out of the sea, which much later evolved into humans, they only had what's known as the "reptilian" brain, which processed the world in only four ways: *do I eat this, ignore it, run away, or mate with it?* This is important.

The reptilian brain is still at the core of our thinking, and as marketers, you must get past this primal reaction to pass into the neocortex, our rational-thinking brain, which evolved last, over a very long time. But you don't want your marketing message getting stuck in the analysis/paralysis part of the neocortex either; it's much better for your prospects to have a core-level gut reaction of, *Yes, I want and need this,* from the reptilian brain right away.

You don't want your marketing message to be ignored or have your prospects "run away" because they either don't understand what you do or how you can help them. Even worse, you don't want potential customers to make a quick judgment that it's not for them. The worst thing you can do with your brand is to confuse someone, because it's well known that *a confused mind says no*, and that's bad.

The final element of our branding formula is the authority or credibility part. Since nobody has heard of Eagle Vision, we added "Labs" to the brand. Dr. Greg has spent many years as an ophthalmologist working in his laboratory, so we felt it would add a level of instant brand credibility. He has an amazing company, which sells supplements that coat the inside of the eye to help block the harmful blue light that comes from computer and mobile phone screens. He also sells specially coated eyeglasses to wear while working in front of a computer all day, which also helps block these damaging rays that can lead to premature vision loss from macular degeneration. Both are great products that we use personally (www.eaglevisionlabs.com).

For more case study examples, download our Creating Your Million-Dollar Brand report and watch the video version *here*: www.clickandgrowrich.com/book/MillionDollarBrand.

Case Study: Ryan Moran, Sheer Strength Labs

Another example of how powerful a strong brand can be is Sheer Strength Labs, which was created by an online entrepreneur named Ryan Moran. Ryan is a friend, and after an internet marketing conference we attended, he reached out and told us about the new workout supplements he created and was selling on Amazon.

The products were great, and many people liked them. Initially, he only had two products, but then, every time it was time to reorder, the product line was larger than the last time—but all with the same packaging and branding. Within a few years, he had grown the product line to over ten different supplements, many of which became Amazon best sellers. He recently sold his company for $15 million. He's been able to leverage his success to build his own personal brand and has started an annual conference of entrepreneurs called the Capitalism Conference, which attracts many very high-level marketers and business leaders.

Buy a Domain Name (URL)

Next, if you don't already have a website, you'll want to look online to see if your ideal website name is available. Many places can confirm this, but godaddy.com is probably the easiest place to start, and you can get started for about $10. If your desired domain isn't available and someone owns it already, you can often acquire the domain from the current owner directly or hire a broker to negotiate for you.

✍ DANIEL STORY

Buying a domain to start your business online can be one of the most exciting parts of owning an internet business. When you create the portal to your business, make sure you don't simply start buying potential domains. You should resist your enthusiasm for buying lots of dot-coms right out of the gate, or it can get very expensive. You might end up with a lot of domains you have to pay to renew each year, and never use.

We had a young lawyer in our live class once who was really good at bankruptcies, but his practice had him doing other things because they didn't have many bankruptcies for him to work on. He decided to craft a personal business around his specialty skill. I remember helping him find a great domain: chapter7bankruptcyinformation.com. It was appraised at over $10,000, due to traffic and keywords. I was able to bid on the property and buy it for only $15. That would be like picking up a corner lot on a great city street for only $1,500—when it was actually worth $1 Million. Who wouldn't like to have that as a starting point for creating a business?

Being smart with your money is a big part of building your business, and unless you have a rich uncle or investor who doesn't care how you spend their funds, it's probably best to deploy your business building capital as wisely as possible. Do your research and follow our steps carefully before buying a domain name.

We recently used the GoDaddy domain brokerage service to buy the domain ClickSales.com. GoDaddy charged a small fee to handle the transaction, but it was well worth it to us. However, when you're first starting out, don't worry too much about having your "million-dollar dot.com." At this stage, you'll just want to focus on getting your business started and making money.

Build Your Business Website

The next step is to have your website built. One of the best parts about starting an online business today is that there are many inexpensive resources for getting your website built quickly and inexpensively. You can build it yourself with WordPress, using any number of easy page-builder plugins, or you can hire a professional to build one for you, being mindful of your costs as you start out. Look online as there are many resources for website builders. Always ask for referrals or use a website marketplace that shows past customer reviews. Some good places to look, which we've used in the past, are Fiverr, Upwork, 99 Designs, and Guru, but there are many other places to search.

Create Your Business Entity

Next, you'll set up your legal business entity. Depending on where you live in the world, this could either be as a sole proprietor, limited liability company (LLC), a type of corporation (INC), or another form of company structure. Check with your tax accountant or attorney to find out what he recommends. You can often set these up yourself online, using a paid third-party service. Here in the United States, you'll first need to get an employer identification number (EIN) from the IRS.

Fortunately, an EIN is one thing that is actually *free* from the IRS, and you can find the form online. Once you have your EIN, you can proceed in setting up your company. We have used various online services to set up numerous LLC's over the years. You can either set up a corporation in your own state or out of state. Delaware, Nevada, and Wyoming are popular choices among business owners. Starting out, setting up in your own state (or province) usually makes the most sense, but talk to your legal or tax professional for specific advice and make sure you pay your taxes.

Apply for Your Business License

Once you have your EIN and corporate entity set up, you're ready to apply with your local state taxing authority. Regardless of whether your state charges taxes on internet sales, you'll likely need this anyway, and again, make sure to talk with your tax professional. Note: you must follow a specific progression, so use these steps as your checklist.

Open Your Business Bank Account

Next, you'll need to get a business bank account. Typically, you'll need to have all of the previous elements we've listed in place before you can open a new business bank account. That's why we're giving you all the steps here in a particular order. Completing each requirement can take up to 30 days or longer, so make sure to plan ahead.

Register for Payment Processing

Another reason to follow these steps in the right order is to be able to secure your business bank account so that you can then get a merchant account (to process sales). We'll talk about choosing a payment processor in the next *P* of our formula: *payment.*

Set Up Your Ecommerce System

The final step in preparing to sell online is to set up your ecommerce or shopping cart software. This will tie together with your merchant processing solution; you'll want to find a good solution for listing your products and services for sale online.

This is a very important decision, and many options are available. We've tried them all, and in the end, we weren't happy with any of them. So, we built our own. We've invested well over half a million dollars building a platform that did everything we wanted it to, and it's allowed us to generate the bulk of our sales along the way—over $20 million in sales and climbing.

The platform we created is called Cydec, which stands for "Create Your Dream Entrepreneurial Company," a name we came up with nine years ago, before we had figured out our Million-Dollar-Branding Formula. So in 2018, we purchased the domain clicksales.com, which we'll be building, rebranding, and moving over to in 2019.

Cydec is a simple, fast, and easy-to-use platform that we built for our own use. It doesn't have any of the unnecessary, costly, and confusing features many other systems have, which they try to convince you that you'll need. *You don't need all the bells and whistles.* Keep it simple and keep your costs down, especially when you're starting out. Trust us; we know. We've been there.

For a free 30-day trial of Cydec, visit www.cydec.com/freetrial

In section five, we'll be talking more about Cydec and other amazing technology you can use to grow your business, but when it comes to selling your products online, you won't find a faster, less-expensive, or more-powerful platform that can flat out make you more money than Cydec. With unique features that can literally grow your business ten times, it's a powerful secret weapon to use.

In the Foreword, you heard from Kevin Harrington, one of the original sharks from *Shark Tank*. He's also an investor and advisor to Cydec, which shows he believes in our product. To see a short video from Kevin and to see three of our more powerful features, visit www.clickandgrowrich.com/kevinharrington or find it in the resources area online.

In the bonus section at the back of this book, you can also see a rare, private interview we did with Kevin, in which he talks about why he's moving his business interests from infomercials to online.

The nice thing about selling online is that it's so easy to create new products and order forms, which you can easily customize with your brand logo, colors, videos, etc., without having to spend millions of dollars on advertising with TV or through other expensive media outlets.

Here's a quick quote from our friend Les Brown, best-selling author, and legendary international motivational speaker, about using Cydec:

"People want simple; they want fast; they want easy; they want to be profitable and have more time for themselves. The technology you have created allows them to do that. I'm excited about this because the technology has changed my life. It's changed my business. It took me three years to earn my first million. The technology you've created allows people to do it in a fraction of the time … Einstein said that genius is making the complicated simple, and this technology will help you to win. You deserve to win … Jump on it right now because it's affordable, and it's something that *you can't afford not to have*. Make sure you invest in yourself and your future and get the Cydec technology."

To watch this interview online, go here www.clickandgrowrich.com/lesbrown1

PAYMENT (THE HOW)

N ow, let's talk about *payment*, the *how* of getting paid. Without this
important part of the formula, your business is really just a hobby. Or,
as we've already joked, you might find yourself with an unintentional
nonprofit, and that's not what you're after, is it?

Ultimately, money is just an exchange of value. If you're able to create and
provide value for *people* in your *market*, then they should be willing and eager to
exchange their money with you to get your solution. All you would then need is
a platform for exchange.

Since you'll be selling online, your customer can't physically hand you the
money, so you'll have to have collection systems in place. Fortunately, setting
this up is very easy to do with any number of payment processors and providers.

The traditional way to do this is with a merchant account, and you can
find many options by simply searching online. Now, beware. Not all merchant
accounts are created equal. We'll talk about some of the dangers and important
things to consider in a minute, but for starters, know that you can fairly easily
set up an online merchant processing account within 30 days, one which allows
you to accept credit cards online—assuming you have your business entity and
banking all set up already.

However, a merchant account may not be your best option at first. Monthly fees are usually involved, and you'll have to be PCI compliant, which essentially means your website and ecommerce platform must securely protect your customers' personal and payment information. Fortunately, newer solutions take care of that for you and are very easy to set up. For example, Stripe is one of the best new solutions to easily and quickly start taking payments for your products and services. Visit stripe.com to see if this service is available in your country. We recommend everyone doing business should get a Stripe account, either as the primary option or as a backup; however, you will still need a bank account.

MP⁴MS²

Payment

How To Get Paid
– Receiving Money From Customers
– Processors and Merchant Accts
- **Stripe / Paypal**
- **MC /Visa / Amex**
- **Amazon Pay**
- **NEW – Mobile Payments**
- **FUTURE – Cryptocurrencies / Bitcoin**

Another popular option, which most have heard of, is PayPal. You can sometimes get away with using your personal PayPal account for selling online, but we highly recommend applying online for a PayPal for Business account. One advantage of this type of account is that PayPal is available in most countries around the world and is easy to set up. Another advantage of using PayPal is that many consumers are comfortable using it, and they don't need to have their credit card information to make a purchase as long as they remember their PayPal login information. This makes it easier for them to purchase.

The major disadvantage of using PayPal is that it doesn't work with using upsells and downsells when using most ecommerce systems, and as we've shown, this is where a significant amount of your sales and revenue will be made. Another disadvantage is that with the convenience to set up and use, PayPal charges both a small percentage and a dollar fee with every transaction. While these are tiny (Ex: 2.9% + $0.30 per transaction), they add up.

Still, PayPal is *free* to set up, and we recommend everyone selling online have a PayPal for Business account. PayPal has also come out with other options, like PayPal Adaptive Payments, which is essentially just a merchant account. However, it may not be integrated with your payment platform.

Chances are, you have at least heard of amazon.com, and most likely, you have used it to buy something online. But did you know that you can also set up a free Amazon Pay account and accept payment from your customers who just need to log in to their Amazon account and choose their preferred method of payment stored securely with Amazon? It's a great alternative to PayPal because it adds in the trust and familiarity Amazon users already have with this platform. Similar transaction fees apply, but you can also apply free online. Just do a search online for Amazon Pay and follow the simple steps to get started.

Another exciting new development in the payments world is mobile payments. Currently tied to another form of payment such as a credit card, one-click mobile payments will soon offer consumers a more frictionless sales experience by simply allowing them to select from a list of pre-saved payment methods or credit cards, and then simply entering an easy-to-remember security code or a credit card CVV number (Card Verification Value). As the world moves closer toward a global mobile economy, you don't want your customers to have to enter all their personal data (name, address, phone, credit card, etc.) onto their mobile phones, which leads to mistakes and abandoned orders.

Another currency medium, which you have probably also heard quite a bit about in the past year, is bitcoin and the emergence of cryptocurrencies. It's still not clear exactly how this will play out and who the major players will be. But for now, bitcoin is the leading cryptocurrency used worldwide in transactions and commerce, and a leading company offering merchant services for bitcoin is called BitPay.

✈ BRETT STORY

Back in 2012 I was hanging out with the founder of BitPay in Orlando shortly before they raised their first round of funding. I bought my first bitcoin from him for $20. I was amazed at this new digital form of money, and since he had convinced the bar owner to accept this new currency, I used my bitcoin to buy a round of drinks and an appetizer. That was a very expensive happy hour as my $20 bitcoin would have been worth over $19,500 at its height in December 2017, before losing more than half its value in January. Still, it opened my eyes to the exciting new world of cryptocurrency.

In the long run, the real value of bitcoin and other cryptocurrencies will be in their use as a secure payment medium. People from around the globe will be able to quickly transact with each other, without having to pay expensive currency conversion rates. The newest emerging trend in crypto is "stablecoins," which are cryptocurrencies designed to minimize the effects of price volatility and are essentially a hybrid of blockchain and fiat currency. Facebook has also just announced that it will be introducing its own stablecoin as a payment medium, so at this point it's clear that this form of digital payment is the future. That's exciting for digital marketers, because whenever there is great change, there is the potential for great opportunity.

It's also likely that mobile payments will evolve quickly and ultimately be tied to various cryptocurrencies in your virtual "wallet." Then, you and your future customers will be able to do business anywhere in the world, using cryptocurrency and a mobile device or some other form of wearable technology.

The good news is that we've integrated most these payment forms into Cydec. We were one of the very first online platforms to integrate with BitPay in 2013 to accept BitCoin transactions. We've also integrated Amazon Pay, Stripe, PayPal Pro and Adaptive Pay, and one-click mobile payments. For years, our platform has been a one-stop shop for frictionless global selling. Now, Cydec can allow you to offer multiple payment options and sell more easily. As early adopters of new technology and pioneers when it comes to cutting-edge strategies for selling and making money online, we're usually a few steps ahead of the curve.

Regardless of which payment platform you use, several important considerations should be kept in mind. It's always best to make sure your payment solutions know *in advance* what you are selling and how. They don't like surprises. So, especially before any big product launch or promotion, make sure to call them, if possible, and let them know your launch date, what the product or service is or does, price points, if you'll be offering free trials that rebill later, subscription/recurring billing products, and any high-priced product offers.

MP^4MS^2

Payment

Important Considerations

– Make Sure Your Solution Knows What You Are Selling and How
- Ex: Free Trials, Subscriptions, High Price
- Some Merchants Don't Like Trials or Rebills

– Make Sure To Tell Them About:
- Product Launch Dates and $ Expectations
- What the Price Points Are and Terms
- Why It's a Good Product & Support

Different payment providers have different risk-tolerance for each of these offers, and it's always best to let them know your plans ahead of time so that you can know if there'll be any issues. In this situation, it's *not* better to ask forgiveness rather than permission because, ultimately, your payment processor is taking all the risk. So, if you surprise them with a sudden surge of sales or high-priced sales, they're likely going to wonder if you're up to something and if they are at risk. If red flags like this appear, their Risk or Fraud departments may decide to terminate your account.

If you violate any of their terms, payment providers can hold all of your funds for a period of up to 180 days, and you can even land on a blacklist of problem clients, making it difficult, if not impossible, to get approved elsewhere. To avoid this scenario, it's much better to let them know of unusual activity ahead of time. It works.

Once, a major parent bank of a popular payment provider we were using decided overnight that they didn't like *internet marketers* because it was a "reputational risk" for them. So, they decided to terminate accounts with some of the biggest online marketers in the game. Not only did they give us a mere three months to leave their platform, but we also discovered they were holding over $200,000 of ours—and planning to keep it for nine months. We were able to get the funds released early, but the worst part was that, after this, it was much harder to acquire new merchant accounts with high limits, like we were used to.

MP⁴MS²

Payment

Why Be Proactive?
- They Don't Like Surprises or Risk
- They Can Hold Your Money
- They May Stop You From Selling
- They May Shut You Down Permanently

So Be Upfront
- Best To Call Them To Build Trust

This is an extreme example, and you likely don't need to worry about this scenario happening again. It was pre-2010, when selling online was still considered relatively new and banks were unsure about this new selling environment. Today, ten years later, it's a very established medium, and we have amazing merchant relationships with high limits and flexibility. If you're just starting out, however, and don't have a history with any prior merchant providers, it may be tough to get approved. If you need good referrals for first-time merchant accounts that we have good relationships with, see the resources section in the back of this book or contact us for a referral anywhere in the world.

$$MP^4MS^2$$

Having Trusted Payment Partners

$$=$$

Your Most Valuable Asset As You Grow Bigger!

So, choose your merchant providers with care and always communicate with them. After all, having trusted payment partners who trust you is one of your most valuable assets as you grow your company, especially if you want to scale it to where you're generating hundreds of thousands of dollars, even millions of dollars, per year or per month.

PASSION (THE WHY)

People don't buy what you do. They buy why you do it.
–Simon Sinek

For our final *P* of the MP⁵MS² Formula for Success, we're going to talk about *passion*, which is really your big *why*. Why have you decided to pursue this business direction? Hopefully it is not just for the money. Money doesn't always fulfill people.

In his Ted Talk and his book, *Start with Why*, Simon Sinek discusses the importance of creating your business life around your *why* first, not the *what*. Apple built a great company around their big *why*: they wanted to create a movement. This aim is apparent in their *why* and in their messaging.

According to Sinek, Apple is really saying, "Everything we do, we believe in challenging the status quo. We believe in thinking differently. The way we challenge the status quo is by making our products beautifully designed, simple to use, and user friendly. We just happen to make great computers. Want to buy one?"⁹

This message contrasts with most other computer manufacturers, like Dell, for example. Dell's messaging was predominantly centered around *what* they were selling: discount computers you could customize and have shipped directly to you without having to go to a store. They have also been successful but not nearly as successful as Apple, which has changed the landscape of computing and recently became the first trillion-dollar company in history.[10]

Very few people actually know *why* they do what they do. Most people know *what* they do. Some even know *how* they do what they do. But knowing your why is the most important thing because your passion will fuel your efforts. In order to get through the tough times and challenges you'll face, you must have a why that's big enough to keep you pushing forward in pursuit of your big end goal.

STARTING WITH WHY

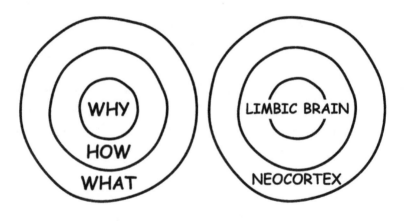

Our why is correlated to our limbic brain, the seat of our emotions, our core drivers. The neocortex evolved over millions of years, around the limbic area, and mostly provides the *how* and the *what*; it plans and executes. But, at our core, the *why* is a more primal desire, housed in an "older" portion of our brain, and it will motivate the more practical tasks the neocortex will carry out. This is all a fancy way of saying what you've likely heard before: follow your passion!

Science tells us it's a good idea to get in touch with your why—both for your satisfaction and the good of the consumer who'll benefit as you grow your brand faster. Now, let's talk about the personal reasons you should spend adequate time thinking about your why. It's very important to identify *your* big why because these reasons will keep you motivated, focused, and grounded. A passionate *why* will keep you from quitting.

We like to use the acronym G-R-O-W-T-H:

- Greater Power
- Relationships
- Outlook
- Wealth
- Time
- Health

Greater Power

Most people believe in some sort of universal power greater than ourselves. Whether you identify with a particular religion, like Christianity, Judaism, Hinduism, Buddhism, or Islam, the way of the Sufi, or just consider yourself spiritual, you may want to give some thought to how your long-term business goals and efforts will affect, impact, or even support your religious or spiritual beliefs and causes. Business can not only be a great vehicle for giving back and raising money for various charities, but it can also create attention and exposure for all worthy causes.

We have used past and present businesses (both online and personally) to support various charities and have raised well over $125,000 for global charities, including the Make a Wish Foundation, American Breast Cancer Foundation, the Red Cross, Wounded Warriors, People for the Ethical Treatment of Animals (PETA), The Leukemia & Lymphoma Society, Virgin Unite, and more. One charity that Daniel is passionate about is a Christian-based charity out of Belize that helps women escape the sex trade, which is a big problem in third-world counties.

Relationships

Having your own business can also be a great relationship builder and open many doors. Whether its meeting celebrities, authority figures, and authors or other influencers and experts in your market niche, you can often leverage your business to align with people you would like to meet but might otherwise never have a chance to. In our various past and present businesses, we've had the opportunity to meet, spend time with, speak on the same stages as, and become friends with celebrities, pro athletes, notable authors, comedians, political figures, public speakers, and more.

Some examples of people we've had the pleasure of meeting, working alongside, and spending time with include: Tony Robbins, Les Brown, Donald Trump, George Ross, Richard Branson, Robert Kiyosaki, T. Harv Ecker, Brian Tracy, Robert Allen, Mark Victor Hansen, among others, including Super Bowl champion Roland Williams, actor Larry the Cable Guy, comedian Ron White, and even Don King, the boxing promoter. One great way to build relationship is to support or raise money for a charity that a public figure supports.

✒ BRETT STORY

I once raised money for Virgin Unite and got to then spend five days on Necker Island with nineteen socially minded and amazing entrepreneurs that I wouldn't have had the opportunity to meet otherwise, including Sir Richard Branson, who owns the island and a few other companies you may have heard of, like Virgin Airways and Virgin Galactic. He was a great host, very down to earth, and I was able to have an interesting a face-to-face conversation with him over dinner one of the evenings there.

We learned a lot about business and met some other world-class entrepreneurs there that I wouldn't have had access to otherwise in the "real world."

The price to attend was a substantial mid-Five figure donation. I really wanted to go, but I didn't have the money at the time. Regardless, I made a decision that I was going to go… and then figured out how. You can see some photos of us hanging out on Necker Island and boating around the BVIs with Richard as our boat captain here: www.brettfogle. com/power-of-decision.

The best part is, I was able to do it in a way that didn't require donating personally or from the company I owned. In fact, it was *primarily because* I owned the business that we were able to raise the money, by having a special sale on several older products that I bundled together and offered at a very reduced price. People weren't buying them anymore anyway, but we had already established the high value for these items in years prior, so the offer was a big success.

It's an amazing feeling to find creative ways to leverage businesses as a vehicle for giving back for the greater good of humanity. Remember, we're all in this incredible journey together. I've actually raised over $125,000 for global charities, using prior businesses as vehicles to generate money for various causes, and each time I was able to do this in ways that created *more* revenue in the business, so everybody benefitted.

When we were being taught by one of our early mentors, John Childers, he talked about the importance of relationships in the GROWTH process.

We know that not all relationships are good ones, and not all are bad. But each one has its place in your personal growth. People do change. So even if you have a bad experience with someone, you should never burn a bridge completely. It's best to forgive people for what they have said or done in the past, because most of them don't even know what they have done. Most people just don't care, and many people only care about themselves, so don't give them the power over your thoughts. It's best to forgive and move on.

The exact opposite can happen as well. You might think everything is great, and a great relationship has started, but those positive feelings of relationship can also be misread. The best relationships often take the most time, but are usually worth it. Some of our best and most profitable business relationships have taken the longest to cultivate and build trust.

Outlook

What is your outlook on life and business? When you look at a glass of water, would you be more likely to say it's "half full" (which means you're more of an optimist) or "half empty" (which means you're more of a pessimist)? Maybe you see yourself as more of a realist, and you think the glass is just half full with water, and half filled with air.

Or maybe you're an engineer like Daniel and you just say the glass is twice as big as it needs to be and should have been designed better! Your outlook will dictate how you respond to these kinds of questions, and how you see the world.

Since your outlook is largely driven by your attitude, our question to you is: How fast can you change your attitude?

⟳ DANIEL STORY

There is a great book by Wallace Wattles called *The Science of Getting Rich.* In it, he talks about the continual effort that people should do each and every day to work on their attitude and outlook. I have had the last few pages taped to my bathroom mirror for over ten years now so I remember it, because I see it multiple times every day.

Even when I'm having a bad day, I'll remember to keep a positive attitude. Since I am at least putting forth this conscious effort, I feel more confident that in the end all will be okay. If you want a *free copy* of the e-book you can download it in our bonus section at the back of this book.

Here's another example that ties well into outlook, the third word in our acronym. Your outlook on life often determines the things you do and how you do them.

⟳ BRETT STORY

A friend and business mentor of mine, Frank McKinney, has a charity called the Caring House. His organization raises money through various fundraising efforts, including Frank's books and the multimillion-dollar beachfront homes he builds in Florida. These funds are used to build schools, shelters, houses, and orphanages in Haiti, one of the poorest countries in the world. Frank's outlook on life, which I share, is that every human should at least have access to the basic necessities in life, like food, water, shelter, and safety. So, I was happy to get involved.

In 2008, we raised $35,000 through a special webinar Frank and I did together, which I marketed to my list of email subscribers. At the unveiling of Frank's new beachfront masterpieces in 2010, I committed to raise money for his charity again and made a decision then and there to raise an additional $50,000. Since a small concrete house can be built in Haiti for just $5,000, my personal and company mantra became "10 in 10," which meant I would raise enough for ten houses in 2010, or $50,000. We were able to accomplish this, even in a beaten-down economy and heading into a severe economic crisis.

To see the actual video of Frank and me, in which I committed to doing this back in 2009, and examples of other charities I've supported (with proof) visit:

www.clickandgrowrich.com/philanthropy/Brett

The greatest part about this and the Necker Island experience was that it taught me the *power of decision*, which has greatly impacted my *outlook* on life. I learned that once you make a decision to do something, circumstances become secondary. Napoleon once said, "Circumstance, hell, I make them," and he was right; when you decide to do something, it's then all about the *how*. And once you switch your focus from *can* I do this to *how* do I do this, everything changes. When you start asking yourself the right questions, magic happens.

How would you like to raise money for your favorite charity or cause, and have your business be the vehicle that lets you do it in a BIG way?

Wealth

Now, on to everybody's seemingly favorite topic: wealth. This is the reason most people start a new business venture, to increase their personal wealth. Some just want to make a few extra thousand dollars per month, while others truly want to build something lasting and leave a legacy. Dan Pena, who wrote the book *Your First Hundred Million*, says "If you think money can't buy happiness, you don't know where to shop." The truth is, it all depends on you and what *you want to achieve.*

✈ DANIEL STORY

Actually, money *can* buy you happiness. A recent study of lottery winners in Sweden and reported by Justin Wolfers of *The New York Times* states that money really *does* lead to a more satisfying life.[11]

Just think about the top ten things you really don't like doing: dishes, diapers, email, driving, cleaning, accounting, mowing the lawn, washing the cars, etc. The good news is, you can hire someone else to do just about anything you don't want to be doing. Money allows the freedom to do what you want.

If you're married, instead of having to do the "Honey Do List," you can pay someone else to do it, and then spend more time with your kids, or significant other. So, you can see that having more *money* freedom can also lead to having more *time* freedom. Once you have more time and money at your disposal, you can start working more heavily on your true passion. So why not start now?

Once we were sitting around in one of our business networking and masterminding sessions on Necker Island, and someone asked Richard Branson if he thought we should all be carving out a portion of our sales to donate to charity. All of us were surprised to hear him say no. He went on to say that we'd be better off building our business up and putting all the money back into the business so that one day we would be able to give back in a bigger way. A lot can be said for that. And the same principle applies if you're truly trying to build something large that can lead to generational wealth. Make sense?

Sometimes you have to take baby steps to get started. Wherever you are now, just take that next step toward the big dream you have. Doing so will get you closer to taking the next big step and the next and the next. Napoleon Hill said, *"Whatever the mind can conceive and believe, the mind can achieve."* This is where you'll want to really think carefully about how much money and wealth you want in life. This number is usually a lot more than what you need, so be sure to think about this in terms of the other important elements in your life.

In either case, clarity is key, and we recommend you set clear financial goals to pursue. There's a reason why they don't have *blind archery* in the Olympics. You have to have a clear target in mind to hit your goals. For a great resource to set financial goals, download our Income Accelerator Worksheet using the link below. Fill in your desired annual sales and income goals. This interactive worksheet will break these numbers down into clear monthly, weekly, and daily targets to achieve your annual income goal, as part of your overarching wealth-building plan.

Download the Income Accelerator Here:
www.clickandgrowrich.com/book/IncomeAccelerator

Time

The next part of the GROWTH acronym is time. Steve Jobs is quoted as saying, "Your time is limited, so don't waste it living somebody else's life." Let that sink in. How many of you are doing this right now, living your life for someone else? Perhaps you're letting personal relationships (family, spouse, siblings), work relationships (your boss or supervisor), or other self-imposed or society-dictated expectations tell you how you should live. Many, if not most, people are living this way, whether they know it or not. The two things we hear most are that people want more time and financial freedom. Does that resonate with you also?

"Your time is limited, so don't waste it living somebody else's life."
–Steve Jobs

Changing your life, designing new life circumstances, and creating true time and money freedom that most people will never experience is what this book is all about. You can do it because now you have a *choice*. In today's society, especially online, more opportunities than ever abound, and it all starts with one idea—the right idea. By executing the principles in this book, you can take inspired action, work hard, and find freedom. *The rewards are well worth it.*

The concept of time freedom and being able to do *what* you want to do, *when* you want to do it, from *wherever* you want to do it is foreign to most people—but not to people with online businesses. This freedom is one of the biggest reasons to start. You can literally run your online business from anywhere in the world, fire your boss, and leave the "office" forever.

This section of the book was actually written on a blueberry farm about 90 miles west of Warsaw, Poland, on a two-week stopover from London on the way to Johannesburg, South Africa. And, yes, we found Wi-Fi every step of the way. As mentioned, we've also been able to get online deep in the South African "bush," wrapping up our day by noon to go see zebras, giraffes, and all sorts of wildlife the rest of the day. And you can too.

Health

Now, let's talk about the final part of our GROWTH acronym for finding and following your passion: health. Most people know their health is important, but you may not realize just how important it is when it comes to running your business.

✒ BRETT STORY

In 2009, I was enjoying success as I had defined it. I had started a business from the kitchen table and within three years had grown it to millions of dollars in annual sales.

Then everything fell apart. In late summer 2009, a perfect storm erupted—with the economy melting down during the early economic crisis—within three months, I lost my business partner and I lost my marriage. Sales were plummeting, so I nearly lost the entire business, too. I somehow survived, moved on, and started another business in the Forex markets with a friend of one of my mentors, Dan Kennedy.

This new venture immediately took off. Shortly thereafter, we acquired the technology that would later become Cydec and started building that as a new business opportunity.

It might sound great, but the reality was that my health was at an all-time low. I wasn't sleeping enough. I wasn't eating well, and my stress was through the roof as I was trying to manage three companies. I was also dealing with toxic people and relationships. At one point, my cardiologist raised my blood pressure medication three times in three months. I then realized it was time to make some changes.

Within the next two years, I sold one company, walked away from another very toxic one—even though it was still generating millions of dollars in sales—and decided to focus on the new software company, which seemed the most fun to me. I closed the office, worked from my beautiful home in Florida, changed my diet, started exercising, lost weight, and within nine months, I was off of all my blood pressure medication.

Is your health important? If you want to be around to enjoy the fruits of your hard work, it should be. If you're not in a positive environment and your health is suffering, then it's likely time to make a serious life change.

You're not getting any younger. We have the best health-extending medicine and technology in history, but you'll have to do your part and put yourself in the right environment. Stress is the biggest killer of all. Experts say that stress is linked to the *six* leading causes of death: heart disease, cancer, lung problems, accidents, cirrhosis of the liver, and suicide. Any of those sound good to you?

So, we've outlined your personal roadmap for finding your true passions: GROWTH. It's time to overlay this with the ideal business that will support your ideal life and allow you to truly fulfill your passion. To help you identify the best business for you individually, we created the I-O-E Worksheet, which we introduced in section one. If you haven't downloaded and filled that out yet, now would be a good time.

Keep in mind, the overlap of the three important areas is the sweet spot where you will likely thrive in your business long term. If you're not interested and *passionate* about an idea, you'll likely quit after the going gets hard. If you don't have any experience, or can't find a credible expert to partner with, people may not trust you enough to buy from you. And, if there is no market opportunity, people won't pay you for your products or services, and you essentially have yourself a hobby.

The four biggest reasons for making sure you're passionate about your business are that it keeps you *motivated, focused, grounded, and not likely to quit.* You don't want to spend six to twelve months of your life working on something, only to abandon it later to head in a new direction that is more in line with your why. At least money replenishes; time does not.

$$MP^5MS^2$$

Passion

Personal Passion (The Why)
Identify Your Reasons Why
 – Keeps You Motivated
 – Keeps You Focused
 – Keeps You Grounded
 – Keeps You From Quitting

We also don't recommend starting more than one business at a time when you're first starting out. FOCUS stands for "Follow One Course Until Successful." Success requires laser focus on a clear goal. In this book, we're giving you the direction and the tools to do that, so make sure to take advantage of every resource we offer. You can't be successful if you're chasing every shiny ball or new opportunity that comes your way. Richard Branson is famous for saying, "Opportunities are like busses; there's always another one coming along." So, resist the urge to jump from bus to bus. It's been the downfall of many new entrepreneurs.

"The person who chases two rabbits, catches neither."
–Confucius

So, there you have it. We've now covered the when, who, what, where, how, and why of starting a successful business online, which is the first part of our MP^{5}MS^2 Formula for Success. Reread any section if it wasn't clear to you because these are important building blocks. You'll want a sound understanding before beginning the second part of our formula: *marketing, selling,* and *staffing.*

9 PROVEN MARKETING STRATEGIES

N ow that we've covered the first half of our proven MP⁵MS² Formula for Success, it's time to dive into our second half, starting with *marketing*. Marketing is *not* the same as sales. Marketing is what brings potential customers closer so you can make the sale. In this section, we're going to talk about 9 Proven Marketing Strategies, both online and offline:

- Joint Venture/Affiliate Marketing
- Paid Media Marketing
- Social Media Marketing
- Webinar Marketing
- Video Marketing
- Viral Marketing
- Email Marketing
- Content Marketing
- Offline Marketing

MP⁵MS²

$$MP^5MS^2$$

Marketing

Key Point:

"Marketing is <u>Not</u> the Same as Sales"

"Marketing Brings Potential Customers So You Can Make the Sale"

Joint Venture Marketing

Also known as affiliate marketing, joint venture marketing is a great way to start out because it's the lowest cost and lowest risk method for getting your product or service out there. With this type of marketing, you're only paying for performance in the form of sales commissions to your affiliates. And the best part is, great affiliates can usually refer you to other great affiliates.

✍ **BRETT STORY**

Affiliate marketing is how I launched Options University from zero to over $200,000 in sales the first year and to over $3 million in sales by the third year. We did this by leveraging the power of joint ventures and affiliates.

This also led to the company being recognized by *Inc.* magazine as one of the fastest-growing privately held companies (#276) in the United States[12] and also as a result, I was featured in *The Official Get-Rich Guide to Information Marketing* by Robert Skrob, which gives a more detailed description of the story.[13]

The power of affiliate marketing lies in the fact that it's the lowest cost and lowest risk way to start out because you can start out as an "unknown" in your market, without customers or prospects, and through a single joint venture potentially generate tens of thousands, even hundreds of thousands or more in sales.

I'll never forget attending an internet marketing seminar one day, introducing myself to the guy next to me, and asking what his business was. It turns out, he and his father were also selling financial education so we formed an ongoing affiliate relationship that generated well over a million dollars in revenue for us, and he also introduced us to other profitable affiliates. It was a win-win for both of us, because we also generated over a million dollars in sales for them.

He and his father have since grown their "family" business to $20 million in gross annual sales online, and now his brother is joining the business. *What's your big idea?*

Joint ventures can be the most effective form of marketing you'll ever do because you are essentially leveraging the relationships other people (your affiliates) already have with the ideal audience you want to get in front of. Since affiliates have a preexisting relationship with an audience who knows, likes, and

$$MP^5MS^2$$

Joint Venture & Affiliate Marketing

- **Best Way to Start Out**
- **Low Cost & Low Risk**
- **Can Be Most Effective**
- **Leverage Relationships**
- **Win-Win For Both Parties**
- **Pay Only For Performance & Sales**
- **Can Lead To Affiliate Referrals**

trust them, when your affiliate partner sends out an email, video, or blog post to their audience recommending your products and services, those subscribers are far more likely to buy from you.

You could also think of this as paid referral marketing, where somebody who doesn't really know you or your products will go out of their way to promote them to an audience they've created a relationship with over time. Why would the affiliate be so generous? Because you offer to split the sales with them. It's a perfect win-win because nobody really loses if it doesn't work.

With paid advertising, which we'll talk about next, if you spend money on an advertisement and it bombs, then you're out all of that money. With affiliate marketing, if the affiliate sends an email to their list or posts on their blog and nobody buys anything, the affiliate may not be happy, but they've only wasted their time and some opportunity cost. If some sales are made, then again you only have to pay them for those sales. So, the affiliate has extra incentive to push harder or maybe even throw in a special bonus of their own so customers will buy your products through their referral link.

This type of paid-referral marketing was relatively difficult to track before the Internet Age. Looking back, it seems almost like the Stone Age when you

consider how far we've come with sales and marketing and being able to track everything today. If we only knew then what we now know today!

To effectively implement an affiliate program of your own, you'll need to use a suitable marketing platform which can track and report things to your affiliate, like how many clicks the affiliate sent, number of sales, sales volume, commissions, and the average "earnings per click" (EPC). Without clear and accurate reporting, tweaking your efforts becomes difficult, but fortunately today, with simple yet powerful software like Cydec, you can easily track this. You can even track sales commissions for affiliates referred by other affiliates so you can incentivize your existing affiliates to make referrals and earn override commissions from them.

For example, let's say Bob has an email list that he's built over years of 10,000 people who trust his judgment as a tennis expert. You find Bob's blog by doing a simple Google search for "tennis affiliate" and see that he has an affiliate program of his own. So, you reach out to tell him about your new video training on how to improve your tennis game and ask him to review it, then promote it to his audience. You also offer him, say, 40% of all the sales. He agrees to send out a few emails to his list, who respond well because of Bob's endorsement, and let's say 100 people buy the online video course at $50 for $5,000 in sales.

Bob's commission would be $5,000 x 40%, or $2,000. He's pretty happy; he just earned $2,000 for maybe an hour or less of work. You're happy because you just made $3,000 for your new product and have 100 new customers you can potentially sell to again.

But now let's say you ask Bob if he has anyone else who might be interested in promoting your tennis program. You offer to pay him 10% for any sales that come from that person. Bob introduces you to Mary, who has a large following of tennis enthusiasts from her Facebook group. She does a video and a series of posts to her group about your program and posts her affiliate link. She generates another 100 sales for you. Now you pay her $2,000 for her sales and pay Bob 10%, or $500, for the sales Mary has made, and everyone is happy. You've paid out a total of 50% of your sales, but you've gained 200 new customers that you can create and sell new programs to in the future, plus you've just earned $5,500.

We've generated millions of dollars in sales using this one type of marketing over the years, and we ran all of it through Cydec, which managed all of our affiliate marketing efforts. It also creates easy-to-use affiliate tracking links, ad creatives, and even affiliate ad-tracking links to use with Facebook, Google, or any other paid-media campaigns.

One of the most effective ways not only to generate large sales quickly but also to build your email prospect list is with a product launch. This strategy has been around for a long time and is also one of the most effective—if not *the* most effective—strategy used. In fact, the first known person to ever generate over $1 million in a 24-hour period used this strategy. His name is John Reese, and in 2004, he set out to generate $1 million in a day.

Just like the late Roger Bannister, who ran the first four-minute mile in history, nobody had ever done this before. In ancient Roman times, they used to set lions loose after people to see if they could get them to run a mile in under four minutes. Let's just say, there were many well-fed lions back then because nobody had ever done it. Experts thought it wasn't possible for a human to run a four-minute mile until Roger Bannister did it. After he did it, people realized it *was* possible and suddenly a bunch of other runners did it also.

When John Reese set out to do $1 million in sales in 24 hours, nobody thought it was possible. He might as well have said he was going to bend a spoon with his mind like Neo in *The Matrix*. But, he did it, and, in fact, he did over $1 million in sales in an 18-hour period. Since then, many other people have done similar and even bigger product launches, usually using affiliates.

John was ahead of his time and realized that if he could just get 1,000 people to buy his $1,000 product ($997 was the exact pricing), then he would generate over $1 million. Here's a *big* secret: when you figure out how much you *want* to make, break it down into a math problem, how many sales you actually need (in a month, week, and day). Then, these numbers become a lot more achievable. Use the Income Accelerator PDF we've given you to visualize your goals.

You can learn more about how to run a product launch online, but here is the basic formula you can use. Again, the power here is in leveraging the existing relationships others have with their email lists already. With more affiliates, you can leverage a lot of people and grow your email subscriber list very quickly, which we'll talk about in more detail soon.

This one strategy has been responsible for literally hundreds of millions of sales on the internet and is still going strong because it works. Even though things are shifting in terms of how much we rely on email as a communication tool, and moving more toward social media, desktop "Push" technologies including messenger bots like Facebook and ManyChat, as well as automated SMS text messaging—the product launch model is still very effective. Why?

As a society, we're busier and have more distractions than ever before. So, as a marketer of your products and services, it's getting harder and harder to get your message across, and to even get noticed in the first place. You must break through people's "distraction barrier," as we call it, just to get your message noticed, and this is why the product launch works. It's a way to put *as many* marketing messages in front of your audience in a relatively short period of time without coming across as pushy and without being ignored.

There's no 100% right or wrong way to do this. As long as you're hitting upon your prospects' most important pain points, fears, frustrations, wants, and aspirations, then you'll be more likely to succeed. For the definitive guide to

$$MP^5MS^2$$

The Product Launch

- Schedule 1-2 Weeks For 'Launch'
- Get Affiliates Committed to Mail
- Build Excitement and Scarcity
- Send To Lead Capture Page
- Build a New List During Pre-Launch
- Make Big Sales on Launch Day
- Stress Scarcity and Fear of Loss
- Close Page and Notify 'Sold Out'
- Re-Launch Later For More Sales

product launches, check out Jeff Walker's book *Launch* and his courses on the Product Launch Formula.

First, schedule a one to two-week window to launch your new product. Again, you want to do this so that people pay attention; you want to get on their radar long enough to generate interest. Here's an example. When Coca-Cola launched New Coke many years ago, did they do it quietly one day, without telling anyone, hoping people would notice? Or, did they do a massive PR campaign, telling the world that New Coke was coming? It turned out to be a huge mistake, but everybody *knew* it was happening and was paying attention. We'll cover the A-I-D-A Formula under *selling*, but the first step in selling is to get people's *attention*. That's what you're doing here also.

Another famous example of a product launch is when Richard Branson was launching Virgin Mobile. He appeared in Times Square in New York City fully naked, all but a Virgin Mobile phone over his privates. Why did he do that? To get people's *attention,* which, most would say, worked. We're not suggesting you go to such an extreme, but, hey, it's your brand, so it's up to you!

Once you've carved out a launch date and time, put it on your calendar and work backwards. You'll want to get in touch with any affiliates you have and ask if they will put it on their marketing calendars. Once they are committed and excited about earning big commissions from promoting your product or service, you're all set. To make it as easy as possible, make sure to give them all the marketing emails and promotional images they'll need to share your offer with their audience. When coordinated and executed well, product launches can generate huge sales for both the product creator and the affiliates.

One of the biggest side benefits of running a product launch is that you can also grow your own email list quickly by having your affiliates promote a free lead-magnet landing page as in the example below. On this page, you offer potential customers a free report, a preview video, or something else of value prior to the launch, to pique their interest.

In this example, we teased consumers with a short Doodle video to get them to opt-in with their email address. After they supplied an address, they got to see how our expert had turned a $5,000 Forex trading account into over $30,000 in just four months. This hook was like throwing red meat to a hungry lion. We knew it would work well to this crowd and also to our affiliates' email lists. It worked, and we captured over 25,000 new-prospect email addresses. We could then email to this list to build excitement and stress scarcity, all building up to launch day.

The way to build excitement is to send a series of emails or post content to your blog—however you communicate with your audience—containing *new* and *interesting* case studies, testimonials, and how-it-works videos to demonstrate how your product or service will create value. Your goal is to convince readers or viewers that your solution can create at least ten times the perceived value of what your potential customer would be spending with you.

Because *fear of loss* is one of the most powerful human motivators, it's useful to have or create a believable reason why you can only offer so many of your product or work with so many new clients at a time. Be ethical and honest, but you can legitimately come up with various reasons why it's in both parties' best interest to limit access to your products.

This can be limited access to ensure quality support and time is spent with new clients. Or, you can roll out a limited release of your software to gain market feedback. Or, you might offer a special, discounted price for the first 50-100 customers, to encourage early buyers or paid beta testers. FOMO stands for "fear of missing out," and it's hardwired into our brains. So, use it where you can.

You may also want to refer to Robert Cialdini's classic books *Influence* and *Pre-Suasion,* which will give you more on this and explain other psychological sales tactics you can add to your sales arsenal.

Going into launch day, continue to stress scarcity and the limited number of copies or limited access you are offering. If all goes well, you'll see your biggest spike in sales as soon as you launch, and you may even sell out, which isn't a bad thing, as we'll talk about shortly.

After and during your launch period, usually the second week of the two weeks you've allocated for the launch, continue to communicate with your audience that time is running out and quantities are scarce. This tactic drives more sales. You'll also want to provide emails with similar language to your affiliates for them to send out, including their affiliate tracking links to get credit for any sales that occur. *Time-bound and quantity-bound scarcity is very powerful.* It's very effective in getting people, who are otherwise hesitant to buy, to get off the fence and buy your products. Nobody likes to miss out on a great deal, do they?

During the first few hours of launch day and going into your prespecified close day and time (also very important), you'll often see the biggest spike in sales. This is normal. Make sure to communicate with your list during the final day and the closing hour to maximize sales. Then announce that your product launch is closed and all available products or client spots are *sold out*—if this is true, as this often happens.

Make sure to review and comply with the latest Federal Trade Commission (FTC) and/or regulatory rules in your region or country to ensure you are complying with all the applicable laws. In the United States, we have laws against stating falsely that you have "limited quantities" or misleading the public in any way about this. So, make sure you are being compliant.

One of the often-overlooked strategies that many marketers miss, leaving potential profits on the table, is to then relaunch your product or service two to four weeks later. This is one way you can pick up anybody who was interested in your offer initially, but, for some reason, didn't buy the first time. If they were experiencing nonbuyer's remorse and high FOMO, they'll be glad to have another chance.

You can send out emails and post online that because many people were still interested and because the launch went well and all orders are now handled, you're releasing another XX number of available spaces, downloads, or copies of your products. That's the launch formula.

Paid Media Marketing

You can also promote your products and product launches using paid media marketing, which is a great way to scale your business fast and take it much further than would be possible with just affiliate marketing alone. Once you've proven your offer is working in the marketplace (again, using affiliates and your "free" in-house list first), then you're ready to start making sales using paid media. The most common and well-known paid media ads are with Google and Facebook PPC, which stands for "pay per click." As the name implies, you'll pay a per-click price, so that every time someone clicks on your ad, you get charged.

This type of online traffic has a virtually unlimited supply, which is great if you have your sales funnel and offer optimized and you know your sales metrics. If you know that you can spend $1 and make $2 or even $1.50 every time someone clicks on your ad, you can get rich online. *Just do the math.*

Imagine if you had a slot machine in your basement, and you knew that every time you put in $1 and pulled the handle, $2 would come out and you would double your money. How often would you pull the handle? Likely as many times as possible until your arm falls off, right? You might even hire other people to sit there and do it for you 24/7. It's a similar concept with perfecting your online advertising and spending the time to optimize your marketing funnel.

This optimization process isn't easy, however, and you'll need to experiment to find what works and how to increase your *average customer value* (ACV) to ensure it's greater than your *cost to acquire a customer* (CAC). It's critically important you know your numbers; you can go broke quickly if you're spending a lot of money on paid ads yet people aren't buying. Your ACV must be greater than your CAC. And, unfortunately, you can't scale zero. If you're just at breakeven, then you're spinning your wheels.

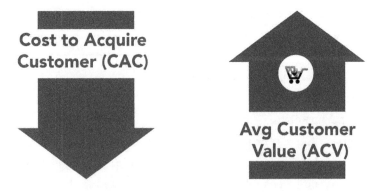

Cost to Acquire Customer (CAC)

Avg Customer Value (ACV)

Let's consider what Google and Facebook can do for you. The days of cheap clicks on Google are, unfortunately, long gone, and it's a more complicated platform than Facebook, with a higher learning curve to get "good" at it. For this reason, we recommend starting out on Facebook, which has come a long way in terms of making its advertising platform more user friendly, even for the beginner. Also consider third-party tools, like Ad Espresso, which offers an easy-to-use interface, along with additional interest layering capabilities—all ideal for beginners. As you grow and learn, Qwaya and other programs for users at the high end offer more advanced advertising capabilities on the Facebook platform.

$$MP^5MS^2$$

Paid Media Marketing

- **Google PPC & You Tube**
  - Learning Curve to Get 'Good'
- **Facebook & Instagram Ads**
  - Best Targeting and ROI
- **Banners & Digital Media**
  - Huge Inventory Available
- **Blog or Content Site Ads & Emails**
  - Hire Agency or Media Buyer

Facebook does have the best targeting capabilities. As of this writing, Facebook still allows for very specific user targeting based on a wide number of interests, demographics, and psychographics. Thus, you can laser-target your ideal audience and show them the perfect ad at the right time, although there is some talk about removing some of these interest categories altogether. It seems Facebook's and Google's artificial intelligence algorithms have become so good they "know" your ideal prospect without your having to tell them. This is both scary and exciting at the same time *(exciting if you are a marketer)*. Never before in history have you been able to effectively target your buyer so easily.

Banners and other digital media are another great way to get your product or service in front of a much wider audience. Banner ads have had an interesting life cycle, starting out as an almost-accidental discovery in the late 1990s by early internet pioneer John Ferber. John created one of the first peer-to-peer video games, where you could play against another player online, even in a remote location. To finance his project, he created the first "banner ad" in his games, and was then approached by someone who wanted to license the technology for $50,000.

To make a long story short, seeing an opportunity, he partnered with his brother who was an attorney and they started a media company, which later became advertising.com. John's one idea essentially created the banner ad industry and his company was acquired by AOL in 2004 for $495 million, in cash.[14] When we tell you, "You are just one idea away," this story is a good example.

Banner ads were everywhere on the internet, being used by major Fortune 500 brands, as well as all across the board, generating hundreds of millions of dollars in revenue and catapulting advertising.com and a few others into the limelight. These ads were so pervasive that people started to ignore them, consciously and unconsciously, and the term "banner blindness" was born. People would see the advertisements out of the corner of their eye and automatically think, "I know what that is, and I'm not even going to look because it's trying to sell me something."

Fortunately, banner ads have become less obnoxious these days and have made a big comeback, largely because prices have come down as well. Dan Kennedy has said, "All advertising works…at some price." If you can get massive exposure in millions of views, then even if only a very small percentage of people look and click on the banners, you can still make money here—if the prices are right and you know your offers are working.

Again, it comes down to optimizing your sales funnel and increasing your ACV vs. your CAC. Almost-unlimited "inventory" is available on a daily basis through advertising networks for you to test. Some are self-service, like SiteScout, which has a daily inventory in the hundreds of millions of topic-specific banner impressions in all kinds of categories, from pets to music and everything in between. Or you can look to the Google Display Network, which also offers massive inventory availability. Both networks can be set to target local areas, including ads by city, state, or zip code. You can even do hyperlocal targeting within as little as a half-mile radius of a specific location or address. You can't do that with newspaper advertising, can you?

Here's an interesting example. The Traffic and Conversion Summit is held each year for internet marketers. One of our competitors, Infusionsoft, has paid approximately $45,000 for being the main sponsor. Instead of spending that kind of money to get in front of the thousands of attendees, we've been buying all the mobile banner inventory within a one-mile radius of the hotel where the event is held every year, for around $500—a lot less than $45,000. One of the fun things you can do in your business is get very creative with your marketing like this, and with available tools today on the internet, you can effectively compete against anyone.

Many options are available for paid-media advertising, so it's best to focus on and master *one* outlet, such as Facebook, until you're profitable enough to branch out. At that point, you may want to hire a media buyer or someone to run your ads for you on Facebook, Instagram, Google, YouTube, etc. Look for someone with good references who won't try to charge you an expensive monthly retainer but will work with you by the hour and within your budget. You can also incentivize them to grow with you by offering performance bonuses or commissions on sales, which is a win-win for both of you and can lead to a profitable, long-term business relationship.

When you have fine-tuned your offer and it's working, you'll want to get it out in front of bigger markets. At this point, you may want to hire a professional who can cost-effectively get in front of as many people as possible. Drew Kossoff of Rainmaker Ventures was the media buyer who helped a company called Peak Performance Golf grow their golf email list from zero to 750,000 in just 18 months, which is pretty amazing.

The company later rebranded and was then acquired by the Golf Channel for an undisclosed amount. The interesting thing is that the founder, Justin Tupper, started the business online from scratch, running it from his Manhattan apartment without any help or outside funding: "Tupper started producing instructional videos on DVDs in 2009, running the business out of his house. Over the next eight years, Revolution Golf invested more than $25 million in advertising to build what is now one of the largest and most-engaged audiences in all of golf."[15]

The point here is that a virtually unlimited amount of media is available to help your business to grow, once you're ready for it by proving you have a solution your market wants and is looking for and that your ads and sales funnel are fully optimized.

Social Media Marketing

Ten years ago, relatively little was happening in the area of social media marketing as we now know it. In 2010, we had hired a full-time person to focus on this new and emerging form of advertising. At the end of a full year, the ROI on this person's social media marketing efforts was a giant 0%. It didn't work for us at all, and we had to move him into a different job entirely. But for a year, this person was posting on early social media platforms, like Digg, Squidoo, StumbleUpon, and Del.icio.us. He might as well have been posting notices on trees out in the forest because nobody was responding to any of it.

$$MP^5MS^2$$

Social Media Marketing

– The 'New' Way of Marketing Online
– Finally Clear How to Make Money

– Built Around Conversations and
Relationships = Building Trust

– People Don't Trust 'Marketers'

– People Do Trust Friends, Friends of
Friends, and People Like Themselves

The social media landscape, like the internet, has gone through many changes. Ten years later, social media has come a long way; it's now abundantly clear how to monetize social media and build massive online followings on platforms like Facebook, YouTube, and Twitter. New, popular social channels have also opened up, like Pinterest, SnapChat, and, of course, Instagram, which was acquired by Facebook for $1 billion.[16]

Social media has become a very effective way to increase and enhance exposure, for not only mainstream celebrities, like the Kardashians, sports figures, playmates, and models, but also for everyday people turned social media celebrity, like Tai Lopez, who has created a social media empire and built an estimated net worth of $5 million using it.[17] These days, you can potentially put yourself in front of the entire world and attract millions of followers using this new form of media—if your message resonates well with your market.

Social media is a large and rapidly evolving media. For the average person, a clear, long-term, profitable, repeatable, and free strategy isn't easy but it's become the "new" way of marketing online, now that it's clear how to make money with social media. The reason it works so well is because it's built around conversations and relationships, which leads to building trust online. Consumers have an inherent distrust of most marketers, but people do trust their friends, friends of their friends, and people like themselves with common interests.

We're not going to dive any deeper here since social media is changing so rapidly, but do keep in mind that as any new media evolves, opportunity is usually there for those creative and bold enough to try something new.

Notice that in the celebrity examples we're referring to "free" social media. Huge opportunity *also exists* for people wanting to use *paid* advertising on social media, as we discussed. Remember, you're just one idea away. *So, what's holding you back?*

> *"A good plan violently executed now is*
> *better than a perfect plan executed next week."*
> **–George S. Patton**

Webinar Marketing

Webinar Marketing is a great way for anyone, regardless of previous experience or expertise, to get started making money online. People often ask us, "If you were to start over today, what would you focus on for making money online?" One answer is with webinars.

We're assuming you've followed the MP^{5}MS^2 Formula for Success and have identified a hot *market*, with *people* in that market who have a problem or pain they are actively seeking a solution for. We're assuming you then either became an expert in that field or found an expert to create your *product* or service with. If you've finished these steps, then you're ready to start giving webinars for profit.

✍ BRETT STORY

Webinars have finally come of age. Back in 2007, when we first had the idea to deliver a presentation online, the technology didn't exist. I had just finished launching an options-trading mastery series, which was 20 video CDs and manuals; it took us eight months to record and edit this series. The product launch was successful, with over $700,000 in sales with an affiliate-driven product launch.

The problem was, we had hired staff and moved into expensive office space at $7,000/month in rent. Plus, much of our income was owed to affiliates in sales commissions, so we didn't *have* another eight months to record a new product. We needed to charge for and deliver content quickly.

I asked my business partner at the time if he had any other material he could "teach online" and deliver live. He said he did, and luckily, I found someone who could build an online delivery system for us. It looked amazing, with our company colors and logo. And with twelve people on the platform, it worked really well. But the thirteenth person crashed it every time. So, we looked for a better solution.

We tried all of the early webinar platforms that were coming out at the time, and they were all terrible. We suffered through every problem, technology glitch, and system crash and made every mistake you could make before cracking the code to webinars, after a *lot* of trial and error. Fortunately, since I was doing webinars before there were "webinars," we had time to figure it out. The result of doing it every wrong way possible is that eventually we got it right.

As we've said, the "pioneers" are the ones with all of the arrows in their backs, and we had plenty of arrows. One of the big breakthroughs we had—enabling us to increase our sales conversions from around 10-15% to over 30% and, in some cases, 35%—was adding time-bound and quantity-bound scarcity to our webinars.

If you've ever watched QVC or the Home Shopping Network (HSN), then you've seen this approach. The TV show host introduces an "amazing watch," for example, and after telling you about the great features of this watch, they put up a timer showing how long this offer will last.

But that's not all. They also claim to only have 100 of these watches available, and as the timer is counting down toward zero, the number of available watches in inventory also goes down. As the timer gets closer to zero, the network magically has just a few watches left (notice they never *sell out*). As they transition to the next item, a wonderful bracelet, they explain it is also only available for a limited time in limited quantities—as you may have guessed.

Even though your rational brain knows they have 10,000 of the watches in the warehouse, you still have the urge to buy so that you don't miss out. As we've said, *fear of loss* is one of the most powerful human motivators to buy, and that's why this tactic works so well with webinars.

We learned this idea from QVC and started calling this the "QVC Close," teaching it only to our private clients and coaching students all over the world. As we've talked about, success leaves clues, so why not borrow something that's been tested and proven to work in the most competitive media possible—live TV?

There are other nuances to making this strategy work that we detail in a special video training as part of our CGR Labs membership area, which you can learn more about below and join for just $1. Inside, we've created dozens of one-hour video trainings on various success strategies and tactics.

Take a $1 Trial of CGR Labs Video Training Here:
www.clickandgrowrich.com/CGRlabs

Webinars are still somewhat new to many, and fortunately the technology has come a long way from the days when we could only have 10-12 people on them before crashing. Now the capacity has finally surpassed the number of people that 99% of marketers could ever put on one. Our record is over 1,900 people for one webinar, which was quite a thrill and led to huge sales as you can imagine. The real magic of webinars is the time you save in getting your message to the masses. You can deliver your sales message from one to many instead of one to one as in traditional selling, and this gives you tremendous leverage.

MP^5MS^2

Webinar Marketing

- Still Relatively New Technology
- Use To Leverage Your Message
  'One to Many' Vs. 'One on One'
- Can Finally Handle Thousands
- Better Because Has Audio & Visual
- Replay as 'Evergreen' Webinars

In the old days, we used teleseminars, which used a similar strategy of sharing your message from one to many. While still effective, the problem was, as the internet grew, so did the number of distractions. With a teleseminar, people weren't usually fully engaged. They were only half listening because they were also checking their emails, watching YouTube, and distracted by Facebook while petting the dog and watching TV. With webinars, you're engaging more of the senses: audio, visual, and kinesthetic (interactive questions, live quizzes, or chat response requests require viewers to type).

Current webinar technology can now handle thousands of people from all over the world tuning in to your live presentation at the same time. This is very exciting! You can sit at home in your underwear and bunny slippers, with a headset or any microphone and an internet connection, and easily and comfortably conduct your webinars, potentially extracting tens of thousands—if not hundreds of thousands—of dollars from a single session. We have done it numerous times.

The future of webinar marketing is where things get *really* exciting. Potentially game-changing technology is coming very soon, likely being developed even now. We've been predicting this for over three years. Invariably, whenever we mention this while speaking in front of an audience, we get goosebumps because of the massive opportunities it will create. You'll soon be able to reach the world in a much bigger way with your message.

If you've ever been to Epcot Center in Orlando, there is a feature attraction inside the giant golf ball structure Epcot is famous for. The ride was a slow-moving adventure through advancements in communications technology. Scenes depict the genesis of important communications breakthroughs, from writing on cave walls to newspapers to the personal computer. In one scene, a young American girl is holding one of those 1970's giant telephone receivers. In the next scene, an Asian girl is also on the phone; they are presumably talking to each other. When visiting Epcot 20 years ago, the narration for this scene said something like, "Someday, you'll be able to speak into the phone in your language and talk to someone else from a different language halfway around the world."

That "someday" is now. The technology exits, and it's only a matter of time before someone puts it into a webinar platform, allowing you to host your webinar to people around the world. Tens of thousands of people could all hear your message in their own language, in real time. *Let that sink in for a moment.*

On Skype right now, a small "globe" icon will allow you to change the language you read your messages in, and there's even a translation option. If you want to have some fun, go in and change the language setting on your friend's Skype to Arabic, then start messaging them—unless, of course, they natively speak Arabic.

Even more exciting, a recent start-up has developed small earbuds you can wear in your ears that translate what you're saying, close to real time, to whatever language the other person you're speaking with wants to communicate in.

So, you will soon be able to sit face-to-face with someone who speaks Italian and carry on a normal conversation, even if you can't speak a word of Italian and they don't speak a word of English. These are amazing times we live in, *don't you agree?*

Current webinar technology doesn't yet support this, but we are talking to a few platform owners about building this. We've tried just about all of them. One we like, both for training webinars and sales webinars (using the QVC Close), is a platform now called Webinato (formerly Omnovia, before they were acquired). Most marketers like to use GoToWebinar for sales webinars and a stable, low-hassle experience. We find it too hard to implement the sales strategies we've developed and described here. Still, it's the most popular platform right now.

Another new development, which works well for people with an evergreen message, is evergreen webinars. These essentially automate and simulate a live webinar but are prerecorded and scheduled as live on several future dates and times. The general rule of thumb is to perfect your live webinar over 20-50 attempts and then select your *best* to use as "evergreen." These are more effective at maximizing people's busy schedules and immediate gratification needs. There are a number of different platforms today that offer this.

Video Marketing

Over the last fifteen years, video marketing has been on the rise and come a long way. In the beginning, YouTube was just a fun way to put various videos online for people to share. The draw was that anybody could do it easily. As YouTube gained popularity and was acquired by Google, more advanced marketing tools were added, like marketing links in the videos and video ads at the beginning of or in the middle of videos people wanted to watch.

You can even create your own channel on YouTube, which is essentially your own TV channel. There, you can self-publish your own show, podcast, or video blog to gain viewers. Many people have taken creative ideas and messages and grown their YouTube channels into hundreds of thousands, even millions of subscribers. What is your million-dollar message that, with the right audience, could turn you into an authority figure and be monetized? Virtually everyone has a message or *some* experience *somebody* else *somewhere* would like to know. And in many cases, that someone will pay you to teach them.

Now if you have a great face for radio or are terrified of the idea of being in front of a camera, you have a few options. One, get over it. Nothing builds trust and relationship with an existing or new audience like a video. The key is authenticity and message. You don't have to become a TV personality to do well with video. In fact, coming across too slick or professional can actually hurt more than it helps. In the end, all people *really want* is a solution to their problem and a person they can trust. So, if you can show you genuinely care and can help them with a problem they are looking to solve, it doesn't matter what you look like, whether you're nervous, or how bad of a hair day you are having. People only care about themselves and improving their situation. If you are genuine and authentic, they're more likely to listen.

> **Pro Tip:** The best way to get better at doing video is to do more video. Trusting that you'll improve over time—and accepting that your first attempts will likely be the worst ones—takes the pressure off so you can *start* doing video. Here's what will happen. You'll watch it and realize the video wasn't nearly as *bad* as you thought. And, gradually, you'll get more comfortable doing them.

Case Study: Suzy Bauer, Red Matchstick Marketing

One of our early mentoring students from South Africa, Suzy Bauer of Red Matchstick Marketing, a social media agency specializing in the hotel/resort industry, wanted to expand her reach in her market. We told her, "Suzy, it's okay.

Your first video will be terrible. It's normal." She recorded a video, and it was terrible. And it was okay. What's great about Suzy is that she doesn't give up, and she kept trying. After a recent Click and Grow Rich live event in Johannesburg, Suzy invited us over to her home for dinner, and we recorded a video. She's now a natural on camera.

Go here to watch Suzy's video:
www.clickandgrowbusiness.com/suzyb

The second option, if you're absolutely against the idea of recording yourself on video, is to pay a video actor to record your video for you. Several good services can be found online, or you can search Google for a local video actor. One service we've had success with is Website Talking Heads, which, for a fee, will professionally shoot your script on a green screen or white background. They allow you to choose from a dozen or so male or female actors with different accents, nationalities, and voices.

A third option, which most lazy marketers use, is to create screen-cast videos. It's okay to be lazy, by the way. Wanting to conserve effort can sometimes lead to easier, less time-consuming, and more effective methods. The "ugly video" or video sales letter (VSL) is widely accredited to Jon Benson, who, as the story

$$MP^5MS^2$$

Video Marketing

- **Gaining in Popularity (YouTube)**
- **Starting to Rank Very Well in SERPS**
- **Video SEO is the Next New Wave**
- **Engaging Way to Tell Company Story**
- **Video Sales Letters**
  (Beat Regular Sales Letters By 2x-10x)
- **Doodle Videos Also Boost Response**

goes, had been sending out weekly live videos of himself to his audience of health and fitness subscribers. One week, his favorite football team was playing, and he didn't want to miss the game. He was wearing his Dallas Cowboy's gear and didn't want to record the video wearing it.

So, instead, he decided to create a quick slideshow presentation of the key points he wanted to share. He recorded his computer screen while speaking the same words on the screen, slide by slide. He was *sure* it would hurt the sales of the offer he typically made at the end of each video. So much so, he was afraid to check the sales results the following day. But to his surprise, sales were four times greater than usual. He shared the method with other top marketers, and they all found this worked just as well!

Pretty soon, many top marketers were using this simple and easy way to "record" a video sales message to send to subscribers. The VSL has become one of the most popular and profitable methods of video marketing of all time, perhaps the greatest breakthrough since the product launch, which we outlined above.

Fortunately, easy-to-use, inexpensive (even free) programs are out there to assist you in creating video. Two of our favorites, as we mentioned, are SnagIt and Camtasia.

One final thing to note. Video search engine optimization (SEO) has also been on the rise. The days of manipulating search engines like Google by keyword-stuffing your website and using similar tricks are over. Google is too smart. But since Google owns YouTube, you're likely seeing a lot more YouTube videos ranking in the top 10 for important keywords. Not to mention, Google knows exactly what your video is about since your video is instantly transcribed during upload. So, if you want to rank well, include a lot of video content on your topic and mention the keywords you want to rank for often in the video. *Google knows.*

If a picture is worth 1,000 words, then a video surely is worth 10,000. So, you'll want to spend time learning how to create video to promote your products or services. The best news is, you can do so much on the editing side that even if you make every mistake you can think of, you can easily fix it in Camtasia or you can easily find a talented video editor to fix it for you.

Some great sites for finding freelancers are Fiverr, Upwork, and Guru. Using Outsourcely, we found an amazing video editor in the Philippines who is very reasonable and does great work. We'll cover more on virtual staffing in the final segment of our MP^{5}MS^2 Formula for Success: *staffing.*

One more creative way to use video is the doodle video, which essentially is a hand-drawn cartoon depiction of an audio message, usually recorded by a voice-over. You can hire professional voice-over talent inexpensively using any of the outsourcing resources above or check out Voices.com whom we've used before and has perhaps the largest database of voice talent around, and you can listen to voice samples there as well. We talked about how we used this in the previous example where we grew our list by over 25,000 people using a doodle video on a Forex product launch opt-in page, which you can see below.

Allowed Me To Grow a $5000 Forex Account To Over $30,000 in Just FOUR Months

EVEN MORE IMPRESSIVE

(An Over 600% Real-Money Gain)
But You're About To See For Yourself...

Enter your best email address below to Discover the
Forex Trading System That Turned $5k into $30k
in Just Four Months....

Get Free Instant Access

We paid several thousand dollars to have this doodle video created, because they are so effective in capturing and keeping the audience's attention, and as we've covered, attention is a critical part of the buying process. The video gave them just enough information to want more, and to leave just their email address, after which we followed up with information on how and when to buy. The good news is, that these days you can find doodle video artists (and even easy-to-use software) to create these types of videos for a much lower price.

Viral Marketing

As people are finally figuring out how to monetize it, viral marketing is also on the rise. Years ago, when the term "going viral" first became popular, it was referring to random ideas, events, messages, posts, or videos that suddenly everybody was talking about and sharing—to the tune of hundreds of thousands, if not millions, of views. One recent example is the "cats and cucumbers" videos on YouTube where one compilation video alone has over 33 million views. Apparently, if you put a cucumber behind a cat while it's eating, upon noticing the cucumber, it will freak out and do various feats of spontaneous acrobatics to get away from the harmless cucumber. For a quick laugh, go have a look.

MP^{5}MS^2
Viral Marketing

- **Can Be Great Exposure Quickly**
- **Video Can Get Millions Views**
  - **Cats & Cucumbers – YouTube**
- **Can Build Huge Email Lists**
- **Monetize List**
  - **Your Own Offers**
  - **Affiliate Offers**
- **Great Exposure**
  - **Dollar Shave Club**

The problem with viral marketing has been that it's very hard to monetize. Consider the cat videos we mention above. Cute pet and animal videos have been some of the most viral videos on the internet, but unless you have your cat wearing a T-shirt with your website URL on it, its spontaneous antics will not likely help your business.

Rare exceptions exist, of course, like Palm Beach, Florida-based ad agency CEO Jim Whelan, who used to wear a $10,000 sequined tuxedo with a cowboy hat and stand front row in crowds to get free TV coverage at the Oscars. It worked. After all, how many 6'3" people do you see wearing a black sequined tuxedo with a cowboy hat? For free advertising, he would then hold up a sign with either a client's site or his own company website on it. That's a bit extreme, but it's one example of how creativity can get you free media.

Viral marketing can, however, be a great way to get lot of exposure to your personal or company brand, even if you're not monetizing it directly. Just look up "girl catches on fire while twerking fail" online and see how many views this had after going viral. The funny thing, which most people don't know, is that it was a Jimmy Kimmel fake. The studio had scripted the scene and hired a professional actress to perform the stunt, which created huge online exposure for the show once the inside story broke.

We have, however, noticed encouraging viral marketing success stories as of late, and several companies who have figured out how to utilize viral video to effectively promote their brand. If you're not familiar with the Dollar Shave Club story, look up their video commercial on YouTube. Not only did they generate over 24 million views, but they also created massive momentum in the disposable razor marketplace, quickly taking over market share from the big-name brands and disrupting the market so much that Gillette purchased them for $1 billion dollars. Not a bad ROI for a low-budget commercial shot in their warehouse for around $10,000.

The success of Dollar Shave Club prompted several other entrepreneurs to follow this model, including a couple of guys who encouraged men to nurture and grow facial hair to its fullest potential, instead of shaving off their beards. Dollar Beard Club was born. These guys shot a series of funny parody videos similar to Dollar Shave Club, and their version also went viral with millions of views, launching a very successful company promoting beard balms and related products.

Two sisters in Canada we know have also recently launched the Dollar Eyelash Club, and we're also talking to one of our platinum mentoring students in South Africa to rebrand his company from The Perfumery to the Dollar Perfume Club.

Another brand we're working with is the Sasquatch Coffee Company, which has a great product with great viral marketing potential. With this brand name, the opportunities are almost endless. We're planning funny Sasquatch sighting videos (coming soon) to promote the brand with Gunnar Monson and his wife, the founders. *Feeling squatchy?* Look them up online.

Email Marketing

While diminishing in popularity and inbox deliverability, email marketing is still the 800-pound gorilla in the digital marketing space. It is still the least expensive and, therefore, the most potentially profitable method of marketing online—*if* you have a responsive email list.

"The money is in the list" saying has largely been gospel among internet marketers for over a decade. The reality these days is that the "money is your relationship with your audience" as we've already talked about. For example, if you have a large subscriber email list but you're not providing value and are, instead, just spamming them all the time with offers, they're not going to be very responsive. In fact, after a while, they'll stop opening your emails. Many marketers have made this mistake and seen their income drop dramatically. This has also contributed to the dramatic drop in email open rates, which has many marketers scrambling.

However, if you're able to nurture and build your relationship with your email list by sending them value in advance, like video trainings, free reports, webinars, and other forms of value (as *they* define value), then you'll likely to still do well. There's a rule of thumb that you should be able to monetize your email list to the tune of $1 per subscriber per month. So, if you have 30,000 email subscribers on your list, you could potentially earn up to $30,000 per month in income or more. These are general guidelines and not any guarantee you will achieve these or similar results because every situation is different, and email is getting harder to get opened.

Although we've given you shortcuts to building your list in the affiliate marketing section, you'll likely spend 90% of your effort, starting out, in building your email subscriber list. But, *wouldn't it be worth it* if, later on, 90% of your income came from just sending out emails to your list, at that point using only 10% of your effort?

$$MP^5MS^2$$

Email Marketing

- Inexpensive and Very Profitable
- "The Money is in the List"
- 90% of Effort in Getting the List
- Then 10% of Effort Emailing List, and Can Generate 90% of Income
- All About Traffic and Conversion
- Mail Your Offers / Affiliate Emails

We used to have between 70,000 and 100,000 email subscribers (primarily generated from affiliates and product launches), which were generating well over $100,000 per month in sales on a consistent monthly basis. How would you like to have even 10,000 on your list? If built and maintained the right way, cross-marketed to on social media, and value created on a regular basis, this audience could support you for a very long time. *Ready to get started?*

Once you've built up your email list, it's all about traffic and conversion. This simply refers to how many subscribers you get to open your emails and click through to see your various offers online (traffic), and what percentage of them convert into buyers (conversion). If your conversion rate is good, you'll make more money. If it's not very good or people aren't taking your upsells on the backend, then your average customer value (ACV) will be lower. Then, you'd want to focus your efforts on improving these areas. That's the beauty of online marketing: you can always improve.

Another added benefit of marketing to your email list is that you can also promote affiliate offers and earn commissions on any sales. Many people don't realize their email can be their greatest asset and a very profitable way of promoting other offers to earn commissions on, without having to deal with customer service or product issues.

One important lesson to remember is to *learn how to make money from people who don't buy from you*. These people are likely still interested in your market and even though they didn't buy from you, they are very likely still buying other companies' products. Why not earn money by referring them to other products they may also get value from (while earning commissions as an affiliate)? This way, you are still monetizing your list, even if they aren't buying from you or, perhaps, have already bought all of your products. Make sense?

The other reason to pursue a good relationship with as large a list as you can is because, at any given time, not all of your emails are going to get delivered,

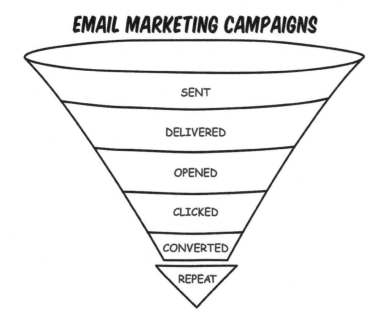

EMAIL MARKETING CAMPAIGNS

SENT

DELIVERED

OPENED

CLICKED

CONVERTED

REPEAT

opened, clicked through, and responded to. That means not every email will produce a sale. Any number of factors affect your conversion rate, from the time of day you're sending, to how busy the readers are, what kind of mood they are in, their current financial situation, family situation, and travel schedule—you name it. So, the point is, keep mailing and keep it interesting. Then, you'll have a better chance of cutting through the clutter and getting through the distraction barrier, like we've talked about.

Some software systems would have you believe that the more times people opened prior emails, watched webinars, or took other actions (displayed by the number of flames next to their names) the more likely they are to buy. But this only shows what that person has done in the past. You still have to catch them in the right moment, with the right message, and the right call to action. So, the more attempts you have, the better—being careful not to upset them by sending the *same* message over and over again. The beauty of the product launch is that you have preset the frame that there's a lot of reasons they should buy your product, and you're going to be sending them lots of different angles for them to make an informed decision vs. blasting them the same "buy it now" message.

One key feature you should have access to is the ability to segment and resend your same email (or even a new one) to everybody who either didn't open or didn't click your prior email. If they didn't even open it, they likely didn't "see" it and, therefore, won't get upset if you send it again a few times. One of the best email subject lines when doing this is, "Just in case you missed this, first name," which lets you off the hook if the recipient did already see it but were too busy to review it, or they may appreciate your resending it if they hadn't seen it.

Content Marketing

Now, let's talk about content marketing. This is one of the newest recognized forms of digital marketing, although people have been doing it for years. This is simply providing valuable information or "content" to your marketplace to build trust, authority, and relationship. Remember, people will buy much more from you if they know, like, and trust you.

These days, it's not enough to just provide a good solution to the readers' or viewers' problem. They need to know who you are and trust you to give them quality information they can benefit from. And, of course, it always helps if they like you, too.

$$MP^5MS^2$$

Content Marketing

- **Provide Valuable Information**
- **Will Build Trust and Relationship**
- **Know, Like and Trust = Sales**
- **People Will Share With Others**
- **Give Away Your Best Content**
- **Secret 'Backdoor' To Selling Online**
- **Repeat Buyers & New Customers**

The way you build a trust relationship is simple; give away some of your *best* information for *free*. Two things will likely happen here: First, readers will likely share your informative, valuable, and helpful information with other people who might also benefit (aka, your target market). Second, they're going to think, "If the *free* information is *this* good, imagine how good everything else being offered must be!" and that will lead to an easier sale and repeat sales later. Try it; it works.

You'll be building tremendous goodwill in the marketplace as well as establishing yourself as an authority figure. Such a reputation can lead to guest appearances on podcasts, radio shows, or TV or result in invitations to write articles for popular blogs, magazines, or groups. It's the secret "back door" to selling. By creating and giving away great information, you'll continue to build a loyal following, which often leads to long-term repeat buyers and customers.

Direct Marketing

To finalize our list of the 9 Proven Marketing Strategies, let's talk about the granddaddy of them all: direct marketing. This is also known as "offline marketing" because this refers to old-school marketing avenues: direct mail, newspapers, magazines, postcards, flyers, and tear sheets—even radio and TV qualify.

$$MP^5MS^2$$

Offline & Direct Marketing

- Take Winning Online Offers Offline
- Magazines, Newspapers, Flyers
- Tearsheets, Direct Mail, Postcards
- Higher Costs But Can Be Worth It
- Less Competition and Clutter
- Test With a Small Budget First
- Big Mistakes Can Kill Your Business

And here's the good news. All of these methods still work and can be even more effective these days because of less competition; most everybody has jumped on the online bandwagon. Have you noticed more or fewer sales letters in your mailbox in the last fifteen years? Depending on how much you actually buy through catalogs and online, you should have seen less. But, increasingly, online marketers are coming back to things like direct mail to send out marketing materials because it still works very well.

One effective strategy is to take your winning online offers offline. Simply convert them to a print sales letter or magazine ad and send them out that way. One example we tested was an offer for a particular type of options-trading software we had created. We had sold it for years on our website and through email marketing promotions. For the most part, we had exhausted all of the buyers. *Or so we thought.*

We converted the online sales letter, word for word, into a print version and *mailed* it to those we had physical mailing addresses for on our same list of customers. We saw a huge increase in sales from the very same people who had repeatedly been seeing it but hadn't bought from our emails. Why? We reasoned that since we had surveyed our audience and discovered they skewed toward aging male baby boomers, they are used to responding mostly through "pre-internet," offline methods. They liked to have something tangible to hold in their hands, to take with them to read later, or to write questions and comments on before making a decision to buy. Whatever the reasons, *it worked extremely well.*

It worked so well we decided to test it out in an industry magazine. We modified the message slightly and hired a copywriter to create four versions from the original sales letter. The interesting thing here was that the first three attempts did *not* produce an immediate ROI. When we modified the call to action on the fourth version, directing them *online* to watch a video overview, this approach *did* work very well. So well, in fact, that it paid for the entire $12,000 expense of running the ads in four consecutive issues.

Here's the most important part and the big surprise. By tracking the visitors and buyers from the four different ads by redirecting the printed URLs to unique Cydec tracking links, we could see how many people actually visited the website and who ultimately bought. What was completely unexpected and a huge surprise—but makes perfect sense—is that the people who originally purchased the $197 software, and made up the $12,000 in initial sales, then purchased an additional $12,000 in product sales from us in the following four months for a total of $24,000. We discovered this accidentally when checking the results a few months later. So, this went from a breakeven campaign to a 100% ROI campaign, which shows the importance of testing and tracking your advertising results.

You can also get very creative with direct mail. One of the challenges, much like with email, is just to get the potential customer to open the mail. However, with email, the only tool you really have is to write a creative subject line. With direct mail, you can include small physical "grabbers" in the mail, which is referred to as "lumpy mail" and can greatly increase your mail-open rate.

✒ **BRETT STORY**

I've sent a lot of direct mail, and with creativity, you can dramatically increase your response. I've mailed letters in see-through "Ziploc" bags so recipients could see the headlines. I've sent plastic *boomerangs* in a shiny blue package with a "We want you back" message inside; those worked tremendously well. I've even sent coconuts through the mail (yes you can do that) with a special offer to a seminar we were having in a tropical destination. As you might imagine, you get a 100%-open rate when you send someone a real coconut.

Oriental Trading Company is a great resource for finding inexpensive direct mail grabbers. Or look online for a company that specializes in "lumpy mail" services, like Handy Mailing Services out of Wichita, Kansas.

Postcards are another inexpensive and effective method to get your message out to people. This works particularly well with a single message, such as a reminder to register for a live event or a "save the date." A simple postcard can drive recipients online to a personalized website to give their name and email address so you can communicate with them online and offline. Most advanced and successful marketers use a combination of multiple methods, an approach called multimodal marketing. We recommend that you initially focus on getting good at *one* first; then, you can branch out to others listed here.

Now that we've covered the 9 Proven Marketing Strategies, it's worth noting that this list is not all-compassing, and marketing strategies are evolving all the time. What this means is that there will always be *new* opportunities. So, keep your eyes open and don't be afraid to try new things. You may just discover the next big breakthrough, which can take you all the way to the bank. Keep in mind *that the creative mind beats the competitive mind* every time. We encourage creativity and innovation as that's what drives opportunity. The first to discover innovative breakthroughs usually reaps the biggest rewards.

SALES TACTICS AND PSYCHOLOGY

N ow that we have established that marketing is not the same as selling, and that marketing essentially covers the first half of the A-I-D-A Formula: creating *attention* and capturing the prospects' *interest*, and maybe a little bit of the *desire* element. It's now up to your sales skills to take care of the last part of the formula: *action*. Without asking for the sale or giving your prospects multiple calls to action, they're not going to know *how* to buy, and all the effort to get them to this point will have been wasted. Wouldn't that be a shame?

You might be saying, "That's silly. Who would do that?" It happens all the time. Marketer's make this mistake regularly and, of course, then blow the sale. Sometimes they miss the opportunity on a webinar; they've done a great job creating attention, interest, and desire, but then either get nervous or don't know how to transition into asking for the sale.

In his book *Speak to Sell*, sales and marketing legend Dan Kennedy calls the ask a "multimillion-dollar secret," and although you may not believe it, it's true. The secret is that your prospect must *actually be told to buy*. Dan states, "They must be told exactly what you want them to do. They must be told to buy... given clear, precise, direct marching orders."

THE AIDA MODEL

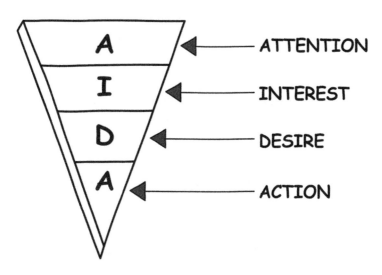

ATTENTION

INTEREST

DESIRE

ACTION

This has been proven especially true with online sales. Often the difference between success and failure is simply giving prospects a clear *call to action*. So, include as many as you can. The more times you ask and the more opportunities you give them, the more sales you will have and the more money you will make. It's well worth making a conscious effort; you must become both comfortable and competent in asking for the sale. *Got it?*

You'll ultimately have to become at least proficient in the selling techniques covered in those books to master online selling. Zig Ziglar is also famous for saying, "Timid sales people raise skinny kids." Fortunately, in the Internet Age, you can use technology to be your silent salesperson by using business automation software, which is pretty awesome, *isn't it?*

At the highest level and before diving into specific strategies and tactics, it's very important that you have absolute clarity and purpose when it comes to your ideal outcome. This can be as simple as creating specific sales goals if "success" is defined in terms of hitting a sales target and that is your intended and purposeful outcome.

People often have several goals or objectives in mind, and this lack of focus and clarity dilutes their energies toward achieving any of their goals. By defining *one* primary objective, you can give more focus to *how* you will achieve this one action. To help you with this, we've created an interactive PDF worksheet called the Focus Wheel:

Download the Focus Wheel Worksheet
www.clickandgrowrich.com/book/FocusWheel

✈ BRETT STORY

When using this same exercise in previous ventures, we were able to regularly hit and exceed aggressive sales goals, simply by identifying clear targets. Remember, there's a reason they don't have blind archery in the Olympics. You can't hit a target you can't clearly see.

Recently, I uncovered several examples of old Focus Wheels where our predetermined monthly sales targets were $100,000 to $150,000 per month, and in each case, we met or exceeded these numbers, reinforcing how valuable and effective focused targets are.

THE FOCUS WHEEL

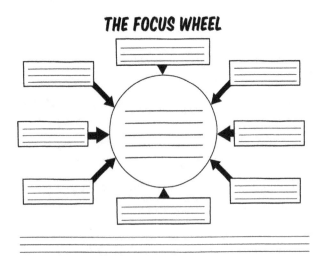

To use the Focus Wheel, simply identify your primary objective—whether purely financial or some other *clearly measurable* goal—and type it into the center of the Focus Wheel. Next, spend time identifying the six to eight specific strategies or activities that will most contribute to hitting the primary focus goal, along with the target contribution of each.

So, for example, if your monthly target income for your online business is $50,000 for the next month (choose a smaller number when starting out, one that is within reach), then in each surrounding box, list an activity, new product, or promotion you can launch along with the sales goals. So, you might estimate you can sell 200 of a $97 new product you're launching for around $20,000 in sales. Maybe you plan a relaunch of a membership site you've already been promoting but haven't mentioned in a while for another $15,000, and then you also have an affiliate promotion for which your commissions might be $10,000. Lastly, you announce a new coaching program at $997, with a goal of five new students.

If you add all this up, it's right around your goal of $50,000. We've found this to be a great way to use the *power of intentionality* to hit higher goals. There is magic to this, to being intentional about hitting your goals. In the book/audiobook *Parallel Universes of Self*, author Frederick Dodson writes of how just giving something your *attention* allows you to become an *observer*, but by giving something your *intention* you are more likely to become the *experiencer* of your clearly defined outcome.

The Intentional Experiencer Worksheet is another important interactive PDF you can use to clarify your intentions and big-picture goals. Again, the power of intentionality is hard to explain, but it can work wonders.

Download the Intentional Experiencer Worksheet
www.clickandgrowrich.com/book/IntentionalExperiencer

You can't be casual about your success and expect it to just "happen" because you work hard. In *Speak to Sell*, Kennedy also says, "Money is repelled by casualness and entitlement. Money flows to people who have great clarity about every detail of the performance of their skill and service and take nothing affecting it for granted." So, we highly recommend using the Business Life Intention Worksheet and updating it once or twice per year.

Now that we've covered some of the high-level strategy considerations, let's talk about the key elements of how to become effective at selling. Before we dive into the actual mechanics of how to do this on the technology side of selling online, let's first talk about the 5 Steps to Effective Selling.

✈ DANIEL STORY

It took me many years of testing and modeling to perfect the *5 Steps to Effective Selling* we teach and implement today. With so many people using what we teach, we know it can be taught, learned, and produce results. While working with a very well-known motivational seminar speaker company, I was able to help them sell without "selling," improving their sales conversions from a 9.2% closing percentage to well over 35%.

During the selling steps it is important to remember that this is a *biological* process, not a series of "techniques" or strategy steps. Everyone who has ever read Zig Ziglar's *Secrets of Closing the Sale* or Brian Tracy's *Sales Mastery* books can model their techniques, which can help you close a solid 10-15% of your sales. But if you want to really blow your numbers up and achieve 25-50% closing rates, or even more, then you should implement the *5 Steps to Effective Selling*.

With this sales process, you can really see the crocodile brain working; how it likes to be approached and *not* approached as we walk you through the Approach, Comfort, Seduction, Open, and Retention steps to effective selling. No matter which of the four personality archetypes you are selling to, remember that *we all are biologically the same*, which is why these principles work so well.

These 5 Steps were adapted from in-person selling. They are equally important concepts to understand when selling online, as they also describe the five phases of human emotion that a new prospect or customer goes through before buying. It's also known as the "customer journey" because your prospect doesn't immediately know, like, or trust you; they need to go through this mental journey before they'll feel comfortable buying from you.

MP⁵MS¹
Selling

Steps To Selling and Opening
- Approach
- Comfort
- Seduction
- Close (The Open)
- Retention

Selling requires a very structured process, so let's review the 5 Steps to Effective Selling.

First, your *approach,* how you first interact with a prospect in the first few seconds or milliseconds, can impact how the rest of the process goes and relationship grows, whether it's fantastic and lasting or terrible and short lived. Next is creating *comfort* with your prospects so they trust you and feel at ease, able to hear and consider your message. Then comes *seduction*; you'll have to romance them a bit before seducing them into becoming a potential customer or buyer. After this, you'll be ready to ask for the order or *close* the prospect with your call to action. This is a bit of a misnomer as what you're really trying to do is *open* up a sales relationship that can lead to future sales. Finally, we have *retention* because it's not about how many sales you manage to make initially; it's how many you keep. If you have a great sales process but poor customer service or products, you may lose many sales in the form of refunds.

Ideally, customers stay around for a long time, becoming repeat customers. In the Internet Age, it's not so much about "closing" the sale. You really want to focus more on *opening* the sale because *closing* sounds like it's the finish line. When you close somebody online, you may win the sale, but what could you be losing? We don't want to finish the sale; we want to *open up the sales relationship* because this is also the ideal time to expose a customer to additional offers in the form of upsells, downsells, free trials, continuity, or membership products, etc. Doesn't that make more sense?

Before the internet, selling was a much different process. Classic movies like *Glengarry Glen Ross*, in which Alec Baldwin immortalized the famous phrase, "Coffee is for closers," glamorized the classic hard-core sales closer of the 1950s. Times have changed, and while people still love to *buy*, most hate to be *sold*. So, you have to be careful about how you're approaching your prospects. You don't want to scare them away. If you haven't seen the movie, watch it, it's a classic.

How many of you have ever gone into a store and had an aggressive salesperson rush up to you? Perhaps they got right in your face, saying something like, "Can I help you? Is there something you're looking for today?" without even introducing themself.

How does that make you feel? What you might really want to say to is, "Go away. Don't pressure me!" But that would be rude. So, you say something nice like, "No, thanks, I'm just looking," even if you might want help. The approach was bad, a little too much in your face, so you pull back into your safe zone. Both sides lose here, don't they?

How many of you have ever gone into a store, wanting to buy something yet nobody comes to help you? That can be upsetting also, can't it? It's another example of a poor approach—in this case, no approach at all. Either the salesperson takes too long or doesn't come at all. As a customer, sometimes you feel like you can't win. We're psychologically taught not to be pushy and also not to ask for help. So, opening up the sales conversation can seem like an unusual dance at first. But, before you despair, consider what a male peacock has to do to approach and attract a female. Consider yourself lucky.

These 5 Steps to Effective Selling have a lot more to do with psychology and biology than sales techniques, but as we learned previously, our reptilian brain has the job of instantly deciding whether to ignore, run away, or pay attention to a new stimulus in our environment. And in this case, if you come on too strong with your sales message, you can trigger two negative responses: ignore or run away. Have you ever wanted to just run away from a pushy salesperson in a store? It's the same thing online, only it's even easier for your prospect to run away, isn't it? All that your prospect has to do is leave your website or close their browser.

One way to engage the reptilian brain is to ask questions that engage your audience. We are taught from an early age to answer questions when asked, so it's natural for us as humans to pay more attention when asked a question, even if we choose not to respond. An even better way to engage your audience, and one of the secrets of mastering selling, is to ask as many yes questions—questions that will likely have a yes answer—as you can. These positive responses serve as microcommitments, *don't they?* Can you see what we're *doing here?* This is starting to make more sense now, *isn't it?* Now, go back and reread this section and count how many "yes questions" we've asked you. That was intentional.

The Four Personality Archetypes

It's also helpful to understand that biology and personality play an important role in how an individual reacts to different sales approaches. Usually the approach that works best is the one that most resonates with an individual's personality. Humans generally fall into four major personality archetypes, which affect how an individual filters the world around them. Have you ever met somebody new and immediately liked them? You had a chemistry together, warm and friendly from the start. As times passes, you feel even more comfortable together. It happens through approach into comfort.

The four personality archetypes we keep in mind when preparing a sales presentation are Lions, Owls, Monkeys, and Cocker Spaniels. Other variations are out there, but we feel you should be aware of these four. Understanding these four personality types can help you in any social situation, especially when trying to communicate with people who have varying perspectives. No one personality is better than others.

Most aren't even aware these types exist, so mastering this concept can give you an advantage. These four groups can be broken down into *extroverts* or *introverts* and according to whether the person is predominantly *feeling* or *thinking* driven.

Lions

As you might imagine, Lions are on the extroverted side of the matrix and are thinkers. They love to be in charge, are confident and not easily discouraged, feel they must correct wrongs and injustices, and are usually independent and self-sufficient.

Lions are proactive in decision-making, typically risk-takers, and competitive. They can also be hostile, dominating, and combative if threatened, even using others to their advantage. In real-life environments, Lions can be more assertive and aggressive, focusing on progress and production. They are able to see the "big picture" and are usually good at finding practical solutions. When talking to Lions, you'll want to get to the point quickly, give direct and honest answers, and speak loudly and clearly.

Owls

Owls, on the other hand, are introverted thinkers. They like to plan and organize and are precise and logical. Owls prefer calm, thorough communication without confrontation or arguments. These types can be seen as overly critical or emotionally unavailable; therefore, they may seem to isolate themselves from others. They are detail-oriented, responsible introverts who take pride in their work. However, Owls can sometimes come across as self-absorbed, eccentric, depressive, and even narcissistic.

Monkeys

Monkeys are fun-loving, enthusiastic, and extroverted feelers. They are personable, expressive, outgoing, and fun. They can be decisive but also impulsive and excessive, not listening well or possibly interrupting. Monkeys like to hear themselves talk, so they may be drawn to public speaking or being the center of attention. They will often disagree with Lions and Owls, who prefer a more structured environment; in contrast, Monkeys enjoy being spontaneous and will make last-minute decisions "on the fly."

Cocker Spaniels

Cocker Spaniels are introverted feelers. They are relationship-oriented supporters who are amiable, trusting, and compassionate. Cocker Spaniels are caring and generous peacemakers, but they can also be fearful, possessive, and high maintenance. They care about how their actions make others feel, so they may not speak up, fearing they might upset another.

THE 4 ARCHETYPES

EXTROVERT (THINKING)	**EXTROVERT (FEELING)**
DRIVERS, CONTROLLERS, RESULTS-ORIENTED	SPONTANEOUS, CREATIVE FUN-LOVING
LIONS	**MONKEYS**
INTROVERT (THINKING)	**INTROVERT (FEELING)**
ANALYTICAL, LOGIC ORIENTED	SUPPORTIVE, RELATIONSHIP ORIENTED
OWLS	**COCKER SPANIEL**

Most people are a combination of two types: one of the above as a dominant archetype, with a secondary archetype to round out their personality. It's easy to see that becoming familiar with the four personality archetypes will benefit you personally, as you better understand your own style, and professionally, as you better understand your potential customer's style.

By better understanding your prospect or being able to identify multiple personality types in a group sales presentation, you will undoubtedly improve your sales. For best results, keep in mind *all four archetypes* as you build your advertising offers and sales presentations. What might appeal to a Lion may not appeal at all to an Owl. Make sense?

Another important concept to understand when selling to prospects is the *5 Levels of Interest*. By knowing these, you can better focus your energy on the levels that are most open and responsive to buying.

The sales pyramid below outlines these 5 Levels. According to the late Chet Holmes, in his book *The Ultimate Sales Machine*, at any given time, only about 3% of your audience arrives at your sales page ready to buy your product or service.[18]

That's it. So, you need to be aware of this low percentage and not get discouraged when you don't see a wave of buyers right away. It takes between seven and ten times of seeing your offer or advertisement before someone is ready to buy. This has been proven.

Knowing this, you can more effectively plan your marketing and sales strategies. Looking at the sales pyramid below, we see that 3% are primed and ready to buy. Another 6-7% are open to the idea of buying but may need additional information. An initial no answer, in this case, doesn't usually mean no forever; it just means they either have questions or need more logical/emotional justification to buy. *It's also well known that people usually make buying decisions based on emotion, then will justify with logic*: "But, honey, the Ferrari really does get good gas mileage around town."

So, looking at the following breakdown, you can surmise that while roughly 10% of potential buyers can be sold with relatively little effort, 90% of your prospects are either not thinking about it, don't think they want it, or know that they don't want it.

SALES PYRAMID

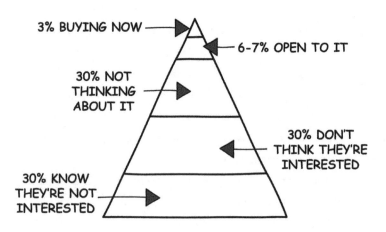

Here's the breakdown:

- 3% are interested in buying now
- 7% are open to buying now
- 30% are not thinking about it
- 30% don't think they are interested
- 30% know they aren't interested

So, where do you think you should spend the most amount of time and sales efforts?

Let's rule out and ignore the 30% who know they're not interested and instead focus on the largest section of people that could potentially be brought around to buying your product: the 60% of people who either aren't yet thinking about buying or think they aren't interested (based on the information they currently have). One of the reasons product launches and retargeted advertising are so effective is that both let you effectively "drip" new information to your prospects over time. *Because new information = new decision.* This means that every time you give someone *new* and potentially interesting content, they have the basis to form a new decision about whether it makes sense for them to buy.

We've already talked about the concept of V-Selling and how everybody's price/value equation is different *for them.* So, you have the greatest potential for increasing your sales in this 60% (people who either aren't yet thinking about buying or think they aren't interested). One of the best ways is to simply educate these would-be customers.

Using the simple "How to X, without Y" headline or advertisement header leads with a big benefit (X) and tells readers they won't have to do the thing they don't want (Y). You'll likely capture their attention. Remembering the A-I-D-A Formula, we know *attention* is the first step in the process of landing a sale, so it's very important (and not easy).

According to *The Ultimate Sales Machine*, "The hardest thing we need to do today is grab the attention of potential buyers and keep their attention long enough to help them buy your product. This approach of offering some education of value to them gives you a significant opportunity to attract more buyers and build more credibility." Chet Holmes calls this "education-based marketing" and also says, "You will attract way more buyers if you are offering to teach something of value to them than you will ever attract by simply trying to sell them your product or service." Makes perfect sense, doesn't it?

To help you attract attention and interest to your products and services, we've created the Headline Generator, an interactive PDF worksheet you can use in your advertising and on your sales pages. It features simple, fill-in-the-blank fields to capture your prospect's attention and interest. It's a great resource that our students love to use, and you can find it here:

Download the Headline Generator
www.clickandgrowrich.com/book/HeadlineGenerator

Hopefully you've gained a better understanding of how effective selling occurs. This is an ever-expanding area, and we've just scratched the surface here, giving you the most important high-level concepts. For more information, search online, but you now have the core concepts you'll need most. These tactics are most effective when used with the other strategies in this book to create your online sales ads, landing pages, promotions, webinars, order forms, and upsells.

DANIEL STORY

About ten years ago, Tony Robbins and Chet Holmes were running radio ads in major radio markets for a program they had created called Business Mastery in which they would ask business owners if they wanted help growing their businesses and increasing sales.

Initially, their sales of the program were not great. It was the first real time that they had used webinars to sell the product, and every day they were producing multiple webinars using hired teachers that had never been taught how to sell well. They mistakenly thought anyone could be effective selling their programs because of their widespread name recognition.

The management team decided to bring on some help to turn things around, and I was one of the first people they contacted. Initially I said no, but I had been retired for some time, I was getting tired of playing golf, and was driving my fiancée crazy being around, all the time. Since I was burning to get back into sales, I joined the team, and one of the first things we did was get rid of all the underperforming webinar presenters.

I then modeled the process for the best performing webinar they had tried. Once we had it performing better, we brought on additional presenters and grew to a team of four of us that were presenting the webinars. Over the course of a few months we had perfected their webinar model, and dramatically increased their sales conversions because we followed a proven sales process. This shows the importance of understanding *how* to sell, which is sometimes *more important* than who is behind the product being sold.

OUTSOURCING AND VIRTUAL STAFFING

N ow let's talk about *staffing*, the last component—yet one of most important parts—of our MP⁵MS² Formula. When speaking to groups around the world, we usually start by saying, "There's nothing inherently difficult about doing *any* of this. It's trying to do it *all* yourself that becomes difficult, if not impossible." That's where virtual staffing comes in. You must find other people who can do what you don't have time to do and *shouldn't* be doing.

In the classic book *The E-Myth*, Michael Gerber writes about the importance of "Working on your business, instead of *in* your business." This distinction is especially crucial today. There's simply too much to do yourself. Fortunately, in the Internet Age, you can find highly qualified "virtual" people (often more qualified than you) to do just about anything for pennies on the dollar, without having to hire them as full-time or even part-time employees.

Think about that concept for a moment. Imagine if you could hire the most qualified person for the job out of hundreds of applicants, see their ratings and reviews for previous work, and pay them either by the hour or by the project— roughly 75% less than what you would pay for a comparable US-based contractor because of lower costs of living in other countries.

And, here's the big one. You don't have to keep them on as an expensive monthly employee or worry about letting them go and how that may impact their livelihood. Most business owners don't like firing people. The problem with "employees" is that it's a major financial and emotional commitment. Experts estimate the cost of a "mis-hire" can be very high if you make the wrong choice.

According to the US Department of Labor, the price of a bad hire is at least 30% of the employee's first-year earnings.[19] So, if their annual salary is going to be $60,000 USD, the "cost" of keeping them on, letting them go, and finding someone else to replace them could cost you around $18,000.

That's a significant amount of money for a solopreneur or even a small company, so imagine not having to worry about making that mistake. With virtual staffing, you can hire by the project or by the hour, and if things aren't working out, you can just discontinue the project. Freelancers usually have other clients and work to do and won't be unemployed. Plus, you don't have to have look people in the eye and say, "You're fired."

The concept of hiring overseas "virtual employees" was first popularized by Tim Ferris in his book *The 4-Hour Workweek,* which became an international best seller and global phenomenon. It also allowed him to launch other successful products under the 4-Hour brand, which made him rich and famous. The funny thing is that we heard he was initially spending about 60-80 hours a week promoting his book *The 4-Hour Workweek,* but, obviously, it turned out well for him. The good news is, *you're also just one idea away!*

This concept of "working less, enjoying more" is understandably very popular. As Freedom Fighters, you are becoming empowered through this book on how to do this, building your own Laptop Lifestyle as we have and as hundreds of our students around the world are working toward now. If you haven't started yet, we invite you to join us!

Another great book in this category was just released by our good friend Nik Halik, *The 5-Day Weekend.* Nik is an amazing example of living the Laptop Lifestyle. He's been to over 150 countries, travelled to space, had lunch on the Titanic in a hired Russian submarine, and climbed into live volcanoes. He has a Guinness World Record and owns real estate around the world—all a result of carefully crafting the kind of life and lifestyle he wanted. Nik joined us for an amazing Mastermind we held in 2017 in an exotic mansion on a secret private beach (actually named Playa de Secreto) in Playa Del Carmen, Mexico, where he shared with us some of the core principles he lives by. Nik is a multimillionaire with residences around the world.

This incredible trip was also a tax write-off for everybody, including several of our students—another reason to have your own online business. And the best part is, we kept our businesses running with our virtual staff in various parts of the world. All we needed was a Wi-Fi signal or a cellular connection, which today is nearly everywhere.

During that trip, we were able to stay in contact with our team leader in the Philippines while sitting on the beach in Mexico, touring the pyramids in Chichen Itza, swimming in a Cenote, and just about everywhere in between. Talk about taking your "office" with you! Never before have you been able to do this, yet we've been doing it around the globe for years. *And now it's your turn.*

So, let's talk about why you should use virtual staffing as you grow. Once you start getting leads and customers and your business starts to expand, you'll need to have some help. There's too much to do alone. Plus, why would you want to? Outsourcing allows you to find people who are happy to take things like customer service, emails, phone calls, bookkeeping, and just about everything else you don't want to do or have time to do.

Plus, you should be focusing on your highest core values and the best use of your time, which is usually sales, strategy, content, and marketing. Everything else should be delegated so you can focus on the most important things in your business. Time is your most valuable asset.

✍ DANIEL STORY

If you want to create the goal to have a million-dollar-per-year income, then break it down to how much per hour do you need to make? Then do the math. $1,000,000 divided by 2010 working hours in the normal work year equals $497/hr.

Now act like you already have a millionaire mindset and focus on only doing things that make you at least $497/hr. Start moving away from the things that do not make you that much per hour and hire someone else to do those other tasks, for less.

If you're saying "But I only make $20 or $40 or $60 per hour now, how do I make the transition?" As you follow our process, and start earning more in your business, then hand off the less important things you are currently doing.

It's sometimes hard to give up tasks at first, but once you start to do it, you will notice that you're getting closer to your real goals, and making bigger changes in your life.

Think about it. How much time to do you waste every day sending and answering emails, one of the biggest time-wasting activities? Yes, it can and should be delegated.

Let's start by talking about the two biggest areas in which you'll need help as you grow your business: *customer service* and *operational support*. For basic customer service, whether by email or, preferably, an online support ticket system, customers will often need help with things like lost passwords, product

MP⁵MS²

Virtual Staffing

How to Support Your <u>Customers</u>

- **Basic Support**
  - **How To Login & Passwords**
  - **How To Download Products**
  - **Billing Questions and Subscriptions**

- **Technical Support**
  - **How to Use Product or Software**
  - **Upgrades and Technical Issues**

access, help with downloads, billing questions, technical support (including usage issues), upgrades, and everything in between. Don't make the mistake of doing all of this yourself, running the business all day and then staying up until two o'clock in the morning answering customer support emails.

Don't do that. It's a terrible use of your time.

There are really only 3 Kinds of Time: Unproductive Time, Productive Time, and Leveraged Time. An example of Unproductive Time is eating pizza and Cheetos, drinking a beer while sitting on the couch, and watching *Game of Thrones*. It can certainly be good to relax every now and then to recharge, but this won't move you ahead in your business. An example of Productive Time is doing things like answering business emails, having calls with your team, recording and editing videos, etc. This *will* advance your business, but some of this is repetitive and should be avoided or delegated. You should try to focus 80% of your time on things that *only you can do*, things you do better than anyone in your company!

Train someone to do everything else for you, which is where Leveraged Time comes in, which can also be called super-productive time. An example would be using your time to record training videos for your virtual assistants so they can refer back to them or so you can use them in training a new assistant. The worst feeling is when you've spent three to six months training a key virtual assistant and she leaves. You have to start all over again, unless you've used this Leveraged Time technique. You do the work *once* and then don't have to do it again. Another example of Leveraged Time is writing an FAQ section for your website. As we go through this section, think of *everything* you could be training someone else to do for you.

The other area where you'll likely want to outsource and hire virtual assistants (VAs) is with operational support. You'll definitely need a team as you grow bigger, unless you're happy being a small-time solopreneur, and that's not what this book is about. Why not aim much higher? Why not aim for the stars and see how far you can go? In this book, we're giving you the tools, strategies, and resources to go far. When you're just starting out, you may not need help with these key functions in your business, but keep these tips in mind for when you do. Plan ahead for hiring help. Some key roles you may eventually need help with are team management/operations, accounting and financial, a support team or manager, and even marketing. Some of these positions are high level and will come much later.

MP⁵MS²

Virtual Staffing

How to Support Your <u>Business</u>
- **Accounting & Bookkeeping**
- **Billing & Sales**
- **Graphic Design**
- **Lead Generation**
- **Email List Management**
- **Affiliate Management**

More immediate areas you may want to hire for are graphic design, video editing, copywriting, social media, content writing, voice talent, and Facebook or Google advertising. These positions are crucial as you begin. Now, not all virtual staff are of the same quality, so you may go through several before you find someone you really like, who does superior work for you. The key is to keep the best, fire the rest. This is very important. Your business depends on it.

Where do you find the best resources? Fortunately, many great online resources are available these days; you can find quality virtual help fairly easily. A popular website for finding outsourced help for just about any project small or large is Fiverr. Fiverr has grown quickly worldwide because of its unique selling proposition (USP): you can find people to do things for you for, you guessed it, five bucks.

That's how it started, but now you might expect to pay a little more with add-ons and upcharges. Even so, it's still a great place to get started, and you can find quality workers here. For example, we've used Fiverr for creating things like graphics, video animations, free PDF reports, logos, and artwork. In fact, many of the graphics in this book were created on Fiverr. You'll be amazed what you can find on this site.

You can find other sites online with a Google search. Another resource we like is called Guru.com, which helps you either look for someone local or search anywhere in the world. One of the nice things is that you can view the workers' ratings and overall score from previous people they've worked for, along with examples of previous work to get a better idea of the quality of their work. This is a great way to try someone out, before committing to hire them. If you're not happy with the work, you can either request revisions or choose not to work with them again. Typically, if you choose carefully the first time, workers do a very good job so that you will rate them well.

MP^5MS^2

Staffing

Where To Find Virtual Staff

– **Look Online**

– **Long-Term**

• Outsourcely
• 123 Employee

– **Per Project**

• Fiverr
• Upwork
• Guru.com

To find a more permanent virtual assistant, like an executive assistant, for example, other websites can match you with the ideal candidate. 123 Employee is a good example. The founder and CEO Daven Michaels is a friend of ours, so he's offered to give anyone reading our book 10 *free* hours of virtual assistant time to see if his company is a good fit for you. Who says there's no such thing as a *free* lunch these days?

To get 10 free hours with a virtual assistant visit:
www.clickandgrowrich.com/123employee

One of our favorite little-known resources worth mentioning is Outsourcely. This site charges a monthly fee for unlimited job posting and searching, but you can then communicate directly with and hire the virtual contractors found there. We've found great VA's on Outsourcely, like video editors, SEO, and executive assistants. The work quality is high, and the cost is much lower than you would expect to find in many parts of the world. When you're beginning your business, saving money should be one of your primary objectives so you can stay in the game and invest it in better things like advertising your business.

Now, you might be saying, "But my sister/cousin/neighbor/friend does graphic design, so I'll just hire them." We don't recommend hiring people close to you because often you won't get the best quality work at the best price, and it can make Thanksgiving dinner really awkward if you have to fire a relative or it doesn't work out. So, use outsourcers until you've grown your business to a point where you're ready for a full-time hire or you need a real office, although this is still a huge and unnecessary expense in most cases. We run our multimillion-dollar businesses with a 100% virtual staff from all over the world, from Puerto Rico to the Philippines, and it's awesome.

When you do branch out to hire "real" employees, just keep in mind that you only want to hire *A* players, the very best that you can find. In *Topgrading*, Bradford Smart describes what happens if you're hiring *B*s and *C*s in your business. If you already have any *A* players, they will eventually get pulled down to the lower *B* and *C* levels because they see that they don't have to work that hard, and you don't want that. One exceptional *A* employee is worth three or more of the rest. So, choose wisely, hire slowly, and fire quickly. It takes practice, but your business (and your livelihood) depends on it!

In terms of finding local staff, things have definitely changed over the last 20 years. Back then, you might run an ad in the newspaper. These days, you would be better off asking for referrals from people you know, posting on one of the many jobs websites, or listing the position on Craigslist, one of our favorites. It's inexpensive and easy to post jobs online, and you'll start getting responses almost immediately. The only drawback is sometimes you'll get too many responses; going through them can become a full-time job. Usually, many are looking for jobs, and some use the "spray and pray" method, not reading ads but, instead, just sending out their résumé all over the place, hoping for a reply.

Whenever running an ad for a new hire, whether looking for a local or virtual worker, consider using this strategy. In the ad, insert something like, "In your application, make sure to tell us the answer to 11+7 so we'll know that you actually read our ad." If an applicant doesn't respond with 18, then delete the application. It doesn't matter how qualified they are, if they're not taking the time to read the ad carefully, they aren't going to give your business the attention it deserves. At the very least, communication issues and confusion will likely arise.

This rule is *especially* true when hiring bookkeepers or people in financial positions. Countless horror stories recount business owners hiring the wrong people and losing tens to hundreds of thousands of dollars in outright theft and embezzlement. It's happened to us, and it's not a fun experience. Check references carefully, always run an online background check, and watch them like a hawk. There's no worse feeling than having money stolen by people you trusted, especially if you realize too late you didn't have your eyes open and weren't paying attention. We've been there, so if this paragraph helps prevent even one of you from going through it, our warning was worth it.

Another important operational-level area where you simply can't do it all yourself is staying on top of and managing key business functions, such as billing and sales reporting, monthly subscribers, customer management, email list management, affiliate commissions reporting, and monitoring your key performance indicators (KPIs) of the business. The days of using day planners and spreadsheets are long gone. In today's world, you need to use online software and business automation tools to run your business effectively. If you're going to succeed and compete, it's not optional. You must use technology to automate your business. The good news is, it's easier than ever to find and use simple software like Cydec, which can automate many of the functions we've mentioned.

One of our favorite and relatively *new* software platforms to use is called Zapier, which effectively communicates with nearly 1,000 other software platforms, from accounting software to SMS and voice broadcast software, CRMs and spreadsheets, and everything in between. Using Zapier, you can quickly "connect" all of these elements together, so any action in any program can trigger a follow-up action in another, giving you a real business automation experience.

For example, you can easily set up a workflow whereby a new email subscriber in Cydec can immediately trigger a SMS message being sent out via a program called ClickSend; a contact record gets created in ZohoCRM; the appropriate team members are notified via Slack; a new follow-up project is added to Trello; and Cydec can still send out automated email messages on set daily delays that follow up on specific dates and times. Thousands of combinations can be created, and almost anything you'd like to automate, is possible.

So, if you've ever wished you could clone yourself or have another you to do all the work, now you can do almost that with automation in the Internet Age.

How do you know it's time for a virtual assistant? The answer is, "as soon as possible," so here's what we recommend: keep a notebook by your desk for one

MP⁵MS² Virtual Staffing

How To Support <u>Yourself</u>
- Clean and Sort Email Inbox
- Report Important Emails by Skype
- Reply To Non-Essential Emails
- Learn To Use Marketing Software
- Schedule & Coordinate Appointments
- Coordinate & Manage Projects
- Handle Administrative Tasks

week and every time you do something that's not the best use of your time, write down the task. By the end of the week (or possibly two), you'll have a list of five to ten things, and that's proof it's time to seek virtual help.

Some of the things you can have your virtual assistant do for you to save time include cleaning and sorting your inbox, reporting important messages by Skype, using your marketing software, doing blog posts, managing social media and Facebook groups, coordinating and scheduling meetings and appointments, being a project manager and coordinating project teams, as well as handling administrative tasks. After delegating these tasks, you simply show up to do only the things you do best.

Email is, perhaps, the most important task to hand off first. Think of how much time you spend (unnecessarily) every day reading and replying to email. And, the more emails you send out, the more you receive. It's a never-ending cycle that only gets worse. So stop doing it.

Have you ever used a "To Do" list? It's time to start creating a "Not to Do List" and start writing things down on this list whenever you say to yourself, "I shouldn't be doing this." As soon as you find yourself with five or more items on this list, hire a VA to take these off your plate.

✒ BRETT STORY

Starting out, I used to be at my office until well past midnight because I spent most of the day on email. Mondays were the worst, so they became known as "Midnight Mondays" because 12-14-hour days were common. Why? The first thing I would do was to dive into emails and search for any "important" emails. Isn't that the reason most people open email first, to see if anything urgent needs attention as they begin their day? From there, it snowballed and the whole day disappeared.

The problem with following this strategy is, you'll also see other emails—seemingly important matters and quick replies you can make. So, you'll take care of those also. A few of them will turn into conversations, a flurry of emails going back and forth. Then, of course, you start sending out other important emails to staff and contractors and anyone else who needs your direction for the week—all the big ideas you had over the weekend that you want to get going on. This turns into a never-ending cycle, and the only way to stop the email treadmill is either to restrict checking emails to certain times of the day, or to stay up well past any reasonable hour. From experience, the latter only results in burnout and not getting anything important done.

How do you free yourself from the email treadmill? Hire a VA and train them to tidy your inbox every morning before you get online and to repeat the process throughout the day. You train them to log in to your business email and delete all the obvious spam or move it to an "unsubscribe" folder so they can remove you from those lists later; either way, they get it out of your inbox. Next, they'll move anything that looks important into a "priority" folder, which is the only folder you'll check. From here, they should message you on Skype every morning before you start *your* day to tell you the top five most important emails requiring your response. You can also advise your VA on how to respond on your behalf to noncritical emails.

Believe it or not, the thirty seconds here and there that it takes you to reply to email definitely adds up, and it not only burns through your day but it will also exhaust you mentally. You should ruthlessly guard your early-morning mental energy and focus, allocating it to your most important projects, your *biggest* domino for the day. The morning is your "hour of power" and should not be interrupted. We've created a useful worksheet for maximizing this time of day. Fill out the Power Hour Worksheet the day before, at the day's end, writing the most important task or project you will work on first thing the next day, *without exception*. Commit to the task on the worksheet. It works.

Download the Power Hour worksheet here:
www.clickandgrowrich.com/book/PowerHour

Another book we recommend to our students is *The One Thing*, which essentially asks the question, "What is the *one* thing you could be doing that will make everything else easier or unnecessary?" They recommend blocking out the first four hours of your day to focus exclusively on that one thing. This is harder than it sounds, but to start with even *one* hour, you'll need to clear your plate of other little distractions, like email. In Latin, clean slate is *tabula rasa*, a term you'll see on the Power Hour Worksheet.

Your VA should list everything important in Skype once per morning, including crucial emails, your important meetings for the day, contact methods, and anything else important for you to review. Then, you delegate to the VA the emails to which they can reply. This way, you won't get sucked into emails and derail your whole day. The next most difficult skill is learning to time-block your day to get work done on your most important projects.

To help with this, we've created powerful interactive worksheets to help you clarify your biggest projects to focus on for the quarter, month, week, or day. We've even "gamified" these to-do lists to make it fun.

The first worksheet is called the Big Rocks Worksheet. Have you heard the story about the teacher who had a large jar and asked her students to tell her when the jar was full? She filled the jar with large rocks, all the way to the top. She asked, "Is it full?" Her students said yes. She then poured gravel into the jar, until it could hold no more. Again, she asked, "Is it full?" Again, the students said, "Yes, now it's full." She then picked up a bucket of sand and poured the sand over the jar until it was overflowing; it filled in all the space between the rocks and gravel. She asked once more, "Is it full?"

The students, starting to catch on, reluctantly said, "Yes, now it has to be full." She replied by picking up a bucket of water and filling the jar to the rim. "Now the jar is full," she said.

As this story illustrates, if you're spending your energies and time filling your jar full of little things—sand, gravel, and water—you'll never get the Big Rocks in the jar. So, you start with the big, must-do items first; then, you add the next-most important tasks to your jar. The Big Rocks Worksheet asks you to list your six most important projects first, then the five to six tasks you'll do to finish the big things. Remember, you really can't focus on more than six big projects at a time without experiencing overwhelm.

BIG 'ROCKS' WORKSHEET
LIST YOUR BIGGEST LONG-TERM GOALS

Download the Big Rocks Worksheet Here:
www.clickandgrowrich.com/book/BigRocks

To break larger tasks down even more, we've included a Weekly Planner that lets you segment out what you'll work on each week and each day, including a self-designated reward for actually doing it.

Download the Weekly Planner Here:
www.clickandgrowrich.com/book/WeeklyPlanner

And, to really get focused each day, we've created an interactive Daily To-Do List PDF. We use this worksheet daily. Not only do you list your top-10 things to do each day, but you can check off tasks as you complete them, seeing the progress bar at the bottom move closer toward 100% in 10% increments. Tracking your progress makes the worksheet fun (and a little addictive). Plus, at the end of the day, with the push of a button, it will clear and sort your completed tasks, removing what's done and moving all the incomplete tasks up the list and advancing the day of the week automatically. You start there the next morning.

THINGS TO DO
TODAY

Day _____   **Completed**

1 _____ ☐

2 _____ ☐

3 _____ ☐

4 _____ ☐

5 _____ ☐

6 _____ ☐

7 _____ ☐

8 _____ ☐

9 _____ ☐

10 _____ ☐

Download the Daily To-Do List Here:
www.clickandgrowrich.com/book/ToDoList

By outsourcing tasks and utilizing the amazing PDF productivity worksheets we've created, you can dramatically increase your output and chances of success. You'll be able to focus on the most important high-level tasks, which will bring you closer to your definition of success. Earlier, we mentioned nothing was inherently difficult with any part of this process, but doing it all yourself is unnecessarily difficult. In fact, it's nearly impossible to do it all yourself. And, why would you want to when you can find top-quality virtual employees who will happily do it for you, often for much less than you could hire someone locally? This frees you up to make the best use of your time and energy.

Everybody has the same amount of time in a day; it's how you use your time that makes all the difference. As an entrepreneur, you'll need to focus your time on the most important areas that can have the biggest impact and create the greatest end result. We've been saying for a long time that there's nothing inherently difficult about any of this, or making money online, but it is very difficult if not impossible to do it all yourself.

To help you stay focused on the things that really matter, typically marketing and sales, we've created this birds-eye visual for you to keep a copy handy. We recommend printing this out and having it pinned to your wall or whiteboard. In the Time and Focus Pyramid below, we've categorized the primary important functions of most businesses into three sections.

Starting from the bottom, you'll see the essential activities that form the foundation of your business and while all very important, these are not things you should be doing and rather training someone else to do, like a virtual employee. These important (yet not critical) functions include: customer support, operations, your back-office tasks, appointment scheduling, accounting, social media, blogging and free content creation, website updates, your CRM or sales platform management, and market research or R&D for new products and services to offer.

You can see all of these listed in Level 3 of the Time and Focus Pyramid. This is where you'll put all of the important functions that keep your business running smoothly, but that can be handed off to someone else to do. These are important functions but aren't directly bringing in revenue, which in 90% of businesses is the core driver of business success.

In Level 2 you'll see three more important areas of most businesses that make up the mid-range of the pyramid. This includes paid content, teams, and systems. Your teams are your managers; people who keep the business running smoothly and oversee your Level 3 staff and virtual employees. They are the ones responsible and accountable for making sure everything is running smoothly, and implementing repeatable systems that you or they have put together. In this section, we've also placed content creation. In contrast to free content like social media or blogging, which can be outsourced (and belongs in Level 3), your primary content will be your products and services that your customers will ultimately pay for.

You may have noticed by now that there is a large circle drawn around the top section of the pyramid, section one, which also has the words Time, Money, and Focus drawn outside the circle with dollar signs just inside the circle. This is to signify that these are typically the highest ROI activities for you to be doing.

TIME AND FOCUS PYRAMID

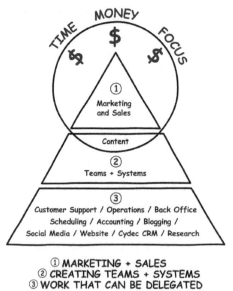

① MARKETING + SALES
② CREATING TEAMS + SYSTEMS
③ WORK THAT CAN BE DELEGATED

Download the Time and Focus Pyramid Here:
www.clickandgrowrich.com/book/TimeAndFocusPyramid

Nothing else comes close in terms of where you should be focusing your time and focus, because these are the actions that will generate the most revenue.

In Level 1, you can see marketing and sales are the only two actions listed. Why? Because everything else is either a management task or "nice to have" function, but at the end of the day for the business to pay its bills and provide income for the staff and owners, sales must occur. Therefore, this is where the bulk of your time as the business owner needs to be spent for you to be successful. We've also drawn the circle around content from level 2, because it's very important that you're producing the best quality information, services and solutions (aka your products), and delivering that to the marketplace. For this reason, it's important that you as the owner and/or expert are also involved in this process, even if you're delegating some of this.

You'll also need to have an intimate familiarity with your products, to be effective at marketing and selling them. So that's why we've drawn the circle this way, and created this helpful visual to help you understand this relationship, and focus your efforts where they count.

So, now that you've just learned our MP^{5}MS^2 Formula for Success, it's all becoming clearer, isn't it? Wouldn't you agree that armed with this simple yet powerful new information, you will have a much better chance of success than when you started reading this book?

You now have a much better framework for moving forward into the next section, in which we'll dive into the different types of online businesses you can consider starting. Ready? Let's go.

Section Three

TYPES OF ONLINE BUSINESS MODELS (THE QUAD-FECTA)

DIGITAL VS. PHYSICAL
INFORMATION PRODUCTS

Now that you understand the MP⁵MS² Formula for Success, our nine-step process of creating your online business, and have a better understanding of how all this works, it's time to figure out what kind of product or service you should create. Ideally, you'll want to create one that resonates with you and reflects your passions and interests; you want it to be fulfilling for the long term. If you haven't yet read section two and filled out your I-O-E worksheet, it's important to do that before moving forward.

Once you've identified the overlap of interests, opportunities, and life experience, you'll see where the biggest potential exists for you in the marketplace. Then, you're ready to figure out the best combination of products or services to sell to the *people* in your chosen *market*. This will largely determine what type of online business you'll want to create. Here's a visual overview of the two primary paths you can take.

To begin, there are two main categories of *products* you can sell: information products and physical products, which are things you actually ship in the mail. The difference is fairly clear, but some overlap exists, so let's have a closer look.

INFORMATION VS. PHYSICAL PRODUCTS & SERVICES

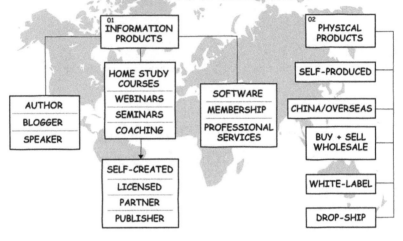

Download the Information vs. Physical Products & Services PDFs Here:
www.clickandgrowrich.com/book/InfovsPhysicalProducts

Often the best place to start out is with information products because they are usually easier and less expensive to create. An information product is anything that delivers value in the form of, well, information. This could include an e-book, a paid webinar, video trainings, audio trainings, software, printed or digital home-study courses, CDs or DVDs, online members-only websites, and everything in between. Because you could choose to ship a physical copy of your course or information product, you can have overlap between information products and physical products. See the detailed diagrams for ideas.

You may want to start by choosing a public outlet for your information. You could write a blog or book or become a public speaker. Or, maybe you'll choose something more private, like paid-only access to your information or content in the form of home-study courses, paid webinars, seminars, or private coaching and mentoring.

The most private forms of information products don't tie your name or personality to the products as much or at all. For example, you can sell software

INFORMATION PRODUCTS

AUTHOR BLOGGER SPEAKER COACHING	VS	ONLINE DIGITAL HOME STUDY COURSES WEBINAR TRAININGS MEMBERSHIP SITES	VS	SOFTWARE BUSINESS/PERSONAL PROFESSIONAL SERVICES

DESCRIPTION:	DESCRIPTION:	DESCRIPTION:
YOU HAVE EXPERIENCE, OR YOU ARE SEEN AS AN EXPERT IN A SPECIFIC AREA, OR WOULD LIKE TO BE A NOTED AUTHORITY EXPERT IN YOUR MARKET. YOU WOULD LIKE TO WRITE A BOOK, BUILD A FOLLOWING WITH A BLOG OR ON SOCIAL MEDIA AND MAKE MONEY SPEAKING TO LIVE AUDIENCES OR AS A SPEAKER, OR AS A PRIVATE COACH/MENTOR.	YOU HAVE SPECIALIZED KNOWLEDGE YOURSELF, OR HAVE IDENTIFIED AN EXPERT TO PARTNER WITH AND CAN CREATE EITHER A DIGITAL TRAINING PRODUCT ONLINE FOR DOWNLOAD, OR A PRINTED HOME STUDY COURSE YOU CAN SHIP. YOU MAY ALSO LIKE THE IDEA OF GIVING LIVE ONLINE TRAININGS BY WEBINAR. ONGOING INCOME CAN ALSO BE MADE WITH A SUBSCRIPTION BASED MEMBERSHIP SITE.	YOU HAVE IDENTIFIED A SOFTWARE OR PROFESSIONAL SERVICES SOLUTION TO A BUSINESS OR PERSONAL PROBLEM. YOU ARE SOMEWHAT TECHIE ORIENTED AND LIKE THE IDEA OF CREATING OR FINDING AN OFFSHORE TEAM OF DEVELOPERS TO CODE YOUR IDEA AND SELL TO THE PUBLIC FOR ONE-TIME OR MONTHLY RECURRING FEES. ALTERNATIVELY YOU WANT TO PROVIDE PROFESSIONAL SERVICES TO THE PUBLIC.

to the public, which either you have written or outsourced to a programmer; create a private, members-only paid membership site, which can be under a generic company or brand name; or you can offer professional services under a personal or company brand name. The best part is, you get to choose.

Obviously, these three "categories" overlap, as you can see in the image above. And within the *information products* category, you can either choose to create and sell *physical information products* (CDs/DVDs) or *digital information products*. The advantages of physical information products are they may carry a higher perceived value and you can charge more for them. But costs for production and delivery also make them more expensive.

The advantages of *digital information products* are that they are easier and often much less expensive to create. Once created, the majority of the cost has already been absorbed, allowing you to simply sell them over and over again via online download.

For many people, digital information is an ideal place to start. Once you have identified a hot, trending market with a clear problem to solve, you can focus on putting together a solution to sell to the people in this market. Again, this can come in the form of e-books (or Kindle), online membership sites, downloadable courses, software, videos, PDFs, or any combination of these.

In the "old" days, around 2004, e-books and e-courses became popular, but eventually the marketplace became more sophisticated. But as we've mentioned, we have seen a recent resurgence in the form of Kindle books, sold on Amazon or repurposed into online courses, which can be sold to the public on portal sites like Lynda. Pricing skews toward the less-expensive side, and while this may not seem very exciting, the reach and potential size of the market is massive.

Selling one to two copies of a $7 Kindle book per day or per month may not seem exciting to you, but selling hundreds or even thousands per month can really add up.

Similarly, people worldwide are creating more advanced information products in the form of home-study courses and digital courses, which are primarily sold direct to consumers via Google or Facebook ads. Or these courses may be offered in one of the major digital product and affiliate marketplaces such as ClickBank, which has grown to over $500 million in annual sales, demonstrating the massive size of the global market for buying information products.

One example of digital information is a product called The Truth About Abs. Creator Mike Geary started this website in the mid-2000s with one simple idea: to show men and women how to get six-pack abs by following simple diet tips and without herculean amounts of exercise. The smartest thing Mike did was to *first* determine that a very big market was there, although he may not have known just *how* big it was.

✍ BRETT STORY

After I sold my last company in 2013, I and fifteen other internet entrepreneurs went to Sweden to stay at the Ice Hotel above the Arctic Circle.

While ice fishing one day, Mike shared with me that his product has been translated into numerous languages and was now selling worldwide. He sold over one million copies of his digital product in English, and then using the profits, started acquiring other companies after his initial success. He now has eight other thriving companies that he's a partial owner of.

The last I heard, he had earned enough from this one product idea to buy part of a ski resort with some friends. That's another point to make here. By building a powerful business brand in in a big enough market, you have the potential to earn enough to invest in other things you enjoy or that can *appreciate* in value, like other businesses.

What's great about discovering a successful information product idea in the right market is that the demand is often strong enough for you to convert it into a monthly membership, with the potential for monthly recurring passive income.

If you can sell someone a $9 product or service that helps them with a problem or pain they are seeking a solution for, you can generally also offer them a chance to receive ongoing monthly information from you for the same price every month.

With some time and effort, you can get 100 people into your membership site or service, and this becomes $900/month. That's enough for a new luxury car payment. With the number of people you can reach online (four billion and growing), getting up to 1,000 customers, or even 10,000, is achievable. Other people are doing it. Why not you? Could you use an extra $9,000 to $90,000 per month? *This book gives you the road map.*

Remember, the bigger the problem you are solving, the more you can charge for a solution. On more than one occasion, we were able to grow revenues into the six-figures-*per-month* range using the strategies in this book.

For example, one time we had exhausted all the buyers on our list for our flagship product, which was a mastery course on how to trade options. We had previously sold it for years at a $997-$1,497 price point and then put it on sale for $497 until there were no more buyers. Since we had put a large amount of time into creating it and had already established the value of the product in the marketplace, it would have been a shame to just stop selling it. So, we decided to *give it away.*

Why would we do that? Because along with the "free" copy of the course, buyers also had to agree to a free 30-day trial of our gold members-only website, which would then rebill every 30 days at $97. The members' area had unique software we had created, other content we didn't create but licensed, and useful educational resources that easily offered $497 in value.

What's interesting is that we had originally only offered 1,000 of these free courses because we were taking a big chance sending out physical packages, including CDs, printed manuals, and workbooks that cost us around $50 each to produce, so our hard costs were around $50,000. When we sold these in days, we decided to offer another 1,000 copies, but this time to save money, we only offered the digital versions of the same materials online. Again, we quickly went through another 1,000.

In the end, we "sold" 2,200 of these free courses that included the 30-day free trials of our $97/month membership site. Roughly 760 people cancelled their free trial during the 30 days before their rebill. But the good news is, 1,440 of them did not cancel and started rebilling the next month at $97, which was just under $140,000 per month. *How would you like to have an extra $140,000 per month?*

This didn't last forever, but it was still a huge windfall. To be candid, we experienced a roughly 20% monthly attrition rate in the program because we didn't cater to their needs as well as we could have. We were too busy with other projects, which, in hindsight, was a huge mistake but a lesson learned. Overall, it was still a very profitable marketing experiment.

One creative way we bundled our digital investing courses and software was to include either a 30- or 60-day trial to our weekly live webinar trainings on how to use the programs. Typically, we would offer 60 days of these training classes for free if they paid in full during the initial launch and only 30 days for free if they opted for the payment plan. This way, both groups felt they were getting all of the tools equally, but they were incentivized to choose the full payment option to get an extra 30 days free.

In either case, because the trainings were very good; we had hundreds of people staying in these subscription services at between $197 and $297 per month, which generated hundreds of thousands of dollars in monthly revenue.

These results aren't typical, but they are certainly possible if you're offering enough market value.

The last example leads us to one of our favorite things to sell online, which is software. If you consider yourself an "idea person," this may be a great place to start because never before has it been easier to come up with a great idea and post it online on one of the many outsourced software development sites. Talented programmers from around the world will bid on your project virtually, and if you search carefully enough, you'll likely find the perfect programmer to bring your vision to reality.

One idea, properly executed, can potentially mean hundreds of thousands of dollars in a relatively short period of time. This is not a guarantee of your results. We're merely talking from experiences we've had personally on more than one occasion.

✒ BRETT STORY

Once in 2003 when blogs first were making their appearance and were getting ranked well in the search engines, I had an idea for how to use software to quickly index large websites in Google. How it worked is a bit complex, but after finding a programmer to actually build this program and somehow getting two of the top internet marketing affiliates around at the time to compete against each other to see who could sell more copies of my software, we sold just over 1,000 copies of the program at $197 in less than two weeks.

It was one of those "in the shower" ideas that turned into over $197,000 in sales. Not average *but possible*, and it all started with just one good idea.

Now that we've covered the different types of information products, let's talk about actually creating information products to sell. You have a number of options for getting this done:

1. Self-Creating
2. Licensing
3. Partnering
4. Publishing

Self-Creating

Let's start with creating your own content for your products or services. "Self-created" also includes hiring someone else to research, write, record, edit, and/or produce part or even all of your final product.

INFORMATION PRODUCTS

SOURCING OPTIONS

① SELF-CREATED CONTENT	② LICENSED CONTENT	③ PARTNER WITH AN EXPERT	④ BE A PUBLISHER OF OTHER PEOPLE'S EXPERT CONTENT
YOU ARE AN EXPERT OR HAVE NECESSARY EXPERIENCE OR INFORMATION TO CREATE, WRITE, RECORD, EDIT, AND PRODUCE CONTENT THAT IS VALUABLE TO THE MARKETPLACE.	YOU ARE NOT AN EXPERT BUT WOULD LIKE TO LICENSE CONTENT THAT IS ALREADY PRODUCED AND AVAILABLE TO USE, RESELL AND/OR REPURPOSE UNDER YOUR OWN NAME OR COMPANY BRAND.	YOU WOULD RATHER FOCUS ON THE MARKETING AND TO LEVERAGE ANOTHER PERSONS' EXPERTISE, KNOWLEDGE OR LIKENESS AS AN EXPERT. YOU EITHER KNOW SOMEONE OR CAN FIND SOMEONE TO PARTNER WITH.	YOU WANT TO FOCUS ON BOTH THE MARKETING, AND FINDING A THIRD PARTY EXPERTS, BUT NOT GIVE UP ANY OWNERSHIP. YOU WANT TOTAL CONTROL OVER INCOME/ EXPENSES, AND WANT TO KEEP 100% OWNERSHIP.

As long as you are using a reputable online outsourcing platform, like Fiverr, Upwork, or Guru, and you require in your project requirements that freelancers agree and accept that the project is "work for hire" and that you solely own all of the deliverables, you should be fine. Most platforms have this already set up, and all providers on the site have already agreed to these terms. So, it's perfectly fine to have help or even have someone else do most of the work for your self-created information products.

But, if you want to build a lasting brand, with long-term customers who will buy from you again and again in the future, then you probably want to be as hands-on as possible to ensure you're offering a quality product. Just don't get stuck in perfectionism; realize that, in the end, *good enough is good enough.* Many dreams have died on the drawing board because the creator procrastinated too long, waiting for it to be perfect (when it never will be). What *is* perfectly acceptable is outsourcing all the parts that don't require your specific expertise, overseeing the final result, and then releasing it as your own product.

Licensing

Another option is to start out by licensing someone else's proven product or idea. If you're not an idea person yourself, but if, for example, you are a huge fan of an existing program, product, or service in the marketplace, then you may want to consider licensing or white-labeling it. You'll skip the hard step of creating a world-class product yourself and can just focus on the marketing. Some people have created massive success online just marketing others' products, either as affiliates or as a licensee.

Pro Tip: "In reality, the marketing of the business is the business."

For example, Dan Roitman, whom we have worked with in the past, created an amazing company called Stroll. Initially, it was simply reselling a premier language-learning program, which they were just licensing from the publisher.

Dan put together a great team and was able to grow his company to $20 million in annual revenues. In his case, however, his success was his downfall because the parent company suddenly decided not to renew his license, in favor of servicing the market themselves. So, this strategy *can* carry some long-term risk. Still, Dan built a great company that was a big success.

Partnering

Another option to consider is partnering with someone else, either as the "expert" or content creator side of your business. Or, if you're the expert, find a partner to handle the sales and marketing. The advantages of this arrangement are that you can both focus on what you're best at and simultaneously grow the company faster. Always consider the *speed to market* factor, especially in a market worth being in. With no shortage of ideas and smart people out there, gaining the *first mover advantage* is huge.

Money loves speed. So, if you're able to find a partner who complements you in the areas you're not passionate about or qualified to do, bringing that person on can save time. We've used this strategy numerous times as it lets you quickly gain leverage in the marketplace.

We've been able to grow Click and Grow Rich quickly, into seven international markets worldwide, speaking and teaching our methods to thousands of people, primarily because we've been able to leverage each other's talents and skill sets. Daniel is an amazing stage speaker, dealmaker, sales trainer, and overall front man. On the 4 archetypes scale, he is an Owl / Monkey. Brett, on the other hand, is a world-class business growth strategist, marketer, and idea guy. He is more of a Lion / Cocker Spaniel on the 4 archetypes scale. So we complement each other well.

Publishing

Another shortcut to creating products and services quickly is by finding a content creator or publisher. Many experts are out there, especially book authors, who don't possess the marketing skills you'll have after reading this book. These days, experts are a dime a dozen, and you can easily find them just about everywhere.

All you have to do is identify and approach one or more book authors or authority figures in your chosen market. Offer to have them on as a guest speaker on a webinar to your list of email subscribers or social media followers. The best part is, your credibility and personal branding goes way up just by association.

You could offer to let the authority figure teach for an hour on the webinar; then let them offer their products for sale at the end on an affiliate basis. You could also promote their online offers to your email list or social followers directly so both of you make money. Another strategy is using celebrities to elevate your status and draw in more customers.

BRETT STORY

Years ago, I approached a well-known author of a unique type of investing analysis called candlestick charting, which he discovered in the Far East. He wasn't even the creator of this method; he merely popularized it in the West. He didn't just write "the book" on the subject; he wrote all five of the leading books. So, he was a very well-known expert in the investing and trading markets.

One year at a financial trading expo, I invited him to present a webinar to our list of email subscribers. He initially said no, but the next year I asked him again, and this time he agreed. We made tens of thousands in sales, which we split in the form of sales commissions. He was very happy, and after that, he would *contact us* on a regular basis to market his products and services and we both made money together for years.

One year, we were putting on a large investor conference in Orlando and were looking for an additional headliner to draw people to attend. A recent reality show had featured a young guy named Tim Sykes, who reportedly turned his $12,415 Bar Mitzvah money into well over a million dollars trading penny stocks.[20]

We reached out, and he agreed to speak at our upcoming live event. Back then, he was brand new to the world of selling information and asked us how we did it. I gave him some advice for starting out, and now he's one of the most widely followed people in his market, which initially was penny stock trading. He's now reportedly worth $20 million and lives in a $5 million mansion in Miami.[21]

All this shows the power of having your own email list to market to and proves why it's worth investing the time to build one. Because once you have this, you can literally publish other experts to your marketplace, *leveraging their expert status and authority to build your own.*

You'll also give tremendous value to your email subscribers and social media audience in the form of sharing the expert's information. It's a great win-win for everybody involved, and remember, you're just one idea away.

PHYSICAL PRODUCTS
AND DROP-SHIPPING

A nother proven way to make money online is to sell physical products. Unlike digital products, these products can't be downloaded; they need to be physically shipped or mailed.

Physical Product Types

Several different types of physical products are available to sell. You could choose to manufacture a product you've developed for a specific market you've identified. Or you could choose to sell an existing brand or product that already exists, having identified a market demand already there. Lastly, you could create the product yourself, either with equipment you own, or, in the case of a physical information product, you could have a local printer create the product.

The self-produced option is often a good way to start, at least until you validate that market demand exists. The last thing you want to do is to invest a lot of money in manufacturing hundreds or even thousands of your products only to find nobody actually wants it. We always recommend starting out with the minimum viable quantity to prove your concept and market demand. If you're able to start manufacturing and selling yourself, until the demand grows and you can later find a more scalable option, this might be a good way to start.

PHYSICAL PRODUCTS

Detail #2

SELF-PRODUCED	CHINA/OVERSEAS	BUY+SELL WHOLESALE	WHITE-LABEL
YOU CAN SELF-PRODUCE OR CREATE YOUR INFO PRODUCTS OR PHYSICAL PRODUCTS YOURSELF, OR FIND A LOCAL SOURCE TO PRODUCE YOUR PRODUCTS TO SELL, AND SHIP DIRECTLY YOURSELF OR USING A LOCAL FULFILL-MENT CENTER.	YOU HAVE A GREAT IDEA OR LIKE THE IDEA OF CREATING A PROBLEM-SOLVING PHYSICAL PRODUCT A SPECIFIC MARKET WILL DESIRE, AND YOU CAN CREATE A LINE OF SIMILAR PRODUCTS UNDER ONE STRONG BRAND. YOU ALSO LIKE THE IDEA OF SOURCING OVERSEAS OR USING CHINA BASED PROVIDERS LIKE ALIBABA.COM.	YOU KNOW OF AN EXISTING BRAND OR LINE OF PRODUCTS THAT YOU CAN SELL, BUYING AT WHOLE-SALE AND SELLING ONLINE AT RETAIL, AND YOU LIKE THE IDEA OF SELLING BRAND-NAME PRODUCTS WHICH ALREADY HAVE PROVEN DEMAND IN THE MRKETPLACE.	YOU HAVE A GREAT IDEA FOR A NEW BRAND OR LINES OF PRODUCTS THAT YOU WANT TO SELL UNDER YOUR OWN BRAND NAME, BUT NOT CREATE OR FORMULATE THEM YOURSELF. YOU PREFER TO WHITE-LABEL OR PRIVATE LABEL FROM AN EX-ISTING COMPANY OR PROFESSIONAL MANUFACTURER AND JUST FOCUS ON THE MARKETING.

DROP-SHIP

YOU LIKE THE IDEA OF SELLING EXISTING LINES OF PRODUCTS, OR CREATING YOUR OWN PRODUCT LINE OR LINES, AND PREFER THAT A 3RD PARTY DISTRIBUTOR SHIPS FOR YOU.

This suggestion also applies to physical information products.

✍ BRETT STORY

When I was first starting out with my financial education company, we were printing 180-page manuals in color on a laser printer, hole punching them, putting them in a binder, burning the CDs, putting the cases together, and printing labels to ship via FedEx.

This was exciting when we had three or four orders per day. It was total chaos when we started getting 40 orders per day. At that point, I had to hand off the production to a professional printer/fulfillment center. They would print 50 at a time, and store them on shelves. When an order came

> in, it was easy to get it right out the door. It was a much less stressful option than assembling it myself, but I didn't want to invest in having 50 courses printed before I knew I could sell them.

In terms of creating physical products, the large and still-growing trend is to produce physical products in China. Many people have started Amazon businesses selling large volumes of products they've identified a market exists for; they produce the goods in China and then ship via an Amazon fulfillment center.

We don't teach this strategy, but it's an option if you are looking to sell physical products. In this case, a great resource to look into is Alibaba and AliExpress as either could manufacture your products and ship them directly to your customers. This strategy has seen explosive growth over the last few years, but it is also becoming very competitive, with thousands of people worldwide getting in on this. As a general rule, we don't like to be in commodity-based businesses; therefore, we prefer to create information products. With these products, the only limitation is your own creativity and market demand, which can be insatiable in the case of hot information-based markets where you're not competing on price but value.

Another option is to find already popular products selling well in the marketplace and become a distributor. You can buy the product at wholesale and then sell it at retail prices online. Think of it this way. You're getting the retail price upfront and then typically have 30 days to pay the manufacturer the wholesale cost, which is essentially an *interest-free loan* that you can use to grow your business. Just look online for your favorite brand and see if they have distributors in your area, region, or country.

Once you have your company set up, contact the established brand and ask the requirements to set up a wholesale account. Typically, brands will also drop-ship the products directly to your customers for you. This is a great option as most people don't have a warehouse or a giant garage they can fill with products.

✒ BRETT STORY

In the online water gardening supply business I started in the early 2000s, we drop-shipped high-priced pond filters and other products for our customers through various regional distributors and manufacturers. I grew this to $500,000+ in annual sales before selling the business. The best part is, I didn't have to invest any of my own money for inventory or manufacturing costs because the distributors shipped the products, then billed us on 30-day terms. I had identified a strong market demand; therefore, was simply satisfying it using products people were already looking for and doing quite well because we didn't have to advertise. People found us online for free, because we had great rankings in the search engines.

The downside of this type of marketing is that the margins are lower, and it doesn't afford as much profit margin to cost-effectively advertise and acquire more customers. This is another reason we like selling information products, which have a much higher ROI. However, if you can find a hot in-demand product or market with good margins and/or you can produce products overseas to reduce costs and increase your return on investment, then physical products might be a good option.

A final option is finding a manufacturer that will allow you to white-label products, supplements, or even skincare that they are already producing. Private-label or white-label supplements and skin care has also been a very hot market in the last ten years and is likely an evergreen market. We have several students in the supplement business, and in each case, they have found a white-labeling manufacturer company to produce these in small quantities to keep the cost down. They then put their brand labels on the bottles.

Here is a visual for you to help keep the different options clear when deciding on which direction you'll be taking.

PRODUCT vs SERVICES

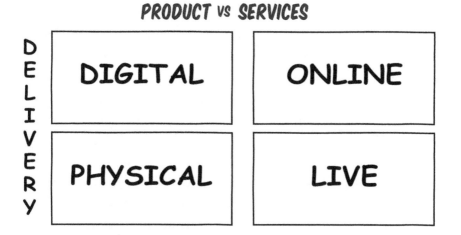

Personal and Professional Services

Another way to make money online is by providing personal or professional services over the internet. This could include personal coaching, mentoring, or consulting, which has been a fast-growing area for the last few years. In 2017, the US consulting market was worth over $58 billion and is growing at over 7%.[22]

Now with the power of Facebook's advertising targeting, you can put yourself in front of the ideal market that could benefit most from your expertise and then potentially charge thousands of dollars per month to deliver your consulting services online. In our business over the last few years, we have generated significant revenue from coaching and consulting fees, all delivered online using Skype. We've also worked with over 200 global clients with an awesome online coaching platform we've discovered that makes it easy to manage and communicate with them.

This platform allows us to effectively interact and lead students from over seven countries through our online training, all at their own pace. Our MP^5MS^2 Formula for Success curriculum and in-depth training modules allow them to go through the material step-by-step, marking each 15-minute module as "complete" before proceeding to the next. Segmentation reduces overwhelm and breaks down the material into manageable and achievable steps.

With this cloud-based platform, students can submit specific questions regarding the materials and get a reply from one of our coaches, who can also share video or images. Each coaching session is tracked, and our coaches can leave session summary notes, key points, and a list of specific agreements and commitments for each student, which is all saved on the cloud.

In the "MindLab" section, we have ten self-paced learning modules, covering everything from setting up your business, getting started, audience building, Facebook and YouTube marketing, marketing and selling strategies, MP^5MS^2, and of course scaling and selling your business. We've also included our CGR Labs video libraries, where students can master a variety of important techniques, all in under an hour per lesson on twenty-four business-building topics like how to run a webinar, affiliate marketing, outsourcing, video production, how to craft a market survey, and more. Online platforms like this can allow you to grow a similar business, generating potentially tens of thousands or hundreds of thousands of dollars per month from your home or from anywhere in the world.

You're just one idea away.

Alternately, using a website like Fiverr.com, you could become a freelancer yourself, and offer your professional or personal services to people looking for help. This may be a good place to start if you're looking to expand your reach as a provider of just about any service you can imagine. If you're just looking to supplement income to start out, this may be a good option. Some virtual outsourcers have been able to earn more working part-time in this way, enjoying the flexibility of working from home, than from being employed full-time.

ONLINE VS. OFFLINE DELIVERY

We've already talked about the different ways to deliver your products. The pros of online (or digital) delivery of your information products are that it's easy, has far lower costs than producing physical products, and is what most people are used to these days. In most cases, buyers are looking for digital delivery. The cons of downloadable products are that people can order and save them, then ask for a refund, and, in some cases, copy your products to give away or even resell on international black markets. This isn't as big of an issue as people think, and in the end, it is simply not worth worrying about or spending energy trying to prevent. Most see it as a cost of doing business. Until and unless you become well known online and web piracy starts really eating into your profits, don't let it concern you.

The pros of physical delivery of your information products is that tangible products can carry a higher perceived value to your customers—especially in a crowded sea of other online marketers, where everybody else is offering digital downloads. So, if you want to stand out or have high-value clients who would be positively influenced by having a quality printed and produced package arrive at their doorstep, physical delivery may be the way to go for you.

Some marketers are still using direct mail and even sending out "shock and awe" packages to their customers to stand out from the crowd. However, the cons of physical delivery are that costs go way up, both with printing costs and shipping. You should weigh both options and usually start with online marketing before venturing out into direct mail and physical delivery. You could even start small with simple postcards.

LIVE VS. VIRTUAL VS. RECORDED

Now that we've talked about the two primary ways you can deliver information products, let's talk about the three options for delivering your services. First, you can either provide your services live and in person at, for example, live seminars or workshops, which can be a highly profitable way to share your expertise and knowledge while generating sales.

In our Click and Grow Rich weekend seminars, we've regularly been able to generate over six figures in sales from our coaching and mentoring programs. The biggest advantage of this type of format is that you have a captive audience for one or two full days and, thus, an ample opportunity to demonstrate your value. An old adage in marketing says, "People won't spend their money with you until they spend their time with you," and this is especially true when selling high-ticket programs like coaching or consulting.

We've perfected this model over the past five years, hosting these events in seven countries and counting. People have recently started asking us to teach our seminar model, so we're now working on a new information product and online course called Six Figure Small Events, which is due out in 2019.

Pro Tip: People will spend typically more money with you, only if they spend more time with you.

The second method for delivering your services is virtual delivery. This could be done with a one-on-one Skype call, a group Zoom videoconference, a real-time webinar to dozens or hundreds of people, a live studio podcast, or even live-event streaming video simulcast to thousands. With today's streaming technology, you now have the ability to share your message to thousands of people all over the world. The latest breakthrough and hottest major trend in 2019 is using live-streaming video marketing on social media. Facebook, Instagram, and YouTube have all added versions of this type of technology, which is making it easier than ever to get your live video message out to the masses.

The third method for delivering your services and sharing your valuable expertise is through video recording. This is a bit of a hybrid method because, in effect, by recording and sharing your live material, you're creating an information product out of it. This is a great way to repurpose your material into other formats. Your live workshop, boot camp, or speaking event can (and should) be recorded and then sold or upsold to seminar attendees, non-attendees, and new customers, then edited and turned into a highlight or "sizzle" reel to be used for future lead generation. The same goes for any of the virtual delivery options mentioned above. Which do you like best?

When you're first starting out, you should choose the options that you're most comfortable with and that resonate with *you*. So, don't be overwhelmed with all of the options we've just listed. This is to let you know what options are out there, so when validating your market, pick and choose a few ideas from above, and overlay it with your IOE worksheet results.

You don't need to do it all…at least not when you're just launching your business.

"Always be yourself, express yourself, have faith in yourself,
do not go out and look for a successful personality and duplicate it."
–Bruce Lee

The Business Quad-Fecta

The "holy grail" of marketing, however, is to achieve what we call the Quad-Fecta in your business. This is where you do have *all* of these different products and services being offered in all (or almost all) of the various delivery methods: digital products, physical products, online services, and live services.

Very few people start out here. It's often a progression, a building process that spans several or many years. While this should be the eventual goal of every smart and savvy marketer truly seeking success online, when first starting out, you should focus on *one* business and delivery model.

Once you're profitable and have some experience, then start branching out into other complimentary formats. For example, if you start out with a digital information product that you're selling online via digital download and sales are good enough to justify hiring a small team to take some of the day-to-day load off of you, then you may want to start offering paid consulting services for your clients who want help implementing your information.

You could then create a membership site to offer weekly live webinar trainings, which you record and include in the online archives for your members who pay you monthly. You could also hire someone to create time-saving software to sell to your past customers and also offer free to your paying members.

For your repeat buyers and better customers, you could put together a higher-priced physical mastery course with printed materials in a binder, a flash drive with instructional videos, and laminated cheat sheets. This is now considered so old-school that it would make you stand out from your competition. This appeals to markets with more aging baby boomers than millennials, but is still worth mentioning.

We've done very well in the past offering online 6- to 12-week *live webinar* mastery series trainings, which sold for $2,497 and offered real-time instruction with an instructor, essentially teaching the same information that was included in the physical mastery series course that we shipped out to other clients who wanted a self-paced, lower-priced option. The interactive class with Q&A allowed us to charge twice the price of the home-study course. Think of how you can apply this in your market.

And lastly, you could advertise having regional or city-specific live events once you have some customers and experience delivering your value. At these events, you could sell your other information products, books, and masterminds or promote your coaching and mentoring services.

This is when you've arrived and have achieved the Business Quad-Fecta.

My Ideal Business would sell A:

Circle One   PRODUCT | SERVICE | BOTH

My Ideal Delivery method would be:

Circle All That Apply   DIGITAL│ONLINE│PHYSICAL│LIVE

The 4 pillars of an ideal mature business includes all 4 types:

THE Q U A D	F E C T A	
	Digital Products - (software, information, videos, etc)	
	Physical Products - (Device, gadget, printed courses)	
	Online Services - (Coaching, membership site, webinars)	
	Live Services - (Seminars, speaking, media, mentoring)	

Download the Business Quad-Fecta Here:
www.clickandgrowrich.com/book/BusinessQuadFecta

BUSINESS LIFE CYCLES

During your business life cycle you'll likely go through *4 phases of growth*. Typically, when starting out, you'll be ***struggling*** to put all the important foundational pieces in place and to validate your business model.

Then you'll be ***grinding*** to grow your business to get it profitable and working hard to build more consistency in the business. In the next phase, you'll be ***surviving***, but not where you want to be in terms of quality of life in the income you want just yet, so you'll be working toward the ultimate goal of ***thriving*** in your business and enjoying true time and financial freedom.

Let's take a closer look at these four scenarios, and also talk about the actions to take in each phase to move closer toward the goal of thriving in your business. We can also look at these as the solutions to the immediate problems at hand.

In the first phase, where you're *struggling* to get the business off the ground and maybe you're still at the "idea" stage or have a product ready but really have no leads or sales coming in to speak of. You have your business foundation in place in terms of company structure, the brand or product idea, but you haven't found your product / market fit yet which you'll need to figure out to move ahead.

In this book we've talked a lot about the importance of identifying a strong *market* first, and then moving forward with your product or service concept. So, the first step here is to analyze the marketplace to see if there is one already and if it's strong enough to support your entry into that market.

Once you've verified the market exists, it's time to validate your proof of concept and prove your idea will work. The best way to do this, as we've talked about, is to survey the market and actually ask them what they are looking for when it comes to solving a known problem. The key here is that they are *already looking* for a solution. Armed with this information, you can now put your product or service (the solution) in front of them and see if there are any buyers.

If you generate some sales, you can continue to ask your buyers and the market as a whole, questions about how to improve your products or services and optimize your product market fit. As you do this, you'll naturally start to make more sales.

In the next scenario you're generating some leads and sales, but there's uncertainty in the business because your results are inconsistent and you don't have predictable sales coming in. You're excited the business is growing, but exhausted from all the work, and this is the *grinding* phase.

To move past this vulnerable time in your business, you should be focusing on optimizing your sales funnels and on getting more qualified leads to them. You can do this through starting to find affiliates to promote your products and get leads, as well as using online advertising which we'll cover in the next section.

You'll want to focus on building your email list and social media audiences, and driving more customers into memberships or subscription-based services to generate monthly recurring revenue, while starting to outsource tedious tasks.

Once you're generating more predicable lead-flow and consistent sales revenues you'll have stabilized the business. But at this point, you're not growing significantly and not at your full potential. This is the *survival* phase.

To get past this, you'll need to start automating your business more, with technology and virtual assistants who can do work you shouldn't be doing. Start delegating the time-consuming tasks that someone else can be doing, so you can focus on scaling up your advertising efforts, creating processes and systems, as well as identifying key performance indicators that will help you grow your business faster.

Watch your KPIs as you increase your online traffic, grow your social media presence, and start doing more video marketing to build authority in your marketplace. As you start to become seen as a trusted authority in your market, you'll be able to add more high-ticket products and services to your business.

This is where things become fun, as you're enjoying true time and money freedom. You feel accomplished and are now running your business at your full potential, with much of the company running on autopilot as you've automated the key business functions and have predictable outcomes. Now you're *thriving…*

In this phase of business, you're working less and earning more. You have built a solid outsourced team of virtual *A* players and systematized all the important processes, so your sales are running smoothly as you scale and grow the company.

To help you visualize this process, we've created a PDF called the Business Life Cycle, which you can download below:

Download the Business Life Cycle PDF Here:
www.clickandgrowrich.com/book/LifeCycle

BUSINESS LIFE-CYCLE

SCENARIO	HAVE AN IDEA NO LEADS OVERWHELMED	SOME LEADS AND SALES UNCERTAIN & INCONSISTENT EXCITED BUT EXHAUSTED	PREDICTABLE LEAD FLOW CONSISTENT SALES NOT GROWING NOT AT FULL POTENTIAL	ACCOMPLISHED AUTOMATED TIME FREEDOM FINANCIAL FREEDOM AT FULL POTENTIAL
PHASE	STRUGGLING	GRINDING	SURVIVING	THRIVING
SOLUTIONS	ANALYZE MARKET PROVE IDEA BUILD FUNNEL SURVEY PROSPECTS FIND MARKET FIT MAKE MORE SALES	OPTIMIZE FUNNEL START ADVERTISING FIND AFFILIATES GROW LEADS ADD MEMBERSHIPS LIST BUILDING OUTSOURCING	START AUTOMATING SCALE ADVERTISING PROCESSES + SYSTEMS WATCH KPI'S INCREASE TRAFFIC SOCIAL MEDIA VIDEO MARKETING HIGH-TICKET SALES	OUTSOURCED TEAM WORKING LESS EARNING MORE SYSTEMIZED AUTOMATED SALES HIRE "A" PLAYERS SCALING AND GROWING

Now that you know more about the different types of products and services you can sell online, along with different types of delivery methods, and phases of business… In the next section we're going to dive into more of the specifics of *how* you can implement various strategies for growing your business quickly.

Section Four

HOW TO GET RICH ONLINE

(HOW TO) MAKE MONEY NOW

You now have a thorough understanding of what it takes to succeed online, including the most important step of determining a viable market with people already actively looking for a solution. You also now know the different types of products and services you can sell. So, you're probably wondering, what's next?

Unfortunately, many people start with this mindset, and after conjuring up a half-baked product concept, they immediately start thinking, "Okay, how can I make money with this right now?" But despite the title of this section and although everyday people around the globe are doing it, getting rich online doesn't come with an easy shortcut.

As we've talked about, the "easy way" is the wrong way to go about it and will result in failure. So, if you've picked up this book, skipped everything else, and jumped right to this section about making a profit *now*, we strongly advise you to go back and read everything up until this point.

If making money online were easy, every half-wit amateur would be flooding the internet with poorly produced products and services by the thousands, offering little real value to the marketplace. And that would be a shame. Fortunately, this does not describe you. You're going to look for a fertile and receptive market environment to share your highest value with the world—and be paid accordingly.

That being said, once you've determined your highest value to offer, *who* you will offer it to, and *how* you'll deliver it, you will find some fairly inexpensive and easy ways to get started. Assuming that you've identified a hot, trending, and receptive market—yes, it really is that important, which is why we keep repeating it—you're ready to create your product offer. For the sake of simplicity, we're going to focus on information products in the following examples.

If you're a beginner, just starting out, one of the easiest ways to get started is to list your information product in an affiliate marketplace like ClickBank or JVZoo—assuming you've written and produced it. These are two of the largest worldwide affiliate marketplaces, which essentially allow list owners and affiliates, who are looking for great products to promote and earn commissions from, to find each other. With a massive worldwide market, these sites are like dating websites for information buyers and sellers. Let's face it. We truly live in the Information Age, which is good news for you.

You can also visit ClickBank and JVZoo and similar sites while researching your ideal market; simply go there and register for free. Then visit the existing market categories to see which products already seem to be selling well.

You can gather valuable information just by seeing what others are already selling. Then you can either create something similar or put your unique expertise or spin on it. This is a simplistic approach, of course. To gain a competitive edge, you should still survey your chosen market to find their biggest fears and frustrations, their wants and aspirations, and what their true emotional hot buttons and drivers are.

To help you with this, we've created a simple survey template. The insights, nuances, and language patterns you will gather just by asking the right questions can be invaluable and provide you with shortcuts to closing more sales. This is one of the *big* secrets in this book.

Download the Market Survey Template Here:
www.clickandgrowrich.com/book/MarketSurveyTemplate

Another way to jump-start your business quickly is to search for affiliates in your market niche on Google. Simply type in your "market niche + affiliates" and see what comes up. This will bring up pages and pages of other sites in your niche built by those who are looking for affiliates, which typically means they are potential affiliates for you to consider. People tend to complicate this. We built two multimillion-dollar-per-year information businesses from zero by using affiliates, and it all started with a Google search to find the first one. It's not *easy*, but it is a *simple* process. You just need to do the work or hire someone to do it for you.

Case Study: Mike and Lara Haxa, Eternal Vibrance

Mike and Lara are two of our students from the United Kingdom whom we mentioned earlier in this book. They found a great market by following our advice, and simply typed "Top Trending Products in 2016" into Google, which showed some interesting results. As health practitioners in London, they were already looking for something health related to sell. The top-two items that came up during their online search were "detox products" and "matcha tea."

We actually had no idea what matcha was, but since it was a top-trending product in an evergreen market (health), we encouraged them to move forward and then helped them come up with a great brand name that embodied their direction: Eternal Vibrance (www.eternalvibrance.com).

But that wasn't enough. Through surveying their market and asking the right questions, we discovered that the number one reason people wanted to detox was for weight loss. That might make sense in hindsight but was a total surprise at the time. So, they decided to create and add a weight-loss detox bundle to their existing line of products, which has become their biggest seller to date.

Case Study: Gerard and Nora Belanger, Ageless Beautiful Skin

Gerard and his wife, Nora, are also two of our platinum students from Calgary, Canada. We worked with them to come up with a great brand, Ageless Beautiful Skin, following our Million-Dollar-Branding Formula.

They first identified the skin-care industry as an evergreen market and made plans to later develop hair care products. After coming up with the brand name, finding a white-label company to produce the products for them, and getting the products to market, we decided to then survey the marketplace.

You might think that the market hot buttons for skin care would be obvious: younger skin and minimizing or preventing wrinkles. By using the Market Survey Template, we discovered that the number one market driver was actually mouth wrinkles.

It's a subtle but very important difference. By identifying the core *emotional* drivers and hot buttons of your market, you'll be better able to speak their language and tap into the conversation already going on in their head, which is important.

The bottom line is, if you're able to articulate your market's fears and frustrations, wants and aspirations, and biggest emotional drivers as well (or better) than they can, then they immediately know, like, and trust you more. And that leads to more sales. What you're looking for here are the exact words, phrases, nuances, and language patterns they use because it already resonates with them.

This is why you should *not* use multiple-choice questions in your survey. Using multiple-choice questions is the most common mistake people make and why many people fail with surveys. To be clear, think of how you will actually *use* the information and results that you get.

The smartest and most successful marketers we know all use market surveys. A friend, Ryan Levesque, who is the world's leading expert in using market surveys, has created a process for this called The Ask Method. He also has a great book out called *Ask* if you'd like to learn more about this strategy.

✍ BRETT STORY

When I had my nice office in Florida overlooking the Royal Palm Golf Course and multimillion-dollar homes while running my last online company, I had various framed pieces hanging on my office wall. But the most important message framed there was something I printed on a plain piece of paper: "Find out what they *want* to buy; then *give* it to them. The best way to find out is to *ask* them." This very simple secret was responsible for multiple millions of dollars in sales.

If you don't have an existing list of customers and are still researching your market, one of the best places to use a market survey is with Facebook ads, which we'll touch on shortly. Using the Market Survey Process below, you'll likely be able to build a highly targeted prospect list while also gaining invaluable survey information about your market, and also paying for your advertising using upsells.

Let's have a look at how this process works. In this example, you would simply run inexpensive ads on Facebook targeted at your core market audience, inviting them to take a quiz and offering them a valuable free bonus for doing so.

For example, let's say your market is tennis. You could run several ads on Facebook with a headline caption that reads, "Like Tennis? Take Our Quiz…" This will likely capture the attention of anyone interested in tennis. Now all you have to do is encourage them to take your "tennis quiz" by stating somewhere in the ad description something like: "Discover the 7 biggest mistakes most tennis players make, and 3 little-known tennis 'tricks' you can use to crush your opponent."

The prospect reads your ad, and then is taken to a simple online market survey, which we gave you a template for. After taking the survey, they are taken to a landing page where they can register to download your interesting report above. You capture their name and email address, which gets added to your email list for future marketing and subsequently you drop them on a page with an inexpensive "trip-wire" offer.

This essentially is an irresistible introductory offer designed to give them super high value for a low price, and for you to get a customer. Remember, *the purpose of a sale is to get a customer* because from here they are much more likely to buy again.

MARKET SURVEY PROCESS

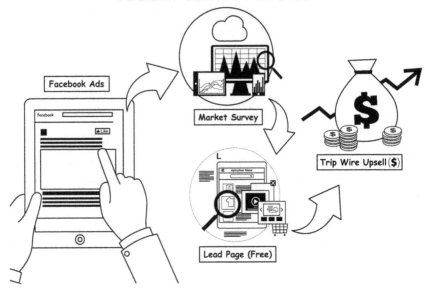

Download the Market Survey Process Here:
www.clickandgrowrich.com/book/MarketSurveyProcess

If you don't yet have ideas for a product or service to offer, the highest and best use of your time would be to create a PDF resource with high perceived value to your marketplace to capture leads. Then drive the leads to schedule a one-on-one session with you, or make outbound calls to them using the internet as a lead source. You goal is getting them on the phone so you can sell your coaching or consulting services. Most everybody has a skill other people will pay to learn.

CREATING YOUR
MILLION-DOLLAR BRAND

The value of a powerful and well-respected brand name in the right market is immeasurable. But how do you get your brand name out to the marketplace when you're just starting out and don't have millions of dollars to do traditional branding on TV or in other more established forms of media?

In the Internet Age, you have access to many new forms of media (social media, video media, email media, etc.). It's easier to advertise now than any other time in history.

But how do you make sure your brand resonates with your market and speaks to them in a way that makes them want to know more? One of the biggest mistakes we see when starting a new business is that people come up with some very unusual (although often creative) names for their new product brand or business. The problem is, if people hearing the product name for the first time are confused, then they will likely ignore your offer. After all, *the confused mind says no*, and that's not what you want.

You want people to immediately recognize the big benefit of using your product or service, and you want them to look into it further. Seeing a logical benefit activates the neocortex, where the final decision will be made, but you only have a split second to get there. The reptile brain will either ignore or, worse, run away from your brand name if it's confusing or not compelling. Too many other competing messages are coming at us these days; we don't have even an instant to focus on something that's not important.

So, while your great, new 15-letter acronym for your brand may sound awesome to you, it's likely not even going to register on the radar of your prospect's mind. To help you create a million-dollar brand, we've come up with a PDF exercise called the Brand Name Generator and a free case study report with more examples.

Download the Brand Name Generator Here:
www.clickandgrowrich.com/book/BrandNameGenerator

Download the Creating Your Million Dollar Brand Report Here:
www.clickandgrowrich.com/book/MillionDollarBrand

This is an invaluable first step. Even if you've already created your business brand name in an existing business, you may be able to adapt or enhance it using the formula we've created.

To see a list of some of the other student brands we've co-created with our clients, as examples, visit www.clickandgrowrich.com/book/Brands.

MODELING SUCCESS
(PROFIT MODELING)

Another mistake we often see is would-be entrepreneurs trying to reinvent the wheel, as they say, with some never-seen-before whatchamagadget or "new" complicated strategy. Or, worse, we've seen some enter a cold market that has no hope of success.

The amateur entrepreneur falls in love with their idea from day one and sees it through rose-colored glasses right up until the day it dies, along with their dream and that's why they never find true success in business.

To avoid this, it's much better not only to follow our MP^5MS^2 Formula for Success but also to research who in your market is *already* successfully selling something similar and profit model them. Sometimes we joke in our live events that R&D stands for "rip off and duplicate," although we never encourage anyone to steal or hack someone else's idea or exact marketing funnel. It is acceptable, however, to watch what other people are doing and then create your own *profit model* based on their successful business strategy.

If someone else online has already proven *how* to sell to that market, that's a valuable first step. In this case, why not let someone else figure it out so you can run with it? One of the tactics we teach in our coaching and mentoring programs is to find a "profit model to model," which is essentially looking at your top competitors and doing what they are doing as a starting point. Your goal is to do it different; do it better, bigger, or bolder; and add more value to capture some of the market share that is already there.

Some people might say that's unethical, that you're taking away potential business from your competition. But that's why it's called *competition*, which, in the end, results in a Darwinian improvement of value and information to the marketplace, and this is good as long as you're not copying or plagiarizing other people's work, which we obviously don't recommend and is illegal.

Plus, if you've chosen a hot, trending, and hungry market like we've been teaching, the demand for products and services is often *insatiable*. So, you're actually offering additional options for consumers. They'll buy as much as they can as long as it leads them closer to the solution they are seeking. You can use this as a good starting point for developing your new sales offer, proving there is a market and demand for your product, and then create something new and unique. Because another *big* secret to this process, is once you know there is a market for your products and services, don't follow what everyone else is doing or looking externally. This is when you'll be better off pivoting in your own direction, and focusing internally on what you want to share with the world, in your unique way. It's a big mental shift, but when you start believing in yourself and what *you* have to offer, you can move mountains.

This may be the hardest step for you, because many people feel inside that they need permission to be successful in a big way, or to be *seen* as an expert. In reality, if you know 10% more than the person next to you, *you're the expert!* The sooner you get over your own limiting beliefs, the faster you can start putting yourself out there in a bigger way and making more money online.

Think of it this way… If you're not actively and aggressively marketing yourself, your brand, and your products and services…then you're doing a huge disservice to your potential customers who are looking for help with their problems, frustrations, and pains…and looking for your solution. It's not only the ticket to big success online, but also your obligation, to the marketplace of people who will benefit from your products and services.

If you want to play small, *and do it your way*…the way that most people do it, by creating a product or service nobody wants or isn't interesting to the market because you've ignored the advice we're giving here…then that's your decision. But wouldn't you rather play big, find huge success online, create true time and money freedom in your life, as you get rich?

Let's put it this way… Which one of these future versions of you would you most like to be along the road to success? The broke, tired loser that's barely paying your bills, because you decided to try and do it *your* way? Or worse, spending eighteen hours a day working *in* your business where the business really owns you? Wouldn't you rather be *financially independent* and heading toward a *rich* retirement when you finally sell your highly successful online business (which is exactly what we're showing you how to do)?

Remember, you're just one idea away…

EMBRACING FAILURE

As with many things in life, not everything in business works the first time you try it. You'll likely encounter and experience many business failures of various degrees along your journey. This is actually something you should welcome and embrace.

The reality is, every successful entrepreneur or business owner has had to overcome adversity and failure to get where they are today. The key difference between them and most other entrepreneurs who quit altogether or fail to reach their true potential is that they have learned to push through and persevere. Persistence is the most important quality to develop when growing your business. Never forget that. The fact that perseverance is required presumes you might fail at first.

Knowing that all great success stories include failure, push forward toward the solution. Embrace failure and do not hide from it. See it as a temporary setback and a necessary rite of passage.

In short, don't let fear of failure stop you. If you let fear of appearance, of what people will think, or of not achieving perfection stand in the way of getting your product, service, or yourself out there, into the marketplace, then you'll never make it.

Realize that every success story had to break through the barrier and so will you. But you have to be prepared for failure, expect setbacks, and embrace uncertainty. That way, you won't be easily deterred. Instead, you'll realize you're just following in the footsteps of giants.

"Nothing in the world can take the place of persistence. Talent will not; the world is filled with unsuccessful men with talent. Education will not; the world is full of educated derelicts. And genius will not; unrewarded genius is almost a proverb. The slogan 'press-on' has solved, and always will solve, the problems of the human race."

–Calvin Coolidge

TESTING (TRIAL AND ERROR)

As not everything works the first time, developing and marketing your product is an ongoing process. As you gain experience, you'll get better at knowing what's more likely to work, and you'll add more marketing skills to your arsenal as you gain better judgment. But as they say, "Good judgment comes from experience, and experience comes from bad judgment."

Fortunately, in the Internet Age, you can get away with making many small mistakes that don't lead up to catastrophic failure. In the brick-and-mortar world of business, you're assuming a huge amount at risk in signing a lease and buying inventory. You're taking a chance that a local market exists and will buy your products. And, of course, you have to invest in comparably expensive advertising that may not work.

With online advertising, the name of the game is testing and tracking your results or, essentially, trial and error. Conceptually, it's very simple: try a variety of things, and if any of them work, keep doing them; if they don't work, stop doing them. Since the internet is so big and the people and personalities you'll be potentially showing your ads to varies so much, it's a bit like finding a needle in a haystack. Fortunately, the advertising platforms on Facebook and Google have evolved and now use very sophisticated machine-learning and artificial intelligence algorithms to "learn" which of your ads will appeal the most to your target audience.

Plenty of free information and training is on YouTube that will show you how to set up and run ads on Facebook, Google, and YouTube. When you're first starting out, we recommend you spend a week or two learning how to do this yourself or hiring someone inexpensive on Fiverr or Upwork to run your online ads for you. We don't recommend going out and hiring expensive agencies that will typically charge thousands of dollars per month to do it for you—not until your business grows to the point to where you can afford that and you know what messages are working. Plus, many "agencies" are barely qualified and just looking to add more paying clients. How do you know what's working? By testing.

Think of it this way. According to Wikipedia, *kaizen* is the Japanese word for *improvement*. In business, kaizen is a strategy where employees at all levels of a company work together proactively to achieve regular, incremental improvements.[23]

How do you use this principle to grow your business? We've already mentioned that the marketing of the business, often *is* the business, so wouldn't it make sense to focus the majority of your efforts on marketing? Yes, having a great product or service in a great market is also very important, but at this point, we're assuming you have that.

Now, assume that you could continuously and incrementally make your marketing better and better each and every day. Where do you think your business would be in six months? A year? Five years? By making small improvements all the time, you will likely see massive improvements in growth and income over time.

Fortunately, testing and tracking technology has come a long way, and you can easily create simple to sophisticated tracking links to use in your marketing, which will tell you which improvements to make, whether it's testing two different landing pages against each other or two headlines on the same landing page. Maybe you just want to split-test the color of the headline or an image or an order button.

All of these things can have an impact on your sales. Many platforms offer this type of technology, and, of course, we have built a simple testing and tracking tool inside of Cydec. You can easily set up tracking links and test groups to show you which of any one thing or combination is performing better based on clicks, sales, revenues, expenses, and more—all designed to give you a clearer picture of what's working in your business.

Other platforms, which can easily be connected with Cydec and we'll talk about in section five, allow you to easily split-test different landing pages or even specific things like headlines, colors, images, prices, bonuses, offers, guarantees, and more.

Again, it all comes down to testing. And the good news is, you don't need to stress out about making it perfect overnight. Once you've found something that even kind of works, you can begin your process of continual improvement over time by testing.

Then all you have to do is keep doing more of what's working. To give you an analogy, let's say you own a stable of racehorses and you survive off of the winning proceeds from the races. Do you want to race your best horse or rotate them? The answer should be obvious; *keep racing the winning horse*. It's the same in marketing. You'll want to test a variety of marketing campaigns to find what's working the best and then do more of that, as much of it as you can until it stops working. Even winning marketing messages tend to diminish in effectiveness over time and as more and more people have seen them.

ONLINE ADVERTISING STRATEGIES

Advertising has come a long way since the days of print newspapers and magazines. But the principles of effective advertising—and the psychology behind it—are still very much the same. What's changed dramatically is the method of delivery, but remember, the internet is just a new advertising medium.

The best way to get started with online advertising, for most businesses, is with Facebook. The ads are much cheaper than on Google. However, ad costs are rising, so the sooner you get started, the better. To help you with this, we've created several helpful exercises for you.

You'll want to create as many ad variations as possible and let Facebook do the rest. Facebook has sophisticated technology running in the background, and, fortunately, you don't need to understand all that's going on there. You just need to give their ad platform enough options and variables to test and sort to see what works. Facebook has recently added a *learning* graphic to the ad platform to indicate that it's in the learning process and automatically optimizing your ads for you.

To achieve the best results, you should create as many ad variations as you can, but it doesn't have to be as hard as it sounds. To help you get started, we've created a worksheet called the Ad Creation Matrix to help you organize multiple visuals, ads, landing pages, or messages.

Download the Ad Creation Matrix Here:
www.clickandgrowrich.com/book/AdCreationMatrix

Facebook currently allows both image and video ads, but when you're first starting out, we recommend you start with images and create several different ad groups, which each have their own audience.

First, create four images or ad groups for the audience you'll be running ads to. These should be visually attractive and either lifestyle pictures, graphics, or a combination. You can easily hire this out to somebody on Fiverr to get more variety. Don't worry about getting the perfect image at this point. You're mostly testing combinations.

Once you have your graphics created, go ahead and write the descriptions down in the first column of the Ad Angle Creation Matrix. We've also created another worksheet called the Ad Angle Exercise. This exercise will help you create multiple different ad titles, starting with four proven angles you can work from, and there will be videos here showing how to use them.

Download the Ad Angle Exercise Here:
www.clickandgrowrich.com/book/AdAngleExercise

Once you have created your various ad angles and titles, go ahead and write down the ad title in the second column of the Ad Creation Matrix worksheet. In the third column, you will list the landing page URL you want to send people to. When you're just starting out, this could be the same for all ads in that group. In the future, however, you might want to craft custom landing pages to match that ad message.

Now, you'll create your ad groups or audiences. One of the most powerful functions of Facebook is showing your ads to the exact people most likely to respond, based on their unique interests, behaviors, and demographics, including age range, gender, and geographic location. To help you figure out your ideal audiences to create for your ad groups, or "ad sets" as Facebook calls them, we've created another unique exercise for you called the Ad Targeting Exercise.

Using this interactive PDF, fill in everything you know about your ideal prospects: the people they follow, the gurus they respect in your marketplace, what inspires them, what they do for a living, and what activities they do for fun. By having all this written out ahead of time, you'll be able to put a laser target on your ideal prospects in the Facebook Ads Manager.[24]

Download the Ad Targeting Exercise Here:
www.clickandgrowrich.com/book/AdTargetingExercise

Video advertising has been increasing in popularity in recent years, especially on platforms like Facebook, Instagram (owned by Facebook), and YouTube (owned by Google). This trend will likely continue for many years, so to keep up with this trend and stay relevant in today's world, you'll want to start learning how to create effective marketing videos.

Since many if not most people freak out at the very idea of being in front of a camera, we've created two helpful worksheets and exercises to help you with your video message. And don't worry; if you just don't want to do it, there's still hope. These strategies also apply to making screen capture videos, which we covered under *products*. You can refer back to that section for tools and strategies for making this type of video using the strategies below.

But if you really want to accelerate your reach, authority, and brand, you'll want to practice being on camera. It's the fastest way to get your audience, who doesn't know you, to know, like, and trust you—the starting point of all sales. Video is the shortcut to being known and liked. And we can tell you from experience, almost everybody is terrible at first. It's okay. Just keep doing more video, and you'll realize, "It's really not *that* bad." From there, you'll build confidence and skill.

To help you with your video messaging, either for YouTube, Instagram, or Facebook ads, or even to start sharing your message free on their social media platforms, we've created the Video Ad Exercise and the Video Planner Worksheet. These are both fairly self-explanatory, but you should start with crafting your video ad message. First download the Video Ad Exercise below. You can fill this out online, but we recommend that you print it out and take pen to paper. You'll only need to come up with five short paragraphs. That's it!

Download the Video Ad Exercise Here:
www.clickandgrowrich.com/book/VideoAdExercise

Start out by filling in the short teaser intro; then, write a one- or two-sentence bio, including any big accomplishments your market will care about. Then tell them briefly what you have to share with them today. Remember: all buyers really care about is what's in it for them. Next, tell them how what you're sharing will help them and then tell them what to do.

It may take some practice, but that's pretty much all there is to it. Having this template and framework will help you break down your message into a simple one you can remember and convey to your audience concisely. Be sure to include a clear call to action.

Once you have your video ads done and ready, it's helpful to create multiple versions of them. One reason, as we've talked about, is that Facebook likes to see variety when figuring out what combination of ad visual and ad copy works best for your campaign.

Pro Tip: It isn't about submitting a single "perfect" ad. By creating a wide variety of ads, Facebook will show more ads to more people, essentially "learning" the best performing combinations of ads and audiences more quickly.

Another reason it's helpful to have multiple ads ready is "ad fatigue," which simply means that a great ad can and will stop working over time because everybody has already seen it. And people like variety.

With this in mind, create a number of different video ads to test and use in your marketing. To help with creating these, we've created an exercise called the Video Planner Worksheet. This will help you plan out your various locations (where you're going to film and the background you'll use), your ad angles (created using the Ad Angle Exercise), and the specific actions you're going to mention in your video, like registering for a webinar, buying your book, or downloading a free report.

Download the Video Planner Worksheet Here:
www.clickandgrowrich.com/book/VideoPlannerWorksheet

These resources will help you when planning out your video ads on most ad platforms. Although subtle nuances exist between each, we won't go into those here.

If all of this sounds completely overwhelming and you would like help with your ad strategy and planning, feel free to contact us for help to get you there faster. You can book a free discovery call online, and we'll have a 45-minute, no-pressure call to see if we can help you.

Book your strategy call here: www.clickandgrowrich.com/Discovery

GROWING YOUR BUSINESS
(THE GAS PEDAL)

Anyone can start a business online, but few people create businesses that generate millions of dollars per year in revenue. Even fewer will create and build a business online that provides over $1 million in annual net income. The sad fact is, according to *The Huffington Post*, over 90% of online businesses fail in the first 120 days.[25] That's an alarming statistic that you should be well aware of.

At a basic level, it takes just *three things* to build a business with the potential to generate millions of dollars in revenue annually and provide the owners with $1 million a year or more in spendable, personal income.

These three things are the same three things you need to drive a car successfully: the gas pedal, the steering wheel, and the dashboard.

The Gas Pedal

The speed at which your business grows is determined by how many new customers you are adding to your business every day, every week, every month, and every year. Your customer acquisition process is the gas pedal that determines the speed with which your business grows. How adept you are at integrating new customers into your business will determine your growth rate.

The gas pedal determines how fast your car goes. While many other factors also determine whether or not you'll get to your destination, the gas pedal provides the speed for getting there.

Without giving the car gas, you'll coast down the highway at 10 mph, at risk of getting passed by everyone else. You're going to get there but not nearly as quickly. If you invest the time and money in building a proven, optimized customer acquisition and sales systems for your business, you will have the opportunity to build a million-dollar business and get there faster. Think of the gas pedal as your *advertising, sales, and marketing process.*

The Steering Wheel

The steering wheel in your car helps you direct your speed and momentum toward your desired destination. Similarly, the steering wheel in your business is your ability to maximize your customer value by increasing: 1) the average sale value per transaction in your business; and 2) the frequency with which your customers come back to buy from your business. Think of the steering wheel as your *testing, optimizing, and upselling process.*

Many business owners equate marketing with simply generating new customer traffic into their businesses. It's true. New customer acquisition is your gas pedal, and it determines the speed at which your business propels itself to its destination. But you can't safely steer around a corner if you're just flying down the road at 70 or 80 mph. And if you aren't steering your business, you are not very likely to arrive at your destination safely, if at all.

For example, if you don't know your numbers and aren't optimizing your advertising and marketing process—instead just throwing more money at growing your business—you might find you're actually going out of business.

What happens when you throw gas on a fire? It burns more quickly, and in a sudden burst of energy, it's all gone. Whereas, giving more gas to a finely tuned business engine can increase your speed and get you there faster in a more controlled way.

To do this, you need to maximize the value of each customer by increasing the average purchase your customers make (using one-click upsell offers, order form bump offers, follow-up email offers, etc.) and the frequency with which they buy from you (offering recurring monthly subscription services, memberships, and other continuity offers).

McDonald's is famous for increasing a customer's average purchase with its Value Meal. Instead of somebody walking in and just getting a hamburger and a drink, if they order a Value Meal, McDonald's increases their average purchase by asking, "Do you want fries with that?" or offering you a "super size."

Simply adding $.79 to the purchase price may not sound like a lot, but it added a 20% increase to each sale and billions of dollars to their bottom line. So, if you can increase the revenue of each sale by 20% in your business, you can potentially create a significant increase in profit, and that can mean the difference between success and failure. With rising advertising costs, it's imperative to have effective strategies for increasing your bottom line.

How can you sell more to the customers you already have? What other products and services can you offer them? Are there impulse items (cheat sheets, templates, top-10 lists, PDFs, etc.) you can easily add to an existing purchase to increase the initial order value? Are there medium- to higher-priced upsells, down-sells, or cross-sell products or services you can offer at the point of purchase? This is when customers are most likely to buy again—just after purchasing.

Do you have or can you create big-ticket items? A certain percentage of your customers will buy more expensive, high-end products if offered. Are you offering those to your customers as part of your mix of products and services? If not, you could be leaving a lot of money on the table.

Next, try to increase the frequency with which your customers are buying from you. Are you communicating regularly with your customers? Do you have an email list of customers who have bought from you in the past, and can you enlist them in a rewards program or offer incentives for repeat sales? Are you sending your customers information and following up with them regularly by email or social media to make sure you stay on their minds?

The Dashboard

If you're speeding down the road and don't know where you are going, how likely is it you're going to get to your destination?

Consider this scary scenario: Nothing looks familiar. You make a turn; you don't know how fast you're going; you don't know how many miles you've gone; and you don't know if you're any closer to your destination. It's getting dark, and you don't have any way of telling where you are. You're driving your car down the road. You're able to steer it well, but you have no idea where you are going, where you are, or how fast you're going.

Without the gauges on your dashboard providing you information on miles driven or the amount of gas you have left, you have little chance of ending up where you want to be. This is why business metrics and key performance indicators are so important. They make up the dashboard of your business.

You have to capture information about your business so you can track whether you are heading toward your destination. You may have a finance degree from a university and be able to create an income statement and a balance sheet to tell you how much cash is in the bank and whether or not you made a profit last month. But those financial statements are looking at the past. This is like driving your car only looking in the rearview mirror.

You can't get to your destination if all you are doing is looking behind you. You need forward indicators, telling you in real time how your business is doing.

Here are three key performance indicators (KPI's) people wanting to build million-dollar businesses will need:

1. **Average New Customers (ANC):** This is your speedometer. Business owners need to track their new customer acquisition at all times. How many customers did you get today, this week, and this month? Compare these numbers to your new customer acquisition goals so you will know how fast you are traveling down the road. ANC tells you exactly how quickly you're reaching your goals.

2. **Average Customer Value (ACV):** If you're able to continually increase your average customer value (ACV) or average order value (AOV) in

relation to your cost to acquire a customer (CAC), then you're growing in the right direction.

3. **Average Customer Frequency (ACF):** How often are your customers coming back and buying from you? Tracking this information is like having a "service engine" light on your dashboard. It gives you a warning if a customer hasn't come back in a while. You can then follow up with your customer and find out why or try to fix the problem with a customer re-engagement offer.

It's important to know if a customer has found a new company to buy from, if they had a bad experience, or if they simply lost track of you. If you have a significant number of customers who haven't purchased from you in a while, that's an important warning sign you are steering off the road. If you pay attention to this warning, you can steer around issues you need to fix within your business.

Pro Tip: Increasing *each* of these by a factor of 2x doesn't just improve your business by 6x (2 + 2 + 2), it increases *logarithmically*, so the end result is 8x (2 x 2 x 2), which can mean huge increases to the bottom line.

# of Customers x Average Customer Value
x Frequency of Purchase = Revenue

The best way to monitor these three elements is with technology, which we'll talk about in the next section. What makes running a business enjoyable is a set of business systems to operate your business without your daily and direct supervision.

These kinds of systems also empower employees to run the business without direct daily supervision, which allows the business owners a stress-free lifestyle, without being permanently tied to their business. Running a business without feedback systems can be extremely dangerous, not to mention stressful.

Failing to set up monitoring systems is similar to driving a car without air conditioning on a hot day. You'll still get there, but it will be a miserable ride. Running a business is much like driving a car in the sense that once you learn how to do it, it's a skill you will have forever and can do without thinking of every detail.

Experienced drivers can drive for thirty minutes and then suddenly realize they haven't even been thinking about driving. Maybe you've done this, too. You've been stopping at lights, changing lanes, making turns, and travelling for miles. Then, you realize you haven't been thinking about driving because it's second nature.

You're experienced at regulating the speed of the car, knowing how to safely steer, watching the gauges, and monitoring your speed; you even have the air conditioning on to make sure you are comfortable. You can adjust all of those things at any time without giving it a second thought because you have learned to trust your car's indicators and dashboards.

Also, you've learned the predictable outcomes when you do certain things. A specific action creates a known outcome. You know all you have to do is push a certain button and the window will predictably go up or down. Automation is key here, as it is with any online business. Experienced business owners who create million-dollar businesses are like experienced drivers. They understand how to effectively use the gas pedal of their businesses—marketing—to generate new customers.

They can increase the new customer flow if they need to accelerate a little bit; they can back off when they are going too fast. They keep the flow going because they understand how it works, and they know what is necessary to achieve their goals.

The most successful and experienced business owners know how to handle the steering wheel of their businesses like a seasoned race car driver. They watch the average sale value and the frequency of sales. When the average customer value gets off track, they make changes.

If customers aren't coming back frequently, they correct their steering. These business owners keep an eye on their dashboards and the information they need to know to succeed, and you can, too. Not only can you, but *you must* if you're going to achieve sustainable success in your business.

There's no better feeling in business than knowing that every dollar you spend or invest will result in $2, $3, or $5 in return. If you know your numbers and know the variables that result in bottom-line revenue improvements for your business, you have control of your destiny.

FUNDING YOUR NEW BUSINESS

Besides not properly researching or choosing the wrong market, another leading cause of business failure is not having enough funding or running out of money. Business owners are notoriously bad at accurately predicting how much money it will take to start and maintain a business. Also, unforeseen surprises and emergencies often come up. Just ask any business owner. So, it's a good idea to have some extra cash available.

The simplest and easiest way to shore up funding is to get a line of credit with your bank. When you open your new business bank account, ask your banker if he can also set up a line of credit for you. You may want to ask this question before opening the account and use it as a leverage point; the bank wants your financial deposits, as that's how they make money, so they are more likely to honor your request.

If your credit is not ideal, you can also open a line of credit with cash deposits, which they will hold. This helps you build a history of on-time payments, such that they might loan you more money in the future without requiring a secure deposit.

Once your business is up and running and you have a history of incoming sales history for more than three months, another good option is opening a third-party line of credit with Kabbage.com. The amount they approve will depend on your monthly income and the online accounts you can link to them, including banking and social media. You can usually get set up and approved very quickly.

One more option is to use a cash advance company that will advance you funds based on your monthly cash flow, setting up either a daily or weekly ACH withdrawal directly from your account. It can be expensive money to borrow, so be sure to understand the interest rate you'll be paying and shop around.

If you want to scale a proven advertising campaign that is already profitable or add another campaign that could generate significant cash flow, this might be a good option if the time value of money is in your favor. We have used these before to scale marketing or host live events because we knew we would generate sizable sales.

Of course, getting a Small Business Administration (SBA) loan is always an option. However, these can be difficult to obtain unless you have excellent credit and/or a business history. You may be required to guarantee the loan personally, which puts your personal credit score at risk, so make sure to consider the chance you are taking. SBA microloans are now available also, which can fund up to $50,000. Both are worth looking into. Just do your homework and find a good SBA loan adviser you feel comfortable with. Or, look online.

A newer and, in many cases, better option would be to use crowdfunding, especially if you have a physical product or gadget, something tangible that would appeal to early adopters in the marketplace. Crowdfunding usually does not work for software or information products. However, if you have a great physical product or gadget idea that people have shown strong interest in but you just need money to market and produce it, look into Kickstarter or Indiegogo.

Third-party companies specialize in helping you create successful company campaigns on crowdfunding platforms. For example, we've worked with FundedToday, and they've successfully raised over $220 million for other entrepreneurs. Though they will take their fees mostly out of funds raised, there is an upfront fee to engage them. Still, this form of rewards-based crowdfunding is ideal because you get money from the marketplace upfront, which allows you to then go create your products. Plus, you're not giving up any of your equity under this type of crowdfunding. For help with your project, contact us for valuable insights on how this works.

Another interesting company that has emerged on the scene is StartEngine, which uses a combination of different types of investment vehicles, from equity-based crowdfunding to traditional Reg A financing. Be sure to check with a qualified legal professional when it comes to raising funds using any of these vehicles.

The good news is that the marketplace is becoming more creative and entrepreneur friendly. Thus, entrepreneurs don't have to go through an arduous underwriting or due diligence process when trying to raise capital from investors.

Once your company is up and running and generating sizable, growing revenues, you might want to turn to private equity or angel investors to grow your business and inject needed growth capital. This isn't easy but can be worth it. Just be prepared to give up equity in your business.

When you're at the point where you want to really grow big, you may want to look into venture capital (VC). Many entrepreneurs who have done this later wished they hadn't given up control of their company and had self-funded growth through sales versus VC money, but it's still an option. Many books cover this topic in detail, so we will not cover it further here.

And there are exceptions. Cofounders Aaron Houghton and Ryan Allis started a company in college after meeting in the student union at The University of North Carolina, Chapel Hill. They turned their initial idea into an email company called iContact that would later be acquired by Vocus Holdings (Nasdaq: VOCS) for $169 million after raising multiple rounds of angel and VC funding.[26] Ryan wrote a great book about this experience called *Zero to One Million: How I Built a Company to $1 Million in Sales... And How You Can, Too.*

But the very best way to grow your business without having to spend time chasing investors or giving up part of your company is to figure out a marketing and sales funnel that can bring *more money in than it costs to acquire the customer.* This allows a company to self-fund and grow without looking for outside investors.

When you're first starting out, many people use credit cards to build their business and cover start-up costs. Just be very careful and resist the urge to buy unnecessary things or services as an excuse for doing the work.

Many people confuse *activity* with *productivity* and wind up maxing out their credit cards, which you don't want to do because then you won't have any money left for advertising and marketing. This can cripple a young business that needs to grow.

You'll need funds to run advertising. Start small until you can consistently do so at a profit. Then you can scale your ad spend more, which is the best way to grow your business and personal income.

INTERNATIONAL MARKETS

Another often-overlooked way to grow your online business is to expand into international markets. Many English-speaking countries outside the United States could also benefit from your products and services, and these locations are often less competitive and less expensive markets to advertise in. For example, we have been speaking and selling in several international companies, from Hong Kong to South Africa to the United Kingdom and Canada, just to name a few.

But you don't have to stop there.

Today, it's very easy to hire an outsourced transcription service to convert your information programs into other languages. Huge opportunity awaits in countries just starting to become comfortable with buying information online. We recommend starting out in the United States and then, once your product or service marketing message is working, you can test it in other parts of the world, especially if you have firsthand knowledge of the culture and/or have friends and relatives there.

Mike Geary dramatically increased his business by taking his very successful digital product, which was selling well on ClickBank, and converting it into German and a few other languages. Human nature is human nature, so consumers all over the world share similarities. He chose excellent new markets to go into, experienced much less competition, and generated new revenue.

If you have friends or family in another culture or country, you might enlist their help to identify market gaps. Ask about successful products here in the United States that may not be offered in that country, then convert your offering into the local language, being careful to consider cultural nuances.

According to WeAreSocial.com (owned by Hootsuite), "Users in Africa are up by more than 20% year-on-year" and the growing userbase in developing countries "will have a profound influence on the future of the internet."[27] So, if you've ever wished you had a crystal ball to predict success, now you do. If something has already proven successful here in America, it will likely work in other countries. People's core desires are virtually the same—or at least similar—everywhere.

SELLING YOUR BUSINESS

O nce your business is consistently profitable and making money, you may have a sellable business. One thing we've never understood is why some people will spend years building up their online business, only to get bored and start doing something else. What many people don't realize is that eager buyers are looking for and wanting to buy already profitable online business.

Online marketplaces, like flippa.com, allow people to list their online business for sale, and buyers go there looking for businesses to buy every day. This marketplace is quite active.

So, keep this variable in mind as you're investing your time and money into building your online business. It's not only about creating an amazing lifestyle now and being able to make money from anywhere you choose, working whenever you choose, it's also about building equity in your business. When you are ready and want to sell, you could potentially put hundreds of thousands of dollars away for retirement or for reinvesting into a new business or real estate opportunity—really for any purpose you want. You could even treat yourself and your family to an epic worldwide vacation.

Selling for a large profit is an often-overlooked reason for starting an online business. If you don't feel you have enough time, you can start slow, working part-time, keeping the future financial benefits top of mind. In fact, one of the best strategies for building wealth over time and securing your family's financial future and your retirement is to learn how to invest your time and money for the long term. You can potentially build multiple online businesses over the next five or ten years, then sell them to people or companies who don't have the skills you've learned in this book.

If you have a business that's generating over six figures per year, we recommend using a business broker who can locate larger buyers capable of investing bigger amounts, including international private equity firms or private investors.

Did you know that the *primary purpose* of a private equity firm is to *invest money* in cash-producing businesses or investments that provide a positive ROI for their investors? If they are not investing their money, *they're not doing their job*. So, they are actively looking for deals, like yours, to invest in or acquire entirely. They typically have millions, if not hundreds of millions, of dollars to do so.

✍ BRETT STORY

After selling my company in 2013, a friend of mine who owned a successful online Forex brokerage company mentioned that he was no longer happy owning the business, and wanted to start doing something else. I asked him why didn't he consider selling the company, but he didn't think anybody could pay him what it was worth to him, since he was earning around $500,000 per year.

He was only considering potential buyers in our market niche, mostly the other marketers we knew. While there were some very successful people, none had the interest or extra capital available to give him what he wanted. I then introduced him to my business broker who had sold my company, and within 90 days he had sold his company to a Chinese private equity firm for a reported $1.9 Million dollars.

So, it pays to consider all of your options in the larger global market.

That's good for you because they don't have the time, interest, or knowledge to create profitable online businesses themselves. They would rather buy yours as an investment. Imagine spending the next few years building your online business and having it acquired for six figures or more.

If you're currently running a business that you're no longer passionate about and want to do something else but feel stuck, consider selling it and investing the money in starting a new business in a new market you love. Contact us if you want help; we've done this multiple times, and have reputable business brokers we work with.

Another exciting option is to buy an *underperforming* business that's already established and, using the skills you're learning in this book, increase the revenues. Then, you could sell it to someone else for a bigger multiple of what you paid for it. This is a very powerful strategy, since the internet is here to stay...

"We need to rethink our strategy of hoping the Internet will just go away."

Consider the possibilities and how you can leverage these actionable ideas in your life. What could your life look like over the next three to five years if you invest time and energy in building your own online business or mini-empire?

Just remember that if you don't do it, somebody else will! So, why not you?

Section Five

AUTOMATING YOUR BUSINESS

ONLINE TECHNOLOGY AND TOOLS

Never before in history has the everyday person had so many opportunities to start, grow, and sell a new business in a relatively short period of time. The incredible tools that have become available to the public on the internet over the last 10 to 15 years have made this new business model possible. Prior to this phenomenon, people would typically have to invest tens of thousands, if not hundreds of thousands, to start a new business—with no guarantee of success and a high likelihood of failure. The risk vs. reward ratio of starting an online business versus a traditional brick-and-mortar business is definitely in your favor.

In this day and age, you can start an online business for less than $100, and for under $1,000 dollars, you can access tools and technologies formally reserved for much bigger companies with huge resources to invest and spend. The internet has leveled the playing field for the small business owner, solopreneur, and average person looking to make money.

In the online marketing world, technology costs have come down dramatically. From CRMs to SMS and voice broadcast systems; from project management to team-collaboration software; from sales and email systems to social media management tools, it's now all within your reach.

CROSS-PLATFORM AUTOMATION

The ability to automate your business cross-functionality between numerous different time-saving tools and platforms is a huge opportunity.

One of the tools we love is called Zapier. This amazing automation tool allows you to connect your favorite software to more than 1,000 of the other top online software programs, allowing you to compete at the highest level.

Imagine if you could easily set it up so that if a lead comes in from a simple form on your website, it triggers an automatic response. The potential customer is immediately added to your email platform of choice, which automatically sends an email, while also instantly sending a recorded voicemail message to their phone and a SMS message with a special offer link.

Your new prospect clicks on the link and buys your product, which is processed through your ecommerce or shopping cart platform, and a new members-only account is created. In addition, they are registered for an upcoming free webinar training you're having two days later, while a live alert is also triggered on your project management system telling your virtual team to follow up by phone to welcome them, all happening seamlessly, on various different systems.

Pretty awesome, isn't it? You have an unlimited number of combinations to create using technology like Zapier, eliminating the need for other expensive platforms that force you to use their overpriced "integrated" technology.

A prime example of this is a software platform that costs thousands of dollars per year and is generally known in the industry as "ConfusionSoft." Many people have been convinced they need this because of all of the built-in tools. The problem is that it's too confusing and expensive for most people, especially as much easier and less expensive tools are available now.

We invested in their software ten years ago and found the experience unbearable, so we decided to build our own. After repeatedly having our emails sent out completely blank, except for the "click here to unsubscribe" link at the top, we gave up on it. Then, we asked our office and virtual staff what they wanted to use.

Invariably, they all said they liked the simplicity of the platform we had been using before that. This other platform was a little buggy and needed some work, but it was very easy to use. So, we decided to buy part of the company, simply to add in the features we wanted to use in our businesses, as marketers ourselves. And that's what we did.

Along the way, friends and affiliates started asking if they could try it because they liked some of the promotions and unique marketing we were delivering using this platform. So, we decided to acquire the rest of that platform and invested over $500,000 of our own money to create what is now known as Cydec, which we've already talked about.

The good news is, Cydec integrates perfectly with Zapier and allows people to access all the other amazing tools and technologies available in the marketplace, for a fraction of the price. You don't have to give up the functionality found in these other systems. It can all be connected using Cydec and Zapier.

OUR SECRET WEAPON: CYDEC

Since 2008, and largely because of some of the features we built into the Cydec platform, we've generated well over $17 million in sales. One unique feature allows us to reduce order-form abandonment by up to 80%, which dramatically increases not only our immediate sales but also leads to bigger increases in average customer values when upsells are factored in.

Some experts estimate that as many as 65 out of every 100 people who land on your order page abandon without buying for one reason or another. Imagine if you could essentially *save* as many as 80% of them and at least get them to look at a discounted offer or payment option? Earlier we mentioned there is often a "Price for every person, and a person for every price." The price/value equation is different for every individual. By simply offering a slightly lower price if someone tries to leave, many will actually take the offer.

Then, largely because of a powerful principle called "consistency of commitment," which Robert Cialdini talks about in his book *Influence*, people are far more likely to continue buying after the initial purchase. Essentially, when we make a decision, we like to feel it is the right decision. So, we justify this initial commitment by creating a new rationale in our minds, if needed, to confirm we have made the right choice—even right after making it.

People are funny creatures; all this happens in a fraction of a second in the subconscious mind. We don't want to feel we've just made a bad choice, so when we're faced with the option to make another choice or purchase that's in alignment with the prior one, we're far more likely to say yes again.

For marketers, this means your primary objective is to get your prospect to say yes to you initially, even if you have to discount your offer or even offer a free trial. Then, they will more likely say yes to subsequent offers or upsells, and that is where the real money is made. Does this make sense?

What's critically important—and what everybody else in the marketplace is getting wrong—is *where* to show the secondary offer if the customer tries to leave. The mistake most marketers make is showing a new offer or discount if somebody tries to leave the website or sales page. This is the wrong place to do it. Have you ever tried to leave a website and a box pops up asking you if you'd like a discount or to reconsider your decision to leave? It's annoying, isn't it? That's because you hadn't yet decided you wanted it in the first place.

It's an entirely different mentality, however, if somebody clicks through to the *order page*. They clearly have an interest, but then decide to leave because of a price/value inequality. This is the ideal place to show your prospect a new offer because every new offer *creates a new decision* to buy as we've stated. Once they have seen the new offer, the prospect can reexamine their price vs. value equation to see if makes sense *to them*.

Even if you had to offer your abandoning prospect a free trial or very low-priced offer just to get them to say yes at *any* level, it's still worth it because of the consistency of commitment principle. You now have the ability to then turn them into a buying customer in the near future. People will often say yes to the very same thing they said no to previously *after* they've made a commitment to buy at a smaller level, even if just to validate that their prior decision to purchase was the right one. This is why upsells work so well, and how we generated the bulk of our revenues in our biggest product launches. *The money's in the back end.*

Cydec video exit popups trigger an attractive window, with easy-to-add images or streaming video to show your "save a sale" message if the user attempts to leave. This happens as soon as their mouse pointer crosses the top of the order form in their browser, which is super cool and very effective from our testing. We've shown up to 80% reductions in order form abandonment using this single feature.

To see an example of this in real life, demonstrated by Kevin Harrington, click here: www.cydec.com/kevinharrington.

Why is this so important? If most of the money generated from your sales promotion comes from your upsells, how many people will ever see those offers if they leave on the initial sales page? You're also offering your prospective customer a nice gesture by meeting them where they are in terms of their personal price/value equation.

A second unique feature we've added into Cydec follows another one of Cialdini's important principles: social proof. Our *social sharing discounts* incentivize customers to share on social media that they just purchased your product and why they purchased it. Why would they do this? Because Cydec users can offer their customers discounts for sharing their experience on social media. How cool is that? Cydec was also one of the first platforms in the marketplace—if not the first—that allowed for easy editing and customization of order forms and emails, using a familiar WSYWIG (stands for "what you see is what you get") editor that virtually anyone can use. You can easily customize your order forms to look just like your website, all the way through the upsell sequence to the "Thank You" page.

We've purposely left out all the unnecessary bells and whistles, like drag-and-drop page building templates and other "fancy" technology, because it's easy to integrate with over 1,000 other software platforms using Zapier. Cydec is a simple to use, fast, and inexpensive platform that's ideal for beginners and intermediates, as well as expert marketers wanting to increase sales. It is a great place for you to start. Our students and Cydec users love it also.

It has been our secret weapon for over a decade and has allowed us to generate millions in online sales while building out new campaigns quickly and efficiently.

To register for a free demo of Cydec, visit http://cydec.com/freedemo.

CONCLUSION

FINAL THOUGHTS AND NEXT STEPS

You're just one idea away. That has been the theme of this entire book, and by now you have a much better idea of how to put all the pieces together. Would you agree?

Following our MP⁵MS² Formula for Success, you have a clear roadmap of where to start and how to move forward in building your next online business. As we've shown, online businesses can potentially provide the time and money freedom you seek. You can truly live a Laptop Lifestyle, which, as we've said, is rapidly becoming a "mobile" lifestyle.

Are you ready to get started?

Simply by investing the time to read this book, you have taken the first step toward creating a better future for yourself, your family, and the world. You now have the tools to share your knowledge, experience, and expertise with people who can benefit from *your* solutions to their problems. These customers will happily *pay you* for solutions if you're following the principles we've talked about here.

You have moved your life one step closer to achieving your goals, and that says a lot about you. But success doesn't come easily. It requires focus, determination, time, commitment, and hard work. Most important, it requires you to make good choices. We suggest you keep this book handy, reread it often, and use it as your playbook for success. It will help you make better choices and dramatically increase your chances of success online or in any future business you're involved in.

Anything is possible if you believe in yourself; apply solid, actionable knowledge; and do what's required to achieve your goals. This process isn't easy, but it is simple. If you follow the strategies in this book, in the right order, you can be well on your way to achieving enormous success online. *But you have to put in the work.*

Reading this book proves you want more out of life. It shows you have the desire to learn and advance your situation, whatever that may be. It conveys that you have curiosity and the intellectual capacity to achieve. It confirms you are able to make good choices and decisions. Most of all, it proves you are willing to take action toward improving your life's circumstances.

If you're wondering *where to start,* we recommend that you identify the end results you desire and then work backwards from your end goal. We'll present three scenarios for you to consider, so you can decide which path forward might make the most sense *for you.*

Scenario 1: Extra Income

Let's say you just want to earn an extra $5,000 per month or $60,000 per year. As we have shown, this can be achieved by just selling 3 x $47 products per day.

Do you think you could do that, given some time to implement our process? This could all go toward paying your mortgage or buying a home if you're renting. It could cover a car payment or allow you to take more vacations or invest in education.

Using the Income Accelerator Worksheet provided earlier in this book, you can easily play around with different income scenarios to find one that best suits you.

As we've shown, once you identify a problem in a responsive market—such as health, wealth, or happiness—you can research and create a digital information product and then sell it through an affiliate marketplace, a joint venture partner, or paid advertising.

Many thousands of people are doing this worldwide, and many untapped markets and marketplaces exist, especially in international markets.

Scenario 2: Life Change

Maybe you'd like to fully replace a job or switch up part of what you're currently doing to enjoy more time freedom—all while earning the same amount you're making now or increasing that amount to $10,000-$15,000 per month, thus raising your standard of living. This desire can be motivated by personal freedom, providing for your family, or having more left over for investing, charitable contributions, saving for retirement, or whatever you choose.

To create $10,000 per month income, you only need to sell 7 x $47 products per day or get 100 people into a $100 per month membership program or just retain 10 consulting clients at 1,000 per month. All of these consumers could be found using online advertising.

The possibilities are limited only by your creativity, market demand, and your ability to share your solution to that market. In this book, we've just demonstrated how to do it.

Scenario 3: Business and Wealth Builder

Or let's say you wanted to build a million-dollar-per-year business. This is also achievable using the principles in this book. We've done it *multiple* times, and it's a repeatable process. Again, one of the best parts of this strategy is that you can even potentially sell your business for six or seven figures, then invest that money in other "traditional" vehicles to increase your wealth over time, such as stocks, brick-and-mortar businesses, or real estate.

Your personal income will, of course, depend on how low you keep your expenses. If you do the math and are bringing in $100,000 per month in your business, you have effectively outsourced using virtual staff to keep costs low, thereby eliminating the need for an expensive office somewhere—you could be enjoying 80% margins and netting $80,000 per month as an example. At $20k per week, that's $1,040,000 dollars per year. How does that sound? It all depends on your efforts and choosing the right product/market fit, which we've covered in detail.

If you decide to set your goal to build a million-dollar business, then you'll at least have clarity in your objective, and it then becomes all about the how. If you start asking yourself *how* you'll achieve your goal, you'll get better answers. For example, you could plan to sell 1,000 copies of a $1,000 product or service in a year, and that would get you there.

Other people have done a million dollars *in a day*, so think big and ask the right *how* questions. How could you sell 1,000 copies of your product? First, identify a problem worth solving, one that people will gladly pay you $1,000 to solve, or offer to help them get more clients, earn more money, close more deals, etc.

Who are the people that most fit your ideal profile? It's time to go find them.

If you've enjoyed what you've read so far and feel inspired to do something more with your life to take charge of your financial future and freedom, then we invite you to join our #FreedomFighter movement and help spread the word.

If you haven't already, reserve your complimentary #FreedomFighter T-shirt (just pay shipping and handling), here: www.clickandgrowrich.com/book/FreedomShirt.

If you're ready to begin your online journey to freedom and would like our help in getting started in the right direction or if you already have an online business you're struggling with, you can contact us for help: www.clickandgrowbusiness.com/discovery.

Also, look forward to the future event we're planning called the Internet Freedom Experience, which will be a great place to meet fellow #FreedomFighters and learn alongside them. You can learn from others' challenges, triumphs, and more lessons to help you succeed.

Plus, we'll have world-class speakers and trainers there (including us) to teach you the latest cutting-edge strategies that are working now. Preregister for more information here: www.InternetFredomExperience.com.

You have already taken an important step in preparation for your journey. Your choices and actions from this point forward will determine your destiny. It's now time to summon your courage and make the commitment to achieve your goals. Make a promise to yourself that you'll continue moving forward with determination and a sense of urgency. The rewards can definitely be worth it.

Sometimes people closest to you may become negative influences. Don't let them. If people try to tell you, "It will never work," or "You can't do it," just ignore them and avoid them, if possible. It takes time and practice, but removing negative people and influences that can distract you and hold you back from your goal is one of the most important things you can do for yourself, so be mindful of it.

Exercise control over your negative self-talk and fears. Then plan your next steps. Once you have a plan, work your plan. Surround yourself with positive people who will enrich your life, elevate your chances of success and happiness, and encourage positive action.

This is a process, and it takes time. But with each small task accomplished, you'll be building your confidence and gaining a new skill to build upon. With each challenge you overcome, your competence and commitment will grow. With each step forward, you will gain greater strength, courage, and confidence. People will believe in you and your potential.

Believe in yourself, and remember, *you are just one idea away.*

Bonus Section
PLANNING AND PRODUCTIVITY TOOLS

ELIMINATING OVERWHELM

E arlier in the book we said that there's nothing inherently difficult about the strategies or the process that we've shared with you here. What is difficult, if not impossible, is doing it all yourself. We've shown you how to outsource and find virtual help, but still it can sometimes feel overwhelming and difficult to stay focused and productive.

Throughout the book, we've also been giving you links to some of the same productivity PDFs that we use and created along the way to help stay focused on what matters most. We've previously only shared these business breakthrough PDFs with our private clients and mentoring students. But because these can be so important in "getting things done" and clarifying what the right things to be doing are, we're making these available to you.

BUSINESS BREAKTHROUGH WORKSHEETS
AND BONUS RESOURCES

I f you haven't done so already, register below for complimentary access to more than twenty-five of these invaluable time-saving tools and interactive PDFs that will help you stay motivated, get clear on your directions, remain focused on the most important things that matter most, and become more productive in your business; ultimately finding success faster and easier.

We would also like to invite you to join our free CGR members area where you can access the Business Breakthrough PDFs, as well as other resources and valuable trainings.

Register for the Click and Grow Rich Free Members Area Here:
www.clickandgrowrich.com/Book/Members

Stay in Touch with Us on Facebook:
www.clickandgrowrich.com/Facebook

Kevin Harrington Video Interview

Earlier in the book, we mentioned we recorded a rare, private interview with Kevin Harrington who is a friend, and was nice enough to write the Foreword. In this very interesting interview, Kevin talks about where things are headed online, international markets, mobile, and why as the founder of the "infomercial" he's still moving his attention online.

Watch Kevin Harrington's Video Interview Here:
www.clickandgrowrich.com/book/KevinInterview

Resources

Throughout the book we make reference to various online resources. For an up-to-date list of our recommendations that you might find useful in building your business, visit this page:

www.clickandgrowrich.com/book/Resources

ABOUT THE AUTHORS

Brett Fogle

My journey actually started at age seven. Brett's Mailbox Service was born while riding my bike all over the neighborhood and noticing that some homes had really nice-looking mailboxes while other houses had rusty, beat-up, and ugly ones.

One day I asked my dad, "Why do some people have ugly mailboxes, and why don't we help fix them?" So, my dad helped me design a flyer. We had three options: basic, standard, and deluxe, which had all the options, including large, reflective address numbers, color choices of paint, and an oversized, high-quality box. Dad did most of the work, while I "supervised."

I rode my bike around the neighborhood, putting my flyers in all the ugly mailboxes. Before I had any concept of marketing or selling, I was offering three different packages to choose from, unknowingly upselling my customers.

Apparently, it was very hard for a grown-up to say no to a seven-year-old asking, "Are you sure you don't want to get the deluxe option? It's only $10 more," with a genuine, kid-like curiosity as to why anyone wouldn't want to get the best option. We ran our business for a little over a year and replaced dozens of mailboxes. I was proud of the shiny, new mailboxes we installed around my neighborhood. The customers liked them too.

From there and throughout college, multiple self-started businesses and projects followed. I graduated in 1992 from the University of Maryland, taking five years to complete my degree because I had talked my roommate into dropping out for a semester to move to Cancún to start a photography business.

On a family trip to Mexico, I met an interesting American who claimed to be an heir to the Vlasic Pickle throne. He said his father had started the pickle company, which was acquired by a large grocery store chain for $60 million. He was a trust-fund baby, living off his father's fortune in Mexico.

I pitched him the idea of taking pictures of tourists using a new camera I had heard about that took "instant postcard" pictures, a modified version of a Polaroid. He agreed to finance the venture, and just like that, I had found an investor to fund my idea and buy four cameras. Unfortunately, the idea was a failure because the investor didn't work out, but my roommates and I had a lot of fun. After a few months, I returned to college and finished my undergraduate degree in finance.

Here's the interesting thing about college. I never used any of my finance education. Almost none of what I learned was useful to me in my life. But before switching to a business major, I started out studying psychology because I felt I had figured myself out pretty well and so the topic was interesting. It was exciting to learn what made people tick. When I had the realization that I didn't want to go through life as a psychiatrist listening to other people's problems, I switched to finance. The take away here, however, is that I've made millions and millions of dollars over the years largely because I understood people, not numbers.

Marketing and selling is largely based on human emotion, not decimals.

After graduating college, I helped out at my family's video store offices. My father, who had been a PhD scientist working for the government in Washington, DC for many years, decided to try his hand at entrepreneurship to increase the family income. He timed the market perfectly and opened the first Potomac Video Center in 1981, right at the start of the video rental craze. He grew the company to be the largest privately held chain of video stores in the Washington, DC, Virginia, and Maryland areas, with 24 stores toward the end before Netflix entered the market and changed the industry. This was my first lesson in watching and listening to your market.

At our corporate office building (purchased through profits from the video stores), people kept coming and asking, "What happened to the pet store downstairs?" It had apparently gone out of business, but people kept asking because many pet owners lived in the neighborhood. My dad and a new business partner decided to reopen the pet store—with zero experience other than having a cat or two in the house while I was growing up.

They floundered and realized fairly quickly that they didn't have the time or interest in learning this new market, so they asked me if I would take over. It wasn't a great business, but I made it work by giving my customers what they wanted, ultimately moving the store to a larger location and selling it a few years later to a "recovering" attorney as I call them, for over six-figures.

Two big lessons here. One is to watch and listen closely to your market. Identify if there *is* a market and then focus on what the people in that market actually *want*. The second lesson is to be careful getting into a new business or career you're not truly *passionate* about. More than a few attorneys go to law school to become lawyers so they can earn a large income, only to realize later that they hate being attorneys. It can be the same with business.

Looking back to 1999 when I first heard about the internet, I was still running my pet store. It was very quiet during half of the day, usually the morning. I took up stock trading to pass the time and was swing-trading shares of Netscape, back when E*TRADE was just a green screen and a flashing curser. This was the very beginning of the internet and online trading.

After having some success, turning $3,000 into $30,000 and then into approximately $60,000—I decided to become a day trader, the modern-day version of a gunslinger. It was very dangerous, and I quickly turned $60,000 back into $6,000.

Then I turned to trading options. With leverage, luck, and timing on my side—and being fast on the keyboard—I made all the lost money back in a month by trading naked call options. Seeing a million-dollar opportunity, I went "long" on as many high-flying internet stock options as I could afford, which then all went to zero when the bubble burst in January 2000.

This was both one of the worst and best experiences of my life.

Mostly, I was lucky early on, but I did have a good eye for trading trends. I started a small advisory service, and for a small monthly fee, investors could get my stock and option picks, which did reasonably well. But I hadn't yet developed solid marketing skills, so my small service stayed small. I was, however, able to sell it to a larger publisher a few years later.

This was my first eye-opening lesson that profitable online businesses could be sold for cash money. My interest was piqued, and I watched for other opportunities. So, while still running the pet store, I "accidentally" discovered a great side business. One day a lady came in and asked the manager I hired to clean out her fishpond. It seemed ridiculous to me, but he came back two hours later, a little dirty but $80 richer.

Now, that was pretty good money for two hours of work back then. We discovered this was a hot market, and lots of people had fishponds in their backyard. I grew this business, and at one point I had a van with two full-time guys out servicing 100 ponds a season—all while upselling high-margin pond supplies, including $5,000-$10,000 koi pond filtration systems.

And when people were spending hundreds and, in some cases, thousands of dollars on a fish (like fancy Japanese koi), they usually wanted to keep them alive. So, we had stumbled onto a great market. I later took that business to half a million dollars in annual sales (mostly online) and eventually also sold it for more than six figures.

Before I tell you how, let me tell you a story about a phone call that changed my life.

After moving the pet store to the new location where I was trying to grow it to sell (a prior attempt to sell at the previous location wasn't successful), I received a phone call from a gentleman in Hawaii. A voice on the other line said to me, "Hi, my name is Jonathan Mizel. I'm calling because you signed up on my website for some information about internet marketing, and I'd like to tell you about a seminar that's coming up." Those weren't his exact words, but pretty close. He also said it was going to cost $2,000. That's not a huge amount of money now, but at the time, it was to me. I had payroll, rent, and inventory to pay for.

Yet something inside of me said, "I have to go," and to this day, I'll always appreciate that phone call and the fact that he wasn't salesy about it. Pushiness would have turned me off, and I wouldn't have gone. But this seminar changed my life forever. He and I are still friends, and I'll always be grateful that he opened my eyes to online marketing, which has been a revolution—one that is still in its infancy today.

I went to the seminar and met people like John Reese, who later become the first person to make $1 million in one day online, and Carlos Garcia, who was, at that time, selling $2 million per month of cable descramblers online. These connections led to other lifelong friendships, business opportunities, and experiences, like spending five days with Sir Richard Branson on his private island with 19 other world-class entrepreneurs, including Matt Mullenweg, the founder of WordPress, and a few other very successful businesspeople. Not to mention, personally raising tens of thousands for Virgin Unite, Mr. Branson's global charity, and $447,000 raised collectively among the entire group.

After that first seminar, I sold my pet store and invested some of the money into one of my first early failures. The success principles we teach today—and the millions in revenue I've generated since then—are based on experience and knowledge of what *to do* but also *what not to do*. I left that seminar thinking that I had to come up with a new idea and a *bigger* market—a market as big as the market Carlos was selling to, which, to me, was *everybody*.

I had a new friend who had licensed water filtration technology from NASA. He was using the same water filtration compound they spent millions of dollars to develop for space travel. His company, Aquaspace, was building home water filters for the public, and he agreed to let me sell his products online.

To me, it was a no-brainer. And in the wake of terrorism threats, everyone would *want and need* one of these amazing water filters. He even had an astronaut as a spokesperson! I couldn't lose—or so I thought. I spent over $9,000 on building an amazing website, hiring the best designer I could find, and installing videos on the site, which was unheard of back in 2003. I couldn't wait to go live, and was sure the money would come rolling in. But it didn't. *Nobody cared.* Why? Because the consumers' view was that they could go to Home Depot and buy a water filter for one-fourth of the price.

The big lesson here is that I chose to sell a *product* where no *market* existed.

Then I went back to the drawing board. Based on my early options-trading service success, I knew a market opportunity existed there, so I looked around for quality education on how to trade options. Not finding anything good, I decided to put my feelers out to find someone I could start a business with, in which we'd teach investors how to trade. An early mentor of mine had just experienced success marketing a similar type of trading product and even produced his own physical DVD with a printed manual, which was unique, as most were writing e-books and digital products. He encouraged me to do the same.

In 2004, I found a partner to launch this business with, one who had a lot of experience and credibility in the stock trading market. He was a former floor trader on the Philadelphia options exchange who had been let go because the exchange had gone digital.

It was perfect timing, and the company exploded because we were *in the right market at the right time.* We grew this business from the proverbial "kitchen table" to #276 on the prestigious INC500 list as one of the fastest-growing privately held companies in America and made the list in the top 5,000 three years in a row—another example of the importance of being in a hot market at the right time.

To make a long story short, we generated millions of dollars between 2004 and 2012, creating multiple variations of the original company, and then I expanded into other hot markets, like Forex, selling information products, software, services, and seminars. I learned a lot and made many mistakes. I even suffered failed economies, partner lawsuits, financial fraud, embezzlement, and lost a marriage. But I survived.

A few years later, Daniel Miller and I had met through a mutual friend in New York City. He had achieved a high level of success with another company that had recently been acquired by a large international bank. He was essentially retired at just over 40 years old, but he saw the potential when I shared the opportunity with him, so we became business partners. This was the stepping-stone that later led to us creating the Click and Grow Business and Click and Grow Rich brands, which are the foundation of this book.

E. Daniel Miller

As the youngest in my family, and being adopted, I knew that I was different. There was always a drive to be something bigger, and a desire to be around people, as well as to please them. Maybe it was a fear of abandonment that made me want to be around people, and maybe it was a fear of loss that made me want to make people happy.

I was raised as a part of a wonderful Christian family on a small farm in northern Wisconsin, where throughout my childhood my father and mother instilled in us the meaning of hard work. My father was a local barber and beekeeper, while my mother was a registered nurse and worked mostly nights. We had plenty of chores on the farm, so it was early to rise and early to bed for us kids (AKA unpaid labor). Looking back, it wasn't so bad because we didn't even have a TV set, so I really had no idea what I was missing. While everyone else was talking about watching *Little House on the Prairie*, I was living it. My dad would always say that he wanted me to "live a bigger and better life" and encouraged me throughout my school-age years to get good grades and an education. He also told me that in order to get a good job, I would need to go to college.

Throughout high school I worked as many jobs as I could handle, from day laborer for Nindorf construction, to grill cook at the local Burger King. It was a way to make a little cash and get ready to pay for college. Those jobs taught me many things, but the biggest lesson I learned was that I didn't like working those types of jobs. I knew I had to do something that I liked to do, so I became a tour guide at a local firehouse and at the SS *Meteor Whaleback* ship, where I would make tips for giving presentations to tourists. This was the moment in my life that I realized I liked speaking and talking with people, which makes sense since my dad always told me I had a talent for it. That, and that I never understood the word *no,* which likely led to me becoming so good at sales.

While considering college, I was encouraged to be like the wealthiest guy in my small town, who was an engineer and owned a construction business. My dad cut his hair and would tell me to "become an engineer so you can be like Mr. Johnson." So, I went to college to become an engineer. Like most college students on a budget, I wanted to have more things like a new stereo, a motorcycle, and my own car, but soon realized that just having a job at the school commissary would not afford me these luxuries. So, I decided to team up with two friends to start a business, and stepped into my real first foray as an entrepreneur. We formed a disc jockey business where I was a DJ at a club on Thursday nights, and Fridays through Sundays it was weddings and dances. I mostly enjoyed making everyone happy, and getting them up and dancing, not to mention the money was amazing for a young college kid like myself.

Just before I graduated with a bachelor's degree in engineering, my dad encouraged me to continue on to a master's degree to be more marketable and "make more money." So, I did what he said and went to graduate school, and was fortunately offered a position at a very prestigious engineering firm shortly after I graduated. One day, I told my dad I'd like to be rich and retire early. But he told me that I would likely need to work for that firm for 25-30 years, and then maybe I could retire and live the life I always wanted. So, at this point in my life, I decided *not* to do what he said.

My early experiences as an entrepreneur and salesperson made me realize that I didn't really want to be an engineer. But I was good at it, so I decided give it a shot and then landed a great job working at Bechtel Corporation, a huge international company. While working at Bechtel, I had some great mentors including Riley Bechtel (#259 Forbes 400 2018), who inspired me to be financially successful. At Bechtel, they encouraged us to look at things "outside of the box" and they promoted the use of Six Sigma statistical improvement, and I later earned my Six Sigma Black Belt Certification. Although I realized that I was making the company a lot of money, and saving them even more, deep down I wanted to do these things for a company of my own.

Around this time, and while married to my first wife, I had the opportunity to pursue an audited MBA from Berkeley because at the time they were allowing husbands and wives of enrolled students to audit any classes for an audited degree. I jumped in with both feet and went to every class a full MBA would attend. It was like getting a 2-for-1 MBA! While pursuing this opportunity, I became the president of the Haas Partners club and a staple member in the community with C4C charity and March of Dimes. I entered every business plan competition I could at Berkeley, Stanford, and Columbia. I learned a lot, and was even offered a cool position at a little-known start-up called *Alibaba*.com, which ended up becoming a multibillion-dollar IPO, the largest in global history, and a company that has changed the landscape of online selling. But I turned it down.

I decided that I wanted to get in at the ground floor and began shopping for a start-up company that would allow me a piece of the action, and a bigger part of their growth. Thankfully, I stumbled onto a start-up financial software company that had just moved onto the pink sheets, and needed help growing. I reached out to one of the founders on a whim and told him I would be great at selling their products. I can even remember my first meeting with him in an airport arrivals hall when I flew up for a two-hour layover, and we talked the whole time. I felt at home, and I was happy that at the end of the meeting he said to me, "Let your wife know you won't be with Bechtel any longer." Needless to say, I flew home with a big smile on my face, because I knew I would be working with a great team of successful entrepreneurs.

I left my cushy engineering job and decided to tell my parents that I was resigning and going to be an entrepreneur. They were mortified that I was leaving the security of my job and taking my chances with entrepreneurship. But one thing I know for sure is that even though I had failed in the past, it never really bothered me. I would just keep going, probably learning my tenaciousness from all those times I would ask the cutest girls out on a date, and if they said, "no thanks," I would just go ask someone else that I was interested in. I realized that nos are just part of life, and they get you closer to YES. Like water off of a duck's back, people should just let their "nos" bounce off and keep on paddling.

Once in the start-up sector, you really can't reliably depend on others. It's "do or die," because often you're the only one that can do it. You and your cohorts are like kindred entrepreneurs, all working towards the same goal…the IPO. There were a few other people at the company that were good at selling our products, but I don't think any of them believed in the product like I did. I had seen it firsthand and had used the software successfully with my own personal finances. So, when I spoke about it, my passion rang through to the audience, and they responded very well. I sold tens of millions of dollars of the program for the company, helping them break $100 million in sales for the first time, and I personally trained some of the other top sales people working there.

Soon enough, the company was on a meteoric rise, which continued for the next 4.5 years, including seven mergers and acquisitions. The company had its ups and downs, but the team and I helped it to grow to over 700 employees, and because of this success, we were later acquired by a large international bank for $606 million. While this was great for me financially, both the company and my personal life ended up in turmoil, and led to my divorce.

I recall meeting with Robert Kiyosaki once, where he said that one should "retire before you're 40 and write a book," so that was my plan. It was at this time that I decided to retire early and invest in a few businesses. I liked fine cigars, so I invested in an ultrapremium cigar manufacturing company called Payne Mason Cigars, and I also opened an upscale cigar club with a few partners. That didn't end well and taught me a valuable lesson about working with the wrong people, and was an expensive life lesson. Since I liked traveling in Central America, I also invested in a few resorts in Costa Rica, which I'm still holding on to. Then I moved from my home on the beach in San Diego, and moved to Florida like all good retirees do, where I purchased a great home on the water with a big dock and a boat. I was planning on just relaxing, playing golf, boating, and finding a new wife, then finally have some kids.

After a few months of the retired life, however, I began to feel restless. I shrugged it off and kept to my retirement plans, while I continued looking for a wife and decided I didn't like golfing that much, so I boated more. Then one day I realized that a body in motion stays in motion, and that a body at rest stays at rest. It was during this time that I received a call from an old friend who told me to "get out of bed and hire a new assistant" that would show up at the home office every morning and give me no excuse but to start something new.

I heeded that advice, and soon after I started helping a company called Business Breakthroughs, created by Tony Robbins and the late Chet Holmes, turn their company around. It was also at this time that I met my current business partner Brett Fogle at a big internet marketing summit in New York City. We have now been partners for almost a decade, doing the things we love to do, like helping hundreds of aspiring entrepreneurs and business owners around the world pursue their passions online, under the Click and Grow Rich brand.

We've also been creating a simple, yet powerful online software that helps people sell their products and services.

I'm proud to say that out of turmoil came triumph, as I now have a new wife and some amazing, beautiful kids. My oldest daughter at the age of five told me she wanted to become a "YouTuber," I think because I encourage her and her sisters to do much better than I ever have, like my father did for me. Heck, she already has more followers than I do on one of her social media channels. I guess that is why parents are on this earth: to help their kids be bigger and better than themselves. I strive for that every day; to set a good example for my children and for the hundreds of entrepreneurs and student partners that we are able to impact with our training.

I believe you will find your freedom inside this book, if that appeals to you, because everything we have done and continue to do is right here in these pages. Blessings to all of you.

ENDNOTES

1 TD Ameritrade to Acquire Thinkorswim, https://www.businesswire.com/news/home/20090108005671/en/TD-AMERITRADE-Acquire-thinkorswim

2 Digital in 2018: World's Internet Users Pass the 4 Billion Mark, https://wearesocial.com/blog/2018/01/global-digital-report-2018

3 US Digital Marketing Spend Will Near $120 Billion By 2021, https://www.forbes.com/sites/forrester/2017/01/26/us-digital-marketing-spend-will-near-120-billion-by-2021/#3fb0885f278b

4 Sears, Kmart And Macy's Will Close More Stores in 2018, https://www.npr.org/sections/thetwo-way/2018/01/05/575932533/sears-kmart-and-macys-will-close-more-stores-in-2018

5 Facebook Revenue Jumps 61% on Mobile Ad Strength, https://www.usatoday.com/story/tech/2014/07/23/facebook-earnings/13045633

6 Market Cycles / E. L. James 50 Shades of Grey, https://en.wikipedia.org/wiki/E._L._James

7 Affiliate Marketing Spending in the United States From 2015-2020, http://mediarails.com/how-fast-is-the-affiliate-marketing-industry-growing

8 Agora Inc. Annual Revenues, https://en.wikipedia.org/wiki/The_Agora

9   Simon Sinek: The Importance of Knowing Your Business Why, https://www.entrepreneur.com/article/284791

10 Apple First Trillion Dollar Company, https://www.washingtonpost.com/business/economy/apple-is-the-first-1-trillion-company-in-history/2018/08/02/ea3e7a02-9599-11e8-a679-b09212fb69c2_story.html

11 Options University INC500 in 2008, http://www.incmagazine-digital.com/incmagazine/200809?pg=78#pg78

12 Options University INC500 in 2008, http://www.incmagazine-digital.com/incmagazine/200809?pg=78#pg78

13 The Official Get Rich Guide to Information Marketing, https://www.goodreads.com/book/show/638809.The_Official_Get_Rich_Guide_to_Information_Marketing

14 John Ferber / AOL Acquires Advertising.com for $435M in Cash, https://www.forbes.com/2004/06/24/cx_tm_0624video1.html#29d25f6d31f7

15 Justin Tupper / Revolution Golf Acquisition by Golf Channel (Golf Channel Public Relations, Aug. 7, 2017), https://www.golfchannel.com/article/press-releases/nbc-sports-group-acquires-revolution-golf-bolsters-digital-portfolio/

16 Facebook Purchase of Instagram, https://techcrunch.com/2012/04/09/facebook-to-acquire-instagram-for-1-billion/

17 Tai Lopez net worth, https://wealthygorilla.com/tai-lopez-net-worth/

18 Sales Triangle—Chet Holmes, https://chetholmes.com/wp-content/uploads/2018/01/NEW-Chapter-4-1-1.pdf

19 The True Cost of a Bad Hire—It's More Than You Think, https://www.forbes.com/sites/falonfatemi/2016/09/28/the-true-cost-of-a-bad-hire-its-more-than-you-think/#49fbcee04aa4

20 Tim Sykes $12k to $1M+, https://www.huffingtonpost.com/eric-kuhn/from-bar-mitzvah-thousand_b_100061.html

21 Tim Sykes net worth, https://pennystockwhizzkid.com/tim-sykes-net-worth

22 Size of US Consulting Market, https://www.sourceglobalresearch.com/report/3025/the-us-consulting-market-in-2017

23 Kaizen—Wikipedia Definition, https://en.wikipedia.org/wiki/Kaizen

24 Facebook Ads Manager, https://www.facebook.com/business/tools/ads-manager *We are not affiliated with Facebook. We are merely referencing various features of their advertising platform.

25 10 Reasons Why Your New Online Business Will Fail and How to Avoid Having These Things Happen, Huffington Post, April 13, 2015, updated Jun 13, 2015, https://www.huffingtonpost.com/greer-wignall/10-reasons-why-your-new-online-business-will-fail_b_7053610.html

26 iContact $169 Million Dollar Exit, https://www.bizjournals.com/triangle/blog/techflash/2014/05/icontact-founder-houghton-opens-up-about-169m-exit.html

27 Users in Africa are up by more than 20% year-on-year, https://wearesocial.com/blog/2018/01/global-digital-report-2018